Historical Fiction Writi
A practical guide and tool-kit

Myfanwy Cook
www.myfanwycook.com

With contributions from:
Professor Bernard Knight, CBE
Andrew Thompson

With tips from:
Malcolm Archibald, Carole Baldock, Edmund Bohan, Jane Borodale,
Edwin Buckhalter, Mary Andrea Clarke, Barbara Cleverly,
Bernard Cornwell, Tania Crosse, Lindsey Davis, Simon Dell,
Margaret Donsbach, Margaret Duffy, Carola Dunn,
Ariana Franklin, Tess Gerritsen, Susanna Gregory, Andrew F. Gulli,
Simon Hall, Feona J. Hamilton, Darryl Harrison, Lilian Harry,
Susan Higginbotham, C.C. Humphreys, Jane Jackson, Michael Jecks,
Sarah L. Johnson, Bernard Knight, Bethany Latham, Richard Lee,
Carole Lllewellyn, Dorothy Lumley, Karen Maitland, Elizabeth Maslen,
Ian Morson, Ann Parker, Glen Phillips, Ann Pulsford, David Roberts,
William Ryan, Tim Severin, Harry Sidebottom, Julian Stockwin,
Frank Tallis, Andrew Taylor, Andrew Thompson, E.V. Thompson,
Nicola Thorne, Marilyn Todd, Christine Trent, Jacqueline Winspear,
Stephanie Grace Whitson, Sally Zigmond

Proof Reading and encouragement:
Carolyn Escott
Linda Kennedy
Printing and technical assistance:
Carol Harrison
Additional assistance:
Elizabeth Cole and Ewa Thompson

ActiveSprite Press
www.activesprite.co.uk

Historical Fiction Writing –
A practical guide and tool-kit

copyright © 2011 Myfanwy Cook

First edition published 2011 by ActiveSprite Press
www.activesprite.co.uk

ISBN: **978-0-9567654-0-6**

Cover design and typesetting by ActiveSprite Press

Typeset in Calibri

Printed in the UK by MPG Biddles Ltd, King's Lynn

Foreword

The purpose of this historical writers' guide and tool-kit is to introduce aspiring historical fiction writers to the skills needed to write both historical novels and short stories. It also provides the opportunity for more experienced writers to revisit these skills, or make the transition from general to historical fiction writing. It is a step by step guide based on activities that provide an opportunity to practise and experiment with the skills and techniques needed to write authentic and satisfying historical fiction, which is both entertaining and engrossing.

This practical handbook is designed to be used sequentially, but as with any good 'tool-kit' each chapter is a complete entity designed to highlight a particular skill or purpose, or writing 'tool' that will enhance your writing skills. Each group of skills that you need has been grouped together under seven main headings. The activities in each chapter focus on one aspect of the craft of writing historical fiction and can be used independently to clarify a particular problem or to reinforce the techniques and suggestions you are introduced to in the chapter. The objective of this how to write creative fiction guide is to provide you with the tools that that you will need to write your own work of historical fiction in an historical subgenre of your choice such as historical crime fiction.

The tips and suggestions which have been generously contributed to this project sometimes complement and sometimes contradict the activities provided. They provide a fascinating glimpse into the way some of the most noteworthy and popular historical fiction writers and professionals within the field view their craft and the genre.

The activities are based on the innovative workshop activities designed and used successfully by Myfanwy Cook (**www.myfanwycook.com**) over the past 15 years. Myfanwy has had over one hundred short stories published both in the UK and Australia. She has won national prizes and had her stories broadcast on the radio. Currently she is features editor of the Historical Novel Society's HNR magazine (**www.historicalnovelsociety.org**).

Myfanwy believes that mastering the art of writing is like becoming an apprentice. It is a craft and demands certain practical skills alongside imagination, creative flair, the desire to write and above all a love and commitment to writing. The workshops that she's run have confirmed that what often holds aspiring writers back is their lack of confidence and fear that they lack certain practical skills such as how to write dialogue. What she is constantly amazed about is the richness of the imagination and the heartfelt aspiration to write historical fiction.

It is hoped that this guide book will fill in some of the gaps and act as a tool-kit to provide you the aspiring writer with some of the skills that you haven't yet mastered, but also that you will find it an interesting and useful introduction to the historical fiction writing genre.

Acknowledgements

The activities in this book were created for writing workshops which I have run for over 15 years to assist aspiring writers of historical and other genres of fiction. The book has been written for all those who have taken part in her workshops and asked her to write a tool-kit for them. A big thankyou to all those who have attended these workshops for their courage in wanting to learn, master new skills and to write for the sheer sense of creative satisfaction that the process brings.

The editing, proof reading and tips have all been contributed free to this project by two very special and loyal friends who have spent hours proof reading – Linda Kennedy and Carolyn Escott. In addition a word of thanks to Carol Harrison for her input, Darryl Harrison for his technical wizardry, and to Elizabeth Cole for casting her eye over the final proof.

A heart-felt thanks to all the authors, professional writers, agents and magazine editors who have generously agreed to share their practical expertise with aspiring writers who are interested in how to approach writing historical fiction and above all to Bernard Knight for his encouragement.

Dedication

In celebration of those who aspire to write and who are willing to spend hours in solitude trying to create fascinating works of fiction that will entertain, inform and provide escapism for their readers.

I would like to thank my wonderful friends, Christian my great son, and my amazing parents Arthur Thomas Cook and Gwyneth Megan Cook, who taught me the solace, comfort and delight that is to be found in fiction, and who until their deaths always loved to read fiction set in times past.

How this book is organised

This practical guide and tool-kit is divided into seven sections. Each chapter will contain relevant tips from professional historical novelists to match the chapter heading. The chapters are designed to be used on either a 'pick and mix' basis or sequentially. Each chapter consists of activities, tips and suggestions, but the format varies from chapter to chapter, as does the spelling. There are tips provided by authors from America, Australia, Canada, New Zealand, the UK and the USA and local spelling has not been changed.

The web site and references to useful publications were correct at the time of printing, but may have changed by the time this is read. Nothing is ever perfect, and so despite the best efforts of the proof readers there will be faults.

CONTENTS

Introduction

SECTION 1 – What do you need to get started?

Chapter 1 – What is Historical Fiction?
* The history of historical fiction
* The different *genres*

Chapter 2 – Which Period?
* Selecting your subject
* Checking out the competition

Chapter 3 – Researching Your Market
* Who are you writing for?
* Market research
* Pre-planning

SECTION 2 – The Essential Ingredients

Chapter 4 – The Essential Ingredients
* Novel or short story?
* Series or saga?

Chapter 5 – Theme, Plot and Synopsis
* Which is which?
* Identifying themes
* Cause and effect
* From inspiration to plot and sub-plot
* Twists and double twists
* Flash fiction

Chapter 6 – Settings
* Physical setting: the role of places and landscape in historical fiction writing
* A sense of place

Chapter 7 – Characters
* Creating characters
* Personality plus
* Dressing up your character
* Less a blemish more a trademark

Contents

Contents

SECTION 7 – Mixing all your ingredients together to produce a mouth-watering piece of historical fiction

Introduction

Look in most bookshops and you won't find a separate historical fiction section, but look under crime, romance, fantasy, slipstream and horror instead. There you will find that a large proportion of the novels are historical ones. Historical fiction and the authors who write them are big business, and include Pulitzer, Nobel and Orange prize winners.

Historical fiction is similar to all other fiction genres in that it is written to entertain the reader. It opens a door for the author's audience to glimpse different worlds, or to see their own world through different eyes. Historical fiction writers take their readers on journeys into past civilisations and societies. Their creative works provide escapism embedded in historical fact. They are often seasoned with myth, folklore, and anecdotes, handed down through generations in the form of oral history. Therefore, unlike any other form of fiction, you are not only told a story, but you are also being given a guided tour of a specific period in history. The writer crafts in words a picture of the life of famous and ordinary people, set in their own time and against the particular historical landscape which they inhabited, thus creating evocative settings for their own characters to inhabit.

This practical guide and tool-kit is written in a straightforward and accessible style. It has been written for aspiring writers who would like a step by step guide, to provide them with useful, practical information, tips, activities, and the skills required to write effective, enticing, engaging and readable historical fiction. Writers who are already involved in historical fiction writing may also find new approaches to historical fiction that provide them with additional sparks of creativity. *Historical Fiction Writing – A practical guide and tool-kit* is also aimed at giving readers of historical fiction an insight into what ingredients are used to write vivid, memorable historical fiction.

Each chapter focuses on a separate aspect of historical fiction writing. The chapters are organised in themed clusters under a section heading.

This guide has been written sequentially, but is designed so that each chapter is a separate unit, which you can refer to as required. The core content of this tool kit and guide is based on the practical activities that have proved to be useful and beneficial to the participants who have taken part in the workshops that I have mentored over the past ten years. These activities were created to introduce them to the basic practical skills needed to write historical fiction, and to provide an opportunity to experiment with them.

Some of the 21 chapters will vary in their layout. This format has been used to enable different contributors with expertise in particular fields, to write in their own distinctive style rather than to conform to a template.

Introduction

Each chapter will have a selection of activities designed specifically for you to experiment with the skills you are introduced to. It will also contain a selection of tips provided both by historical fiction writers and experts in related fields. However, one essential item that this tool-kit does not contain, is your need to be committed to the past, if your objective is to write high-quality historical fiction. If you aren't already passionate about history and historical fiction, we hope that you will be after reading this self-help guide and carrying out the activities.

Bernard Knight
"If the date of the setting is earlier than the author's own personal experience, then a lot of work has to be done in making it authentic, be it the hair-styles, Norman shields or the model of motor-car! Readers are all too eager to seize upon inaccuracies and anachronisms. You need a genuine interest – indeed, a fascination – with history to make your writing succeed, rather than a general idea that 'something set in the past' might go down well."
www.bernardknight.homestead.com

SECTION 1

What do you need to get started?

Chapter 1 – What is Historical Fiction?

What do you need to get started? You need:
- To be passionate about history, or at least curious about the past;
- To be interested in writing fiction even if you haven't done any form of creative writing before;
- To love reading both fiction and non-fiction books;
- To have a lively and creative imagination even if you've never had the opportunity to use it practically before;
- To be flexible in your approach, and to be willing to try different suggestions and 'tips' even if after you've experimented with them you find that they are not for you;
- To be determined to overcome any difficulties that you might experience in mastering the craft of writing fiction;
- To be able to accept criticism without becoming depressed about it;
- To enjoy your own company;
- To be able to set aside some time to write and read on a regular basis.

What is historical fiction?

The definition of historical fiction has recently been the subject of considerable debate. Is it any novels that are set before the First World War, or the Second World War? Whatever one would like to believe, the reality is that from the publishers' and readers' viewpoint, historical novels can be set within our living memory.

Bernard Knight
"Once the decision has been made to launch into a historical setting, what period are you going to use? These days 'historical' can range from Ancient Egypt up to the nineteen-sixties! Andrew Taylor has won a number of historical awards for his great stories set in the pre- and early post-World War Two era and using these criteria, all Agatha Christie's books are historicals!"
www.bernardknight.homestead.com

Sarah L. Johnson

"I typically define 'historical fiction' as fictional works set more than 50 years in the past, ones in which the author is writing from research rather than personal experience. I include autobiographical novels within this scope if they're set in a time sufficiently distant from our own. That said, I think a case could be made for including some novels with more recent settings if the historical period is a main focal point, such as novels set during the 1960s counterculture or the Vietnam War. This is especially true when speaking of children's or young adult novels, since these readers won't have lived through the time period in question."

Sarah L. Johnson is the author of *Historical Fiction, a Guide to the Genre* and *Historical Fiction II: A Guide to the Genre,*

www.readingthepast.com

The history of historical fiction

Historical fiction has its origins in the oral story-telling tradition. The Viking Sagas such as the *Saga of Eric the Red*, The Celtic, *Mabinogin* and Homer's tales of Odysseus' adventures, like the stories collected under the title of Arabian Nights, are all part of this tradition. The Japanese and Chinese stories play as much of a part in this legacy, as the Arthurian legends and myths, found in works such as the Romances of Chrétien de Troyes. These retellings of daring, tragic, romantic and heroic stories, form one of the cornerstones of the historical fiction that we read today.

The consolidation of these stories into a written form was a gradual process, and the early writers often concentrated on the plot and were not, from the historian's perspective, factually accurate. It wasn't until the nineteenth century that historical fiction started to emerge as an identifiable genre. Sir Walter Scott published *Waverly* in 1814, which was the first of a series of novels about the Jacobite Revolution that occurred sixty years before he published his novel. It is considered by some that Scott's novel is the first of the modern genre of historical fiction.

It also foreshadowed a trend that dominated the historical fiction writing of the 19th and early 20th century; a fascination with national identity and heroism embodied in such novels as Scott's *Rob Roy* and Leo Tolstoy's *War and Peace* published in 1869. One of the most productive of the writers in romanticising nationalism and heroism was G.A. Henty, who died in 1902. He was considered to be one of the best storytellers of his own time. Originally a special (foreign) correspondent who covered the Crimean War amongst others, he wrote over 120 books, many of them historical adventure novels for children, and all set against colourful historical events such as the Spanish Armada, and seasoned with a large dose of patriotic fervour. His legacy can be seen in the wide range of Navy novels featuring characters such Horatio Hornblower created by C.S. Forester, and in the pirate novels of authors like Tim Severin.

Charles Dickens's *A Tale of Two Cities* (1856) also hinged on self-sacrifice and noble deeds, a theme that was taken up by later novelists like Rafael Sabatini in *Scaramouche*, which has had over 50 editions sold world-wide, and was described by the *New York Times*, June 26th, 1921 as "A plot of cunning construction, worked out with finished technique. There is just that amount of suspense which is necessary to charm the imagination of the average reader, just enough heroic gestures to satisfy the child that survives in all of us." Alexander Dumas was the French master of this popular type of 'swashbuckling' historical fiction. *Les Trois Mousquetaires (The Three Musketeers),* first published in serial form in 1844 in *Le Siècle* between March and July 1844, and *The Count of Monte Cristo* are two of his best known works. He was also a writer of romantic historical fiction with novels such as The Regent's Daughter published in 1845.

Other major historical fiction writers of this period were the American Nathaniel Hawthorne whose novel of 1850, *The Scarlet Letter,* was about Puritan New England, and Victor Hugo whose *Notre-Dame de Paris (The Hunchback of Notre-Dame)* was published in 1831. Hugo's novel opens in Paris in 1482, on the day of the 'Festival of Fools' in Paris. This novel helped to create a sub-genre of historical fiction that is one of its most popular sub-genres today: the Middle Ages or the medieval period from c. the 5th century to the 16th century in Europe.

The 20th century saw the popularity of certain types or sub-genre of historical fiction gaining popularity while others waned. Georgette Heyer, with her Regency romances like *Sprig Muslin* (1956) took centre stage, setting a standard of romantic historical fiction writing that many have aspired to reach, but she also achieved an even higher accolade in the eyes of historians and that was factual accuracy (as illustrated in her novel *An Infamous Army* (1937). Heyer's contribution to popularising historical fiction particularly with women readers, was one that she shared with Anya Seton. Anya Seton (Ann Seton) was an American born in New York and whose novels such as *Katherine* (1954) and *Avalon* (1965) are still popular today. Other novelists who made their mark and became popular best selling novelists were Mary Renault, Catherine Cookson and Jean Plaidy (Eleanor Hibbert) who also wrote under following pseudonyms: Victoria Holt, Eleanor Burford, Elbur Ford, Kathleen Kellow, Anne Percival, Ellalice Tate and Phillipa Carr. Writing under the pen name Jean Plaidy her novels grew into sagas such as *The Catherine De Medici Trilogy*, which started with *Madame Serpent* (1951).

Sagas and multi-volume sagas became increasingly popular from the 1930's onwards on both sides of the Atlantic with Elswyth Thanes *Williamsburg Chronicles*, which open during the American Revolution in Virginia, but then move to England during the Second World War, and Mazo De la Roche's *The Whiteoaks of Jalna* set in Ontario, Canada, to Williams R.F. Delderfield's *Swann Family Saga* and *The Poldark Saga* by Winston Graham.

Then in the late 1980's Barbara Erskine published *Lady of Hay*, which opened the door for historical 'time slip' writing to capture the reading public's imagination when Jo Clifford Erskine's central character agrees to be hypnotised and regresses back to a past life. *A Connecticut Yankee in King Arthur's Court* (1889) by Mark Twain, helped to lay the foundations for historical fiction time travel novels. Other similar genres of fiction, such as fantasy, have been grafted with great success to historical fiction to form their own sub-genre, and illustrated by such 21st century novels as *Temeraire* by Naomi Novik.

Historical fiction is increasing in popularity with novelists from around the world finding their novels translated into many languages. It would appear that there is a universal appeal about the cocktail of history, bold characters and stylish writing that travels well. The Polish author Jósef Ignacy Kraszewski during the late 19th century wrote a 29 part multi-period saga based on the history of Poland. Then in 1928 Sigrid Undset won the Nobel Prize for Literature in part for her trilogy set in medieval Norway *Kristin Lavaransdatter*, while during the same period in Australia, Katharine Susannah Prichard was writing novels that would culminate in *The Goldfields Trilogy* that spanned the social history of the Western Australian goldfields from the 1890s to 1936.

Today if you visit your local bookshop you will find that historical fiction covers all historical periods and fictional genre, from crime fiction to time-slip and fantasy. You will also be faced with an array of well-researched and written historical fiction, which often finds its way onto the best seller lists. However, what is even more encouraging for the aspiring writer of historical fiction is that previous 'aspiring' writers of historical fiction's work can also become best-sellers as well ,for example *The Heretic's Daughter* (2008) by Kathleen Kent and *The Company of Liars* by Karen Maitland.

The history of historical novel writing is a story itself , and so rich and complex that if your curiosity has been aroused Sarah L. Johnson's *Historical Fiction, A Guide to the Genre* , and *Historical Fiction II: A Guide to the Genre* provide a detailed and fascinating account of the flowering of historical fiction world-wide as a genre (see **www.readingthepast.com**).

ACTIVITIES

1.1 What is historical fiction and why do readers enjoy it?

Objective To assist you in clarifying what readers are looking for when they buy, or borrow a novel and how they interpret a historical 'good read'. Writing down the key words that readers use when talking to you will also provide you with important information that you can use when trying to 'sell' your novel or story to an agent, magazine or publisher.

Your task **A** Ask all your friends and anyone that you know who reads historical fiction, to define what they think historical fiction is, and then jot down the key words and phrases that they use on the photocopiable questionnaire below.

B Pose the same questions to any or all of the following: the assistants who work in your local book shop, the staff of your local public library and any book groups in the area, and note down what they say.

Group interviewed	Definition of historical fiction and what is defined as 'a good read' Note down the answers as KEY WORDS, PHRASES OR SHORT SENTENCES
Friends, family and colleagues	Examples: exciting adventures, colourful descriptions of clothes and what people ate etc.
Bookshops, Libraries and Book groups	

1.2 Comparing the past and the present

Objective   To enable you to identify the differences between past and present historical fiction writing, and to help you to identify any aspects of past historical fiction writers that you might like to emulate, or avoid.

Your task   To read three novels written by authors who have written historical fiction, but that lived in different centuries e.g. 19th century Victor Hugo, 20th century Georgette Heyer and the 21st century (your choice). Just go to your local bookshop or library and pick one at random on a period that interests you.

After you have read them, write down in the table overleaf why you liked or disliked them. You don't need to write whole sentences, just bullet points. For example was it because the sentences were too long? Were there too many characters? Did the dialogue seem stilted? Do you think it was well-researched? Which voice (I, he, she etc.) was used for the main character? Did it have lots of action and cliff hangers? Do you like the author's style (the way in which it has been written e.g. formal or informal) of writing?

COMPARING THE PAST AND THE PRESENT		
Author details and century	LIKES	DISLIKES
19th		
20th		
21st		

The different genres

Historical fiction can be divided into genres in various ways, one of the most common is chronological. The list given below is a broad one as used by magazines such as the Historical Novel Society[*] and as you research historical fiction more deeply, you may find that you discover much more detailed breakdowns.

[*] **www.historicalnovelsociety.org**

Chronological:

Prehistory
Ancient Egypt
Classical (which includes Greek and Roman history e.g. the Roman Republic, the Trojan Wars etc.)
1st Century (and then by century up to the 20th century)
Multi-period
Timeslip
Historical Fantasy
Alternative History
Children and Young Adult

Another way of breaking down historical fiction is under broad sweeps or bands of history as used by web sites such as *Wikipedia*[*] and *All About Romance*[†] which coincide certain historical periods, topics or subjects:

Historical Bands:

(Please note that c. = circa, which means about or approximately and not exactly).

Examples of main bands, themes, genres or groups of historical fiction:

Adventure
Romantic
Crime, Thriller, Whodunits
Mysteries
Military (including Spy, Wuxia and many others)

Examples of Subgenre:

Arthurian
Medieval (c.938-1485)
Tudor (c.1485-1603)

[*] **www.wikipedia.org**
[†] **www.likesbooks.com**

Elizabethan (during the reign of Elizabeth the 1st (c.1558-1603)
Georgian (c.1714-1810)
Regency (c.1810-1820)
Victorian (c.1832-1901)
Edwardian (c.1901-1914) and La Belle Époque
Sagas
Psychological Thrillers
Gothic (and Horror)
First World War
Second World War
Colonial United States
Colonial
Civil War
American (c.1880-1920) and its subgenre Native American
 Frontier (U.S., Canada, Australia, New Zealand)
Pirate
Naval
Trains

Both types of listing are useful ways of organising the rich array of historical novels and their genre and subgenre. If you would like to understand the hierarchy and full range of historical fiction across the world, then you need to consult an academic study of the subject. For example Sarah Johnson in exemplary *Historical Fiction, A Guide to the Genre* has chapters devoted to traditional, 'Literary' and 'Christian Historical Fiction'. While under 'Sagas' she has 37 sub headings listed, which cover historical sagas written about and by authors from Africa, Asia, the Middle East, Latin America and many others in addition to the traditional sagas.

At this point you may be starting to panic, but don't. The relevance of this information for you as a novice historical author is simple. First of all you need to know which genre your short story or novel will fit into, because when you approach an agent, publisher or magazine they will need this information. Secondly, it enables you to see the massive appeal that historical fiction of all genres and subgenres has world-wide. Thirdly, it should act as a tonic for those moments when you wonder if your writing will ever be published. If reference books with over 800 pages can be compiled on Historical Fiction, then you can cheer yourself with the thought that the opportunity to be published is possible.

ACTIVITIES

1.3 How do bookshops and libraries display their historical fiction?

For example, are the historical romantic fiction novels displayed alphabetically under author, or does the shop or library have a separate section to themselves e.g. 'Regency Romances'? Also check out the non-fiction sections of the book shops. In late 2009 while browsing in Blackwell's bookshop in Oxford, I noticed that the non-fiction Classics department had collected together a wide selection of historical fiction covering Greek and Roman themes, which were displayed as a sub-section within the non-fiction. Check carefully to see if other book shops are emulating Blackwell's creative and practical marketing strategy. Customers interested in non-fiction about specific historical periods should theoretically also be interested in the historical fiction written about their specialist period.

Objective   To discover what genre of historical fiction and subgenre they are displaying on their shelves. If they have any special displays in the shop window or elsewhere highlighting any particular author or genre of historical fiction e.g. a display of naval fiction. The purpose of this activity is firstly to give you an overview of how much historical fiction is available to buy or sell, which demonstrates there is a market. Secondly, it will give you information about which authors are in vogue at the moment, or being promoted by publicists and publishers. It will also give you an insight into the types of historical fiction that are popular with the readers in your local area. You may find that an author who writes historical fiction about the place you live in, is not only on the general fiction shelves, but also displayed in the local history section, and more space is devoted to him (or her) than to authors on the best-seller lists.

Your task   Visit your local library, an independent bookshop and a bookshop which is part of a chain. Make notes on the table below, which you can enlarge and photocopy. The information that you collect will be needed to complete the activities in **Chapter 21**. To save yourself feeling uncomfortable, and because being polite is always a plus, particularly if you ever want the library or bookshop to promote your work at a later date, ask if they mind you carrying out this task and explain why you are doing it.

How do bookshops and libraries display their historical fiction?	
Library	
Independent Bookshop	
Bookshop, which is part of a chain of bookshops.	

1.4 Where else is historical fiction on sale?

Objective   To make a list of other outlets of historical fiction. Add to this list as you discover new potential markets for the future sale of any work that you have published.

Your task   Buy a small notebook and make a list of any places that you come across that sell historical fiction. You could be amazed at how many potential outlets there are, from stately homes and churches to village post offices and cafés. Don't forget to find out who orders or buys the stock, and take down their contact details.

1.5 Who writes what?

Objective   To provide you with an overview of the historical fiction that is currently available set in a period and genre that is of interest to you. To give you a benchmark to help you select a period and subgenre that you will enjoy researching and writing about, and which has an audience of readers willing to buy or borrow books in that subgenre. This piece of mini market research will also provide you with information that you can include in a covering letter to a prospective agent, publisher or funding body (should you be applying for a grant or funding to enable you to write or carry out research for your novel).

Your task   Select any subgenre and a period that interests you and find out who writes in that genre, who publishes the novels and how many titles are on display, such as Medieval crime fiction, multi-period sagas, historical time-slip, or historical fiction set during the First World War etc.

	Name of Author	Title and Publisher
Who writes what?		
1		
2		
3		
4		
5		
6		
7		
8		
9		
10		
11		
12		
13		
14		
15		

Tips

1 Be constantly aware that fashions in historical fiction reading change. Sagas were very popular in the second half of the 20th century, but are currently less popular with readers at the moment, whereas historical crime, fantasy and naval fiction have very strong followings.

2 Ask your friends to save any newspaper and magazine articles, leaflets or guide books that they come across that mention the period you are interested in.

Useful Publications

1 Historical Fiction, A Guide to the Genre and Historical Fiction II: A Guide to the Genre (very similar title!). Both of these books have been written by Sarah L. Johnson of Booth Library, Eastern Illinois University, USA. If you want to order it, the best way is through the publisher's website as they have a UK distributor. Here's the relevant page: http://www.greenwood.com/catalog/LU8624.aspx Readers can also obtain it through Book Depository, which has free shipping and a discount. See www.readingthepast.com

2 The Novels of G.A. Henty including:
The Cornet of Horse, A Tale of Marlborough's Wars (1881)
Under Drake's Flag (1882)
The Dragon and the Raven, The Days of King Alfred, (1886)

Useful Web sites

www.historicalnovelsociety.org
www.readingthepast.com

Chapter 2 – Which Period?

The first decision

Bernard Knight
"Before you even start to think of plots and characters, analyse what you really wish to write. Assuming that the decision to write some type of crime fiction has been made, do you want to persevere with a historical format or stick to a contemporary setting? The latter is easier in many ways, as there is no historical research needed and your daily experience can provide you with every detail, from dress to transport, aided by the profusion of police and forensic procedure churned out by the media.   In addition, a present-day setting has faster action, with mobile phones, the internet and helicopters to keep your story-line rolling – in the twelfth century, getting a coroner in Devon to attend a murder in Barnstaple would take three or four days before you could even start your investigation!   If you are not already addicted to historical mysteries, then read quite a few by different authors, to see how they approach the matters discussed here."
www.bernardknight.homestead.com

Selecting your subject

Why is it so important to select a period, event, place, theme or person that you are interested in to research?

- The accurate use of historical background and details are the hallmarks of the genre.
- You need to be interested in what you are writing about, because if you aren't passionate about it your readers won't be either.
- You are about to invest a large chunk of your life in researching the period, event or person, and it shouldn't be a chore, but an adventure, a challenge that gives you a sense of satisfaction.
- You may already have a fairly comprehensive knowledge of a particular period, but even so there is a difference between knowing something about a century or a particular historical character, and spending hours reading, only to discover that you aren't interested in it after all. You also need to research what

came before the period and after it, which involves additional research.

♦ If you have a specialist knowledge already of a particular subject such as trains, ships, art, fashion, armour or a noteworthy historical figure for example then this may influence the choice of the period that you decide to set your story in. However, remember that this specialist knowledge has to be set in a specific context, and that will still involve a lot of general research about the era you select.

ACTIVITIES

2.1 How to decide?

Objective The following activity is designed to help you clarify how committed you are to writing about a particular period, event, place, theme or person. This activity is also designed to sharpen your skills at writing synopses, which will be focused on in more detail in **Chapter 26.**

Pick a period (era), event, place, theme or person, and write down in one hundred words why you want to write about that particular subject or time. You may wish to try all of the subjects to enable you to pinpoint even more precisely what aspect interests you the most. The models to act as guidelines have been kindly reproduced by participants from past workshops on the theme of historical fiction writing. A space has been provided underneath each example for you to write your reasons. You may prefer to use bullet points or notes; the choice is yours.

Your task In a maximum of one hundred words write down your reasons for choosing to write about one or more of the following:

PERIOD (OR ERA)

> **Model**
>
> The early 19th century was a period of war in Europe, but it was also a period of creativity. Exciting new technology in the form of steam was transforming the pattern of everyday lives, as was the improvement of transport with the building of canals and macadam roads. It also saw the birth of the entrepreneur who used the new inventions to maximize profits, and sometimes to improve working conditions. It was an era of opportunity and change.

Write your reasons in your notebook

EVENT

> **Model**
>
> The French Revolution attempted to sweep away the old order. At the outset it appeared as if it was a people's revolution, fired by the aspirations of the intellectuals and the dire poverty of the ordinary people, but other forces were at play. It was a time when William Wordsworth like many of his generation believed it was, "Bliss to be alive, but to be young was very heaven." Unfortunately, the good intentions of these young intellectuals were not as strong as the greed, revenge and fanaticism which underpinned it, and culminated in Robespierre and the Reign of Terror, when no one was safe from the threat of the guillotine's blade.

Write your reasons in your notebook

PLACE

> **Model**
>
> Pompeii and Herculaneum are now as peaceful and ordered as they must have been at the beginning of August 79AD before Vesuvius erupted, except the sounds are different. They are of distant traffic, tour guides and the babble of voices from every corner of the world, and not the everyday chatter of a town that had grown prosperous on oil and wine. The peristyle of the house of the Vettii family with its garden is dotted with sculptures would once have been filled with music and laughter. Inside the walls are decorated with scenes of domestic daily life, but hidden in the corners are shadows like memories of the past. You can almost hear the whispers of those whose lives and civilization vanished on a hot summer day.

Write your reasons in your notebook

THEME

> **Model**
>
> I am fascinated by the theme of risk, taking chances and gambling with one's own life and that of others for fame, glory, power or monetary gain or as an act of courage. For me the exploration of the Antarctic embodies this theme. Particularly, the story of Priestley, who as one of Shackleton's advance party in 1908, and due to lack of space in the tent, slept outside during a blizzard for three days, just in his sleeping bag and found himself at one point slowly slipping down a glacier and nearly falling to his death. Then in January 1912 the Terra Nova was unable to reach him and his party because of the ice, however he and the five others managed to survive the winter without any provisions or real shelter, and then walk for five weeks to Cape Evans.

Write your reasons in your notebook

PERSON

> ## Model
>
> Benozzo di Lesse (Gozzoli) was not one of the most famous of the early Renaissance artists, but he was one of the fastest workers. His name might never have achieved any kind of fame, except for the procession of kings that he painted, weaving its way around the Medici chapel. Did he realise that he was only second best? Why did he select faces from his own generation for painting the kings and their retinue, instead of creating a cavalcade of Eastern monarchs in the Procession of the Magi? Was he the paragon of virtue that Vasari suggests, or was he a canny businessman who was quite happy to paint anything and everything?

Write your reasons below:

2.2 Checking out the competition

Objective   To investigate the period which interests you to find out which authors are writing at the moment, which specific aspect of that era they are writing about, and what you can learn from them.

When you start to write yourself it will also act as a checklist to which you can refer, to assist you in including all the ingredients you need to write interesting, engaging fiction that can transport the reader in a few sentences into a past time.

Your task   **Complete the Three Novels Comparison Table**

Buy or borrow three novels which have been published during the previous two years, and read them. Two of these should have been published by mainstream publishers and the third by a smaller, or an independent publishing house. While you are reading them you will need to analyse why you think they were accepted by the publishers. Write down an example of each ingredient that you think would interest the reader e.g. "Eliza hated washing day most of all. It made her hands swollen and red. On Monday, in the middle of the day, she'd begin to wash the young ladies' fine things and the gentlemens' shirts and neckclothes." This kind of description might be of interest because it tells the reader something about the character and her life, or because it sets the historical scene, which has been done in this case by adding authentic details from a housekeeping book that was published in 1776.

This activity is not a matter of personal taste. You will need to try to distance yourself from personal likes and dislikes. What you are trying to establish is why the publisher accepted them and why the public buy them. It doesn't matter if you enjoy them or not, for this activity. If you enjoy them it is a bonus. This is simply a piece of market research to help you establish, what if anything, makes these novels stand out enough to enable them to be given space on library shelves and bookshops.

Three Novels Comparison Table			
INGREDIENTS	Mainstream publisher 1	Mainstream publisher 2	Smaller publisher
The author has a strong track record, or the novel is part of a popular series			
Main Characters			
The subgenre type e.g. crime, romance etc.			
Setting e.g. Venice			
Dialogue			
Descriptions e.g. Good action scenes, sense of place			
Does the writer have a particular style that makes their work more alive or memorable?*			
* For example do they use a lot of similes (comparisons) e.g. "Alexander the Great was			
Effective use of historical detail			
Pace e.g. action packed and fast moving			
Any other characteristics of the novel that you think might attract readers and publishers to the novels you have chosen?			

Tips

Once you've selected a period that you are interested in writing about, don't allow yourself to be side-tracked by the allure of another historical period until you've completed your novel or short story.

Jane Jackson
"Choose a period that fascinates you and a theme about which you care deeply. (A theme I enjoy exploring is a woman's place in a man's world) You are going to be working on this story for up to a year, so it's important that you are captivated and absorbed by it. If you aren't, how can you expect the reader to be?!"
www.janejackson.net

Chapter 3 – Researching Your Market

Do I need to know who I'm writing for? Well, if you hope to have a novel or short story published then you need to know who your potential readers are. When you write a letter to an agent or a publisher you will be expected to define the market and readership that you think will buy and enjoy your work of fiction.

Another benefit for some writers is that it helps them to have a picture of a group of readers, or one particular reader fixed in their mind as they write. This can be a real person such as a friend who enjoys that particular genre of writing, or it can be a composite person that you've created and are writing to entertain.

In a similar way, carrying out some simple market research can help you to clarify who buys the type of book or the publication that you want to write for. Then you can pre-plan what you intend to do with your novel or short story when you've completed it. Your ideas may change as your writing progresses, but if you intend to self-publish from the outset, then making a list of possible venues for your launch, and specific details of the local media and press that you've written down in a notebook, or on a spreadsheet, may help you to focus on your ultimate objective. Alternatively, you could draw up a list of agents or publishers who you might submit your manuscript to, when it is completed.

At this point you may be thinking yes, but I just want to write; which is quite understandable. However, if you want to write and be published then by careful pre-preparation you can neutralize some of the anxiety that may swamp you, as you start to write. You will have a plan in place, so that you can concentrate on writing a piece of historical fiction that may appeal to and entertain a group of people, who you already know exist and are keen to read the genre that you are writing in.

Who are you writing for?

Are you writing for yourself? Do you want to share your stories and entertain readers who you've never met? Have you met people who like the genre of fiction that you want to write, or who like novels set in a particular period?

ACTIVITIES

3.1 My Imaginary Fans

Objectives   To enable you to build up a picture of the type of person who will read and buy or borrow what you publish.

To introduce you to a quick way to create character profiles for your stories. (Creating profiles will be referred to again in **Chapter 7**).

Your task   To draw up a profile for a reader that you have made up, created from your imagination. First complete the questionnaire below for your imaginary fan. Later you will be comparing this character profile with the information that you collect after carrying out Activity 3.2 in this chapter —Eavesdropping and Asking Questions.

Model Profile 1

Profile of my imaginary fan for my Crimean War historical adventure fiction novel

Name: Horatio Wellington
Age: 40-55

Physical description: A tall, thin man with fair hair flecked with grey. His hair is cut with military precision and is very short. He has sharp features and might be considered too gaunt and thin to be attractive. He is wearing expensive walking boots, a thick padded jacket and has a battered rucksack, which he is using as a shopping bag. He is wearing a wedding ring and his hands look as if he has spent a lot of time in the sun either gardening, or in some military capacity in a dry, desert area.

Interior description (personality): A man who plans everything, but thrives on challenges.

Job, background and income: Ex-military and now a climbing instructor. Divorced, but with two children. More interested in relationships with his climbing friends and mountains, than with women. He isn't well-off as he is supporting his family, and spends most of his spare cash on climbing holidays.

Interests: Climbing, travelling, rambling and cycling.

What do they like about your writing? The military settings and the element of adventure and danger that the main characters have to overcome.

Anything else? He reads a lot and always takes a novel with him when he goes climbing and travelling.

Model Profile 2

Profile of my imaginary fan for my historical romances set during the First and Second World Wars

Name: Ella Brighton
Age: 30-35

Physical description: She can just squeeze into size 12 clothes. Ella has well-styled ginger hair, which was once chestnut but is now dyed. She walks quickly despite the shoes with very high heels that she wears every day.

Interior description (personality): She is almost never sad, and is content with her busy life. She is a romantic and loves it when her husband brings her home some flowers or pays her a compliment.

Job, background and income: Ella is married with a two year old daughter. She is a part-time receptionist at a dental practice and loves her job.

Interests: She collects old postcards of the part of the city she lives in, and where she has lived since childhood. Ella is also interested in family history, because she comes from a large family.

What do they like about your writing? It's romantic, set in the city she lives in where she can identify the places you describe. The period you write about and the families also appeal to her, because it reminds her of the family anecdotes about the Two World Wars, which she was told as a child.

Anything else? She enjoys fast paced novels with short chapters, so that she can read them at work if she isn't busy, or when her daughter takes a nap.

Your task is to fill in the profile questionnaire below

Your Imaginary Fan Profile

Profile of my imaginary fan for my ...
Name: **Age:**
Physical description:
Interior description (personality):
Job, background and income:
Interests:
What do they like about your writing?
Anything else?

Market research

It is very easy for us to make sweeping generalisations and categorize readers into certain age or income bands, but this does not necessarily take into account factors such as 'recommendations' or 'gifts'. While talking to an assistant recently in a large chain of book sellers, I was introduced to the 'grandparent' factor, which is that on wet days during the school holidays grandparents take their grandchildren into bookshops and buy them books. These are not, as the assistant explained the ones the children want, but the ones the grandparents think are suitable, or the ones that they enjoyed reading when they were young. The assistant went on to explain that there were some customers who bought books because they've been recommended by a friend, or by a TV personality, but added that he wasn't sure how many of these would then swiftly find their way to a charity shop. He also went on to point out that people buy books as gifts, and that for 'get well' gifts usually picked books that looked as if they had happy endings. Pure escapism novels were also bought as presents for friends who were having hard times, and needed to know that adversity could be overcome. Before going back to putting novels on the shelves, he added that of course a lot of people bought novels just because the covers were attractive.

This encounter with an observant assistant re-enforced many of the concepts about readers that I'd already formulated, but it also taught me a lot about the motivation of other book buying customers. In order to find out more about the current market place for historical fiction, you will benefit from 'rolling up your sleeves' and taking a practical approach to finding out who the real people are, who will be reading your work of historical fiction. This involves undercover observation, eavesdropping and asking an occasional question. You have created a profile in words of who you think might read the genre or subgenre of fiction that you would like to write, so your task is now to see if your 'reader' in anyway matches the 'real' readership.

ACTIVITIES

3.2 Eavesdropping and Asking Questions

Objective   To enable you to uncover what 'real' readers look like, and what motivates individuals to buy certain subgenres of historical fiction, or fiction written by a particular author.

Your task   **Eavesdropping**

Try to go to your nearest bookshop as often as possible over a three week period (or longer if you don't feel too uncomfortable about this activity). Spend as long as you can, without getting in the way, near the place that sells historical fiction similar to the kind you think that you might be interested in writing. If you can afford it you might like to buy a novel occasionally as well! If you haven't got a book seller nearby then you might try a library, a supermarket or a charity shop that sells books.

Just observe the type of people who buy the genre that you are keen to write. When you get home jot down notes and keep mini-profiles about the people who have invested their money in buying a novel.

Asking questions

Your task is to ask customers and assistants in book shops or libraries a series of questions, and to find out as much as you can about which customers buy and read the type of fiction you would like to write.

Fellow customers

If the customers look friendly then you might ask them a simple direct question such as:

- Is that author any good?
- Can you recommend that author?
- Do you read a lot of historical novels? Have you got any favourites? What's special about that author?

Quite often people enjoy recommending novels that they are passionate about.

Customer Assistants

The first rule is don't disturb assistants if they are busy, but if they aren't and they are working on re-stocking or tidying the shelves with the books that you are interested in then often you'll find they are quite keen to share their knowledge with you.

If the assistants aren't busy and appear friendly then you might like to ask them questions such as:

+ Excuse me, can you help me? I was wondering which authors writing (e.g. Roman) historical fiction are popular?
+ What sorts of people buy Roman historical fiction, are they mostly my age or older?
+ Excuse me, but do you know who the best selling historical (crime) fiction novelists are at the moment?
+ Is there any one that you'd recommend? Why do you like them?

Remember don't overstay your welcome. A quick question is all that is required to find out what you need and always say thank you. It is amazing how many people forget those two powerful words 'thank you' accompanied by a smile of course! The person you are talking to may be your first customer and become a fan of yours in the future.

If you can't face the prospect of lurking in the corners of bookshops then you might like to join a book group and uncover through their discussions, which ingredients make compelling historical fiction, and which authors use these ingredients effectively.

Your aim is, once you have spent some time observing real customers and book borrowers, and jotted down notes about them, to compare this information with the imaginary reader profile. The objective is for you to have a picture in the back of your mind of not just a faceless target market group of readers, but rather an imprint on your mind of a collection of individuals. All of these readers will be seeking escapism and entertainment in an engrossing read that you are writing just for them.

Pre-planning

If you are an organised person then you may well have an advantage over those who are not. Planning is of utmost importance for the writer of historical fiction. Pre-planning what you intend to do with your writing when you've finished it is important, but even more so is the ability to keep track of your characters and the plot within accurate time frames. Time lines are dealt with in **Chapter 15**, and we suggest that when you've completed the activities below you read **Chapter 15** next.

How am I going to keep track of my characters, my plot and the research that I am going to carry out? Individual preference will determine how you keep track of your research and plot. You may feel comfortable with creating a character database on your computer or a database into which you enter all your notes on background research, or it might suit you better to have a card index (old shoe boxes are great for this if you don't want to invest in plastic file boxes). Some writers prefer to keep their notes in a collection of notebooks. Others prefer to keep track of their plot and characters using *post it notes* with the key information written on them, while others prefer to use a white board and colour code the events, character profiles etc. with different colour marker pens. This system of planning provides you with a constant visual reminder of 'who (whom), what and when'. You may need to experiment to see which suits you best. However, you will need to break down your record keeping into certain key headings and sub-headings. The sub-headings may vary and will be looked at in more detail in **Chapter 17**.

Main Headings:

> Plot
> Main characters profiles
> Background research

Examples of sub-Headings (see Chapter 17 for a more detailed breakdown)

> Chapter by chapter synopsis of the action (storyline)
> Sub-character profiles
> Settings
> Fashion
> Food and drink
> Arms and armour
> Transport

ACTIVITIES

3.3 Which way is best for me to keep track of my research, characters and plot (storyline)?

Objective   To assist you in deciding which is going to be the most comfortable way of planning your historical work of fiction.

Your task   Write a description (in a maximum of 200 words) of what sort of system you think you might set up to enable you to keep track of your research and your story plan, and why you've chosen it.

Below is an example which was written by a participant in a recent workshop

---

Description - Model Example:

I tend to remember things by seeing them and when I visit a new place I can recall even tiny details of what I've seen even years later. I like drawing plans and mind maps, so I will create a visual story board to keep track of my story. I haven't got a white board or even a cork notice board, but I do have an old jigsaw board that folds up and so I thought that I'd use post it notes and stick them on the jigsaw board. That means I can store it when I'm not using it, as I haven't got much room at home. I've also got some large pieces of cardboard from a fridge box that I am going to use as sub-heading boards, which can be easily stacked and I can take out when I need them.

You can write your description in your notebook.

Tips

- Remember that an effective plan is one that has been designed to enable you a degree of flexibility.
- Start saving receipts. If you buy any books, or visit historic houses or make special journeys for research purposes keep your receipts. You may not publish a short story or have your novel accepted within your first year of writing, but you might. If you receive any form of payment for your writing then this will need to be declared on your tax returns. Keeping your receipts will enable you to reduce the amount of tax that you pay. Try to keep the receipts in an easy to access file e.g. a file with plastic pockets in it that are labelled with the name of the month when you made the purchase or paid the visit. If you get into this habit it will make your life a lot less fraught should you start to make a regular income from your writing. Professional writers are usually self-employed and so you may like to check out the websites listed below.
- Whatever you do make certain that you save any work that you do on your computer and copy it on to a memory stick. Saving your work needs to become an automatic habit. It's really upsetting when you've managed to squeeze in a few hours' writing time out of your busy life, and then you forget to save it, or at a later date your computer decides to stop working. At least make certain that you have a hard copy of your work and update this regularly at the end of each writing session.

Julian Stockwin
"Plan your work and work your plan -This adage from the business world is vital for writers. I have a chart which describes my books in terms of the main variables – time, geographical location, the stage in life of the main characters etc. Then for each book I follow this up with a very detailed plan."
Julian Stockwin is author of the Thomas Kydd series. For details of his latest novel *Victory* see ***www.julianstockwin.com***

Useful Websites:

www.adviceguide.org.uk
www.hmrc.gov.uk/selfemployed

SECTION 2

The Essential Ingredients

Chapter 4 – The Essential Ingredients

The basic ingredients that you need to write historical fiction are similar to those that you need to write any other genre of fiction. The extra ingredient is the historical detail that you add to give your story a distinctive flavour of period and place.

What are the basic ingredients and the writing skills that you will need to mix them together to write a 'flavoursome' story? For the purpose of this guide book these include (these have not been listed in order of importance):

Basic Ingredients:

Plot (or story line) and sub-plots if appropriate, theme (e.g. love, greed, revenge), characters (main and subsidiary), dialogue, settings (place and time/historical period), descriptions (external = people, place, time/historical period and internal motivation, psychological make-up, emotional responses/feelings, mood)

What extra ingredients might you need to add extra flavouring to your story?

    a twist
    a double twist

You will also need to have, or to acquire, certain skills to blend the basic ingredients into readable, interesting and captivating fiction. These include technical skills such as selecting an appropriate viewpoint and voice (are you going to use 'he/she' or 'I') for your main character, the ability to write information and interesting dialogue, to be able to change the style and pace of your writing to fit the register[*] of the scene that you are describing. This is sometimes referred to as the 'narrative tone'.

At a recent workshop, the participants drew up the following list of what they considered were the necessary ingredients it was necessary to have, in order to master the art of historical fiction writing. They prioritized the skills that they perceived they needed in the list below:

Good spelling, accurate punctuation, correct grammar, plot/story line (beginning, middle, end), characters with problems, a knowledge of the history of the period, a good imagination, ability to write descriptions, knowledge of how to write dialogue.

---

[*] The word **register** in this context could mean are you writing in a formal or informal way (for further see **Chapter 12**)

What is interesting about this list, is that the group had highlighted the ability to spell and punctuate above the creative ingredients. For them the technical skills came out as of paramount importance.

When asked to analyse why this was, it became clear that for two thirds of the group it was their fear of making technical mistakes, rather than a lack of imagination or an ability to create plots and characters, that was preventing them from writing. This lack of confidence came from two main sources according to their discussion and feedback. The first was that they'd never been taught the basic rules of grammar (syntax) and punctuation at school, and they didn't even have a grasp of the verb tenses (past, present, present continuous etc.). The second was they'd "never been able to spell" certain words or that their "spelling was bad". What was holding them back from writing their novel or short story, was not that they were unaware of the ingredients that they needed. It was rather that they were unsure about the balance of ingredients required. However, their main block was a fear of making mistakes. They were anxious about not being able to spell and not understanding the rules of punctuation. Grammatical skills and having difficulties with spelling are an obstacle, but they are thankfully an obstacle that can be removed or at least circumnavigated. There are strategies that can help aspiring writers to get around their obstacles. The technical skills ingredients that you need can often be acquired (see **Chapter 13**).

Writing is a practical craft and many of the skills can be acquired by being made aware of what is needed, and practising and experimenting with these skills. However, the highest and most challenging hurdle to overcome is 'fear'. Overcoming the fear of 'not' being able to do something, or of 'not' being able to spell, or of people laughing at, or belittling your attempts, is one of the hardest skills to acquire if it doesn't come naturally to you to be able to ignore snide comments and digs. Always try to remember that Michelangelo did not paint the Sistine Chapel ceiling after his first lesson. It took him years to acquire the skills he needed to tackle such a large and complex project. Writing fiction is a craft as well, and artists and writers are all apprentices in the same way as any other craftsperson.

One basic ingredient that isn't on the list above, but which both the novice and the professional writer needs is:

COURAGE

Courage to write, even when you know that whatever you write is going to be found lacking in some respect by a few of your readers. The other ingredient that isn't often mentioned is:

RISK

When you write you are taking a risk. You are investing your time in creating a piece of writing that may not bring you fame and glory. Writing must above all satisfy a need within you. The journey that writing takes you on must be a pleasurable and interesting one, even though it will no doubt also be frustrating on occasions.

The last three vital ingredients are:

INSPIRATION

Inspiration comes in many different forms. It might be a place, a face that you see as you are walking to work, an article in a magazine or an old family photograph. Whatever your source of 'inspiration', it may well niggle at you and pester your thoughts until you start to write. Some writers would argue that inspiration is simply your imagination turning a feeling into a concrete and workable idea. However one defines 'inspiration', what most writers, would agree on is that it can be very useful to them.

IMAGINATION

It has been suggested that an imagination enables you to transform your inspiration into a plot, with characters to people your story. For others it means that the words 'writer's block' do not exist in their vocabulary. Having an imagination that enables you to create stories in your mind whenever you want, and wherever you are, is a characteristic stamp of creative writers. Hand in hand with imagination goes another key tool for the aspiring writer to master, if they haven't already got it, and that is prediction. Being able to predict outcomes to people's actions adds realism to plots and sub-plots. The ability to imagine other times, other worlds than the one we inhabit, is one of the most difficult skills to acquire if it doesn't come naturally to you. One comment that readers will often make to authors is "I love your stories; I wish I had your imagination. My mind just doesn't work like that." The writer of any genre of fiction is simply using their 'imagination' to make up for a shortfall in their readers' ability to 'imagine', and thus acts as a tool by which they can stimulate their own imagination, enabling them to escape from their daily routine.

Nicola Thorne
"Don't attempt to write historical novels, or novels of any kind for that matter, unless you have a strong sense of imagination. A novelist must be like an actor playing a part, in this case several parts. I once researched a book so thoroughly in advance (The Daughters of the House) that I didn't know where to begin and nearly abandoned it."
(See also **Chapter 19**)
www.nicolathorne.com

DETERMINATION

Writing any kind of fiction and completing the project requires determination. You need the desire to keep going until you've finished. Writing for fun and just to amuse yourself is great if that is what satisfies you, but if you want to graduate to becoming a professional writer then you will need to be determined to make time to write, and even to turn down invitations that you'd love to accept, because you have a deadline to meet. You need the marathon runner's determination to cross the finish line whatever happens to you along the course. All the professional writers that I have ever met or interviewed, share the marathon runner's determination to finish what they've started, and to finish it by the deadline given to them by their publishers.

ACTIVITIES:

4.1 Insight

Objective   To provide you with an insight into which ingredients are the ones that make memorable fiction of any genre.

- To enable you to isolate if it is the plot or the character, which you as an individual are attracted to.
- To find out what other readers think are the most important ingredients in making fiction memorable, and the kind of read that they would recommend to their friends

Your tasks   **A**   Which is your own personal favourite story and why? It doesn't have to be a historical novel. It can even be a children's story or a fairy story.

> **Model answer**
>
> I love the story of Cinderella, because it is the best rags to riches story and has great characters especially the ugly sisters.

Your answer:

B   Ask at least three fiction readers who you know what is the 'best' story (novel or short story) that they've ever read and what happened? It doesn't have to be historical fiction. It can even be a children's story. Note down their replies and copy them into the box below e.g. "I love x, because there is something about them that reminds me of me. They get into scrapes and never have enough money."

> **Readers' Comments**

4.2 Imagination and Prediction

Objective   To give you practice in using your imagination and the ability to predict actions and consequences.

Your tasks   **A** Spend as long as you feel comfortable in a book shop or a café, and observe the customers. As soon as you see a customer entering the shop or café try to predict what they are going to buy or order. You may want to try this experiment over several days, but aim to predict the actions of at least ten customers.

You may, or may not have predicted accurately what the customer was going to buy. What you may have noticed is that you automatically stereotyped a person by their physical appearance, and matched them to what you personally assumed they might purchase. We all make these assumptions, but the job of a writer is to use these assumptions in a creative way, to surprise and delight their readers.

B Focus on one of the customers that you observed and the object that they bought and use your imagination to predict what they are going to do with their purchase, or how it affected their mood, and write down your imaginative predictions in fewer than 200 words.

> **Model answer**
>
> **Purchase in a book shop:** *Horse & Pony* magazine and a book *Unsolved Murders*
>
> A woman wearing wellington boots, smelling of the farmyard and wearing a fleece bought a copy of *Horse &Pony* magazine and a book on *Unsolved Murders*. Her great love is her horses, but her hatred of her husband had grown, as he drank and gambled away all the money that she made as a horse breeder. She'd decided it was about time she got rid of him and bought *Unsolved Murders* to pick up a few ideas from the experts.

> **Purchase in a café**: Hot chocolate with whipped cream and marshmallows
>
> A young man with large sad eyes and dressed in a rumpled suit, buys a hot chocolate with whipped cream and marshmallows. He is hoping that he will cheer himself up, and that the sweet taste and comforting aroma will work its magic, and bring back memories of carefree childhood outings with his parents. Losing his job because of his boss's incompetence, and having his girlfriend dump him, both before his lunch break, was just too much.

You can write your description and predictions in your notebook

C   Take one of the scenes that you've just written and transform it by setting the same scene in the past. Don't forget you can change the purchases to suit the period, and you might like to add in a few more details. Try to keep your description below 200 words.

Please read the example below carefully. The description has been altered, but also the tense that has been used has been changed. The description is no longer written using the present tense, but it has been written using the past tense. Write your description using the past tense:

> A young man with large sad eyes and dressed in a rumpled suit ordered a cup of hot sweet tea from the waitress. He would have liked to order a bun as well, but he'd just lost the girl he loved and his job in one morning. Tea and buns always reminded him of carefree childhood outings with his parents, but now he was alone and jobless. He wanted to blame his boss for losing his work as a clerk, but it wasn't his fault. It was 1931 and no one was in safe employment anymore. Industry had ground to a halt and everyone was feeling the pinch. Emigrating to America wasn't even an option as it was even worse over there, from what the newspapers said.

Write your description in your notebook

Novel or short story?

If you ask your friends what they think the difference is between a short story and a novel, the most common answer is that a novel is much longer, which is absolutely right. A short story can be anything from a piece of 'flash fiction', which could be as few as 30 words or even less, to over 5,000. A novella, is longer than a short story, but shorter in length than a novel. Novella is an Italian word which means 'story,' and the form became popular in early Renaissance Italy and France. A novella is sometimes referred to as a 'novelette (or novelet)' and can range from c.7, 500 to as high as 70,000 words, depending on the publishers' definition. According to some publishers a novelette is shorter than a novel, and to complicate matters even further a novel can be anything above 40,000 words. The difference between a short story, novella and novel is however not just a matter of the number of words that you write, but it is a completely different form of fiction writing. It is a form of fiction writing that is currently appreciated and championed in the USA far more than in the UK. Many leading magazines such as the New Yorker, publish short stories (**www.newyorker.com**).

Historically, publishing popular short fiction was part of the apprenticeship of experimenting and mastering the craft of short story writing. First published in 1891, *The Strand Magazine* was a monthly magazine composed of fictional stories and factual articles. It was founded by George Newnes and ceased publication in 1950. There were over seven hundred issues published, many of which contained the original work of some of fiction's best known names such as Arthur Conan Doyle, Agatha Christie, H.G. Wells, Rudyard Kipling, Leo Tolstoy and Georges Simenon.

In his 1924 autobiography, *Memories and Adventures*, Conan Doyle explained that he had written the Holmes short stories with a view towards establishing himself in *The Strand Magazine*: "A number of monthly magazines were coming out at that time, notable among which was the Strand, under the very capable editorship of Greenhough Smith. Considering these various journals with their disconnected stories it had struck me that a single character running through a series, if it only engaged the attention of the reader, would bind that reader to that particular magazine ... Looking around for my central character, I felt that Sherlock Holmes, who I had already handled in two little books, would easily lend himself to a succession of short stories".

The good news is that in December 1988 The Strand Magazine was re-born in the tradition of the original Strand Magazine, and now features a wide selection of stories "from cozy whodunits to hard-boiled detective stories, suspenseful thrillers to humorous mysteries, set in a variety of places from Victorian England, turn of the century Prague, to modern day England, and written by the leading authors of our day, including H.R.F. Keating, Michael Bond, Peter Lovesey, Catherine Aird, and Bill Pronzini." (**www.strandmag.com**)

How are short stories and novels different?

A short story:

- Has fewer characters than a novel, usually just one main character and one or two secondary characters;
- Depending on the word count of your short story you will most probably only have one main plot and possibly a sub-plot, which may reveal itself as a twist or double twist;
- A change should occur within the framework of the story for your character. This does not have to be a major change, but there needs to be a resolution of the problems or conflict that your main character is facing at the outset of your story;
- It is shorter and therefore there is less room for description, and every detail has to count. Anton Pavlovich Chekhov (1860-1904). Chekhov who was a Russian master of the art of short story writing is credited with having have said that if you mention a 'blue shoe' in a short story then that shoe has to be important. It has to have significance in the story line and to the plot. This is one of the fundamental differences. In a novel you can afford to lavish words on descriptions and details, which add flavour and texture to the historical period they are writing about. In a short story the details often have to be pared down to the bare bones. The information that you provide with the details that you include, should enable the reader to fill in the gaps using their own imagination;
- Short stories are compact and often require the writer to use shorter sentences in which every word counts. This is particularly true with dialogue. The dialogue that you incorporate has to carry the story forward, or throw enlightenment on your character's dilemma. You haven't got enough space for polite exchanges;
- You need to plan your short story to fit within a word count framework, or be willing to edit it down after you've finished, to the required number of words.

Andrew F. Gulli

"It's sad to say, but in this day and age only a handful of writers can make a living solely on writing short fiction; that by no means indicates that the short story genre is dead or suffering. Far from it, when I began my job as editor of the Strand, the short story market was in deep trouble; it had fallen out of vogue with authors to the point where even if paid well, bestselling authors were never interested in contributing short fiction to literary journals. Today, authors look at short stories as a skill and exercise to hone the craft of writing, plot, dialogue, and word crafting and the genre is enjoying somewhat of a new lease on life.

My advice has always been for writers to read more than they write. To read the great short story masters, Chekhov, Hemingway, Roald Dahl, Stanley Ellin, Patricia Highsmith, and Daphne du Maurier. I would dissect the short stories of these writers in detail, analyzing their work almost as if you're a spy taking a mental image of a building for your handlers—but with the written word you have the luxury to take your time. See how Hemingway used dialogue to forward his plots, how Ellin was a master of sleight of hand with his twisting plots, how du Maurier's psychological insight made her works gripping. I'm not saying you should copy their styles. I'm often asked by young writers how they can develop their own style and I might say it's rather difficult if you're bogged down in a workshop and handed the same exercise book. The key to developing a unique style is to read like crazy and at first you'll see that you're borrowing too much from a favorite writer, then you'll pause and you'll spend the longest time in that no-man's land where you have no style, and then the greatest thing will happen, without knowing it, you'll develop your unique mark, your work will bear your signature, and that my friends is one of the greatest joys of writing."

Andrew F. Gulli is the Managing Editor of *The Strand Magazine*:
The Strand Magazine, P.O. Box 1418,Birmingham, MI 48012, USA
www.strandmag.com

A novel:

- The chance to write more intricate and complex plots and character conflicts;
- The freedom to use more descriptions and more detail. You can also develop your story over longer time spans without making your plot too contrived;
- The opportunity to introduce a lot more characters and to interweave their stories;
- More cliff hangers are needed to keep the reader's interest;
- You can use more complex and longer sentences more often, as you are not constrained by a word count;
- You can incorporate clues and hints, which enable you to pave the way for a series of novels about one character or a saga about a family;
- You have to invest a lot more time in writing a novel than a short story. If you lead a very hectic life you might find it easier to try writing a few short stories before embarking on a novel, which may take you years to complete. However, if you do this do remember that short stories are a different genre of writing than novels. They are not just a way of limbering up your creative imagination and writing skills before you tackle a novel, but they can be, because they enable you to practise on a smaller canvas the skill of structuring a story. A short story at its best is like a vibrant miniature painting and not like a wall-sized landscape painting.

ACTIVITY

4.3 Write about an artefact you could use as a plot device

Objective

To write about a historical object (artefact) which you might be able to use in a short story or a novel, and which could play a key role in the plot. The item that you pick should be one that you think might influence the destiny of your character or characters.

Model

Recently in a series of writing workshops, which I ran in Devon for aspiring writers entitled *Writing for Publication*, the group picked the object 'a golden torc'[*]. This object they decided could either have good or evil properties, depending on the intent of the wearer. Each member of the group picked a different historical period to write about. They had a limit of 1,500 words and had to leave the torc somewhere on Dartmoor where the next storyteller's character could discover it.

The short stories when completed were then published in the *West Devon Diary* during 2009 as a series of short stories linked by an object (see **www.tavistock-today.co.uk/ tn/specialpubsnew.cfm**). Short stories and novellas linked together are an effective way of combining stories as The Medieval Murderers have demonstrated in their successful series, which includes *Tainted Relic*, *House of Shadows* and *The Last Prophecies* and the *Sacred Stone*. (see **www.michaeljecks.co.uk** and **www.bernardknight.homestead.com**).

Your task

Find an item to write about. It could be a painting, a book, a dress, a trinket box, a walking stick. You might discover it in a museum, an antiques and collectors fair, or in your own loft. While moving house on one occasion, I discovered an empty matchbox in the loft, which dated from the First World War period, and

---

[*] **Torc**, also spelt 'torq' or 'torque': a type of a necklace that is open-ended at the front. It was often made in twisted metal and is associated with the Early Iron Age and in particular with the Scythian and Celtic civilizations. Herodotus mentions the Scythians (or Scyth) in the 8th century BC. They were an ancient Iranian nomadic people who inhabited Scythia (the Pontic-Caspian steppe).

immediately started to build a story around this ordinary discarded item that had once played a part in someone's real life story.

Once you've selected an item, write down where you found it and then in less than 200 words jot down how you think it could be used as part of a story e.g.

Place: Spotted in an Antique shop in Bath

Object: An ornate Georgian silver candlestick – given as a wedding gift, but stolen by the heroine who is being forced to marry a wealthy widower when her heart belonged to a British officer who is presumed dead, in the conflict with America. She is going to sell the candlestick with other items she's taken to fund her trip to America to find him, as she is convinced he is alive.

Your answer:

Using the same object write down another two ways in which the object could be given a key role in a story or novel. Do not use more than 200 words for each description.

You can write your ideas below:

N.B. By now you are perhaps becoming fed up with the prescriptive word counts that you have been given for the activities so far. Naturally, you do not 'have to' stick to them. The reason you are being given them is to make you aware that if you would like to be a professional writer you will have to be able to stick to the word counts that you are given. It should also help you to get into the habit of being able to predict how many words you are writing, and how many you will need to write to complete a piece of writing, or a competition entry.

What is the difference between a series and a saga?

+ A series will often feature one main character and possibly one devoted 'side-kick', which means that you can follow them through their fictional life and develop their characters as they grow older and richer in experience. Ellis Peters' *Brother Cadfael Series* consisting of 21 novels about Brother Cadfael and set in the mid-twelfth century, is one popular example of a series of historical novels.

+ A saga is a story that tells the adventures of a family or hero. It is the narrative form that we associate with the Icelandic Viking Sagas of the 12th to 14th centuries such as the *Greenlanders' Saga*, or the *Saga of Eric the Red,* while in recent times Winston Graham's classic *Poldark Saga* set in Cornwall spans the late eighteenth and nineteenth centuries. Nicola Thorne's *Broken Bough Saga* traces one family's climb out of poverty in early twentieth century Dorset, and the American author Elswyth Thane's Williamsburg Chronicles followed the fortunes of two families – the Spragues and the Days – from the American Revolution until the Second World War. Aaron Fletcher, Collen McCullough and Tamar McKinley are examples of authors that have all written sagas set in Australia.

What both a series and a saga require is meticulous planning and a method by which you can easily check details about characters that have appeared in previous novels in the series or saga. Changing the colour of one's character's hair might be part of your plot, but changing the colour of their eyes, or even their name can and does happen, if you aren't able to refer back to your original character outlines and descriptions of settings, particularly the interior of houses.

Julian Stockwin

"Writing one book, let alone a series, seems incredibly daunting to most would-be authors, and I have to confess that when I first thought about the idea I was very sceptical. Now, ten published books later, I look back on this achievement with both pride and amazement – one million words in print!

A series gives a writer a wonderful opportunity to really develop a character and to grow a readership very loyal to the world you write about. But it also poses great challenges: will you run out of steam after the first two or three titles?; have you chosen a subject that publishers/agents/readers will still care about five or

> more years down the line?; do you have the mental and physical stamina to take on such a commitment?
>
> Master the art of back story
>
> A big challenge in writing a series is to produce each book so that a person new to your work can experience a satisfying read, picking up sufficient information of what has gone before to understand the flow and nuances of the text, while a fan of your earlier books is not bored by too much back story."

For further details on series read Julian Stockwin's tips in full in **Chapter 19**
www.julianstockwin.com

Which is the most important ingredient?

History is the ingredient that hallmarks the genre. Historical settings, places and the research that you will do are vital in writing a work of historical fiction, but is it the most important ingredient in writing effective historical fiction? Below Lindsey Davis provides us with an answer.

Lindsey Davis

"Remember you are not writing history, you are writing a novel. This requires you to master plot, characterisation, dialogue, narrative tone and description. Note that nowhere in my list do the words 'research' or 'history' appear!"

Current novels *Rebels and Traitors* (Century/Arrow)and *Nemesis.
Falco: The Official Companion* was published in June 2010 (Century)
www.lindseydavis.co.uk

Nicola Thorne

"Choose a period that you feel at home in. For instance I would never attempt to write about pre-history, Greeks and Romans, the Dark Ages or the Renaissance even though this latter in particular is a period I love from the point of view of art. My earliest period is the 18th Century (*The Enchantress Saga - Bonnie Prince Charlie*) and I feel comfortable from then on. I also like mid to late 19th Century and the early years of the 20th (*The Askham Chronicles, The People of this Parish* and the *Broken Bough* sagas)."

www.nicolathorne.com

Chapter 5 – Theme, Plot and Synopsis

Before embarking on writing your plot, sometimes referred to as 'story-line' and your synopsis (a condensed version of your plot which consists of an outline of your story, main characters etc.) it may be useful to make certain that you have a clear definition of what these terms mean to an agent or an editor.

Often aspiring and professional writers have an 'idea' for a story or novel that won't go way. It may be a character that niggles them into action. Some authors prefer just to 'start writing' and see where it takes them, but others need a framework, and pre-planning your novel (see **Chapter 3**) may save you time and anxiety later.

Which is which?

Theme	This is often defined as a recurrent idea in a story, for example 'revenge'
Narrative	A written or spoken account of a series of events in the order in which they happen. It is also used to mean the part of a story that describes events and action as opposed to the dialogue (a conversation between two or more people).
Outline	The main features leaving out the details, but demonstrating the structure, progression and arrangement.
Plot	The story or scheme of events that run though your novel or work of short fiction.
Scene	This isn't just where an event takes place, but it is a sub-division of a continuous narrative, which focuses on an event or action in which something happens to move your plot forward.
Story-line (storyline)	The main plot of your story, or the line along which the plot is to develop.
Synopsis	A condensed version of your story.

Theme

Certain themes occur more frequently than others, they are often related to a quest of some kind such as overcoming hardship or adversity. The themes often also act as motivation for your characters such as love, jealousy, revenge, greed, envy. Themes act as 'moral' messages just like the ones that are found in children's fairy stories. For example Hansel and Gretel teaches us about overcoming adversity and how careful planning can result in a successful outcome. Novels and short stories may have more than one message or theme. A popular theme for a sub-plot is love in some form e.g. for family or friends. Shakespeare was a master at incorporating these 'universal' messages into his plays, and should you ever need inspiration for a theme Shakespeare's plays make a great starting point, even if you only read summarised versions of the plots. Stories such as those told by the Persian Queen Scheherazadea (Scheherazade) in *One Thousand and One Nights*, which was first published in English in 1706 are equally inspiring.* However, it is useful to remember when deciding on a central theme that often the simpler the theme the wider the appeal, for instance themes such as the battle between 'good' and 'evil', which are at the core of many riveting reads.

---

* These stories are of significance as well for the aspiring writer, because they are one of the earliest examples of the use of a 'framing device'. This enables the writer to write a story within a story. This means for example that an event, setting, action, or place is used to both open and close a story.

ACTIVITY

5.1 Identifying themes

Objective   To practise identifying themes and messages, which you may wish to use when writing your own stories.

Your task
- To select three historical novels written about any past time and to match the themes in them to the list of themes given below.
- To add any other themes or messages that you come across to the list.

List of themes

Ambition, madness, loyalty, deception, revenge, all is not what it appears to be, love, temptation, guilt, power, fate/destiny, heroism, hope, coming of age, death, loss, friendship, patriotism ...

Write any other themes that you discover below:

Write the names of the novels you've selected and the main and sub-themes that you've identified below:

Plot

A plot is constructed from significant events in a story. These events must have important consequences for your characters. They result in change, cause things to alter and are vital to the development of your story.

These events do not have to be of 'earthquake proportions'. You might use a major event such as the eruption of a volcano and the destruction of Pompeii as a catalyst, the consequences of the event acting as a pivot from which your story-line or plot can move forwards.

You can use the actions of your characters expressed through what they think, feel, say or do to move your plot forward. Even everyday happenings can have major repercussions and play a decisive part in your plot.

ACTIVITES

5.2 Cause and Effect

Objective   To show how ordinary, everyday events can lead to creating exciting and intriguing plots.

Your task   Transform what might appear to be an ordinary, or even a trivial happening into a significant event that you could use as a starting point for a chain of events to create a plot from. Read the example below and then describe what effects will be caused on the world around her (friends and family) by this 'trivial' event and how you might be able to transform this incident into a starting point as a plot for a novel or a short story.

> **Example: The Fan**
>
> **Background:** Japanese fans originated in Kyoto in c. 670 AD. They were made from paper and bamboo. In the Middle Ages they were used to write love poems on, which were given as tokens of love and affection.
>
> **Everyday event:** A lady during the medieval period (any nationality) loses a fan that has been given to her with a love poem written on it.

Your plot:

5.3 The role of small events that have altered history

Objective   To understand the value of using small, but significant incidents and events in providing a basis for a plot.

Your task   Tiny incidents, coincidences and discoveries have changed history. Your task is to make a list of five such events.

Example: Discovering the source of cholera

Dr John Snow (1813-1856) made significant progress in the field of anaesthesia, but the 'small' incident with which his name is most associated is the 1854 Broad Street (now Broadwick Street), Soho, London outbreak of cholera. Until then it had been assumed that it had been spread by 'bad air', but having investigated the water supply in the area and with the help of Reverend Henry Whitehead, he was able to pinpoint the source of the outbreak to a pump in Broad Street. By locating the source of the outbreak he was able to establish a link between cholera and water.

Write your examples below:

5.4 The first sparks

Objective   To create three different story-lines from three sources.

Your task   To find ideas from different sources that you could base a story-line on. Your plots or story-lines might be sparked off by:

* Research that you've carried out into a particular period, movement or person;
* Reading an article, novel, letter, old newspaper cutting, theatre programme, wedding invitation or a diary extract;
* Research into family history;
* Visiting a place e.g. a city, ancient site, cemetery, house, museum, battlefield, derelict walled garden etc. ;
* Overhearing a story or an anecdote that someone else tells;
* A myth or a legend;
* A specialist course or a talk that you go on that teaches you about the history of the subject e.g. carpentry, pottery etc.;
* Watching a film or documentary or listening to a radio programme;
* An artefact such as an old farming tool, an evening bag, a battered deck of cards, an ancient instrument like a crump horn or an old coin
* A piece of music, play etc.;
* A theme or recurrent problem that keeps appearing in the news that would have been equally as important in the past e.g. greed, water shortages and drought;
* An old photograph, painting, etching, tapestry, or piece of embroidery;
* An article of clothing e.g. a child's shoe
* An idea just appearing in your mind that won't leave you alone until you weave it into a story.

Collect your ideas and write them down. They don't have to come from the period that you are writing about. An example of an historical novel that was sparked off by an historical event is *Lorna Doone: A Romance of Exmoor* by Richard Doddridge Blackmore which was first published in 1869. Set in the 17th century mainly on Exmoor it was based on a real event that took place in Chagford on the edge of Dartmoor. In 1641 Mary Whiddon had just been married and was leaving the church of St. Michael when she was killed. Blackmore just took a real event and transferred it to a different setting and gave it a happy ending, which the real event tragically didn't have.

5.5 From inspiration to plot and sub-plot

Objective To transform 'the first spark' into a main and sub-plot.

Your tasks (To be completed in your note book, or computer file using no more than **100 words**)

A Pick one of the following sources to finds a 'spark of inspiration' that you can use as the basis to write a synopsis for a short story or novel.

Sources:

- An event in the local history of the place that you live in
- An old photograph, picture or engraving of an 'event' e.g. a horse race, a battle, a fair etc.

Model

Source of inspiration for your plot: An article in a newspaper

Theme: Overcoming adversity

Draft synopsis of a linear (no sub-plots) story:

Maggie is left to look after John and Ann while her father goes to a family funeral. Maggie's mother died when she was 14. Since then she's been responsible for her brother and sister. Cholera breaks out in the street that they live in. Maggie is assured that even though her neighbours are already ill she needn't worry, as her home will be fumigated. Her instincts tell her to leave the village. She walks ten miles to the mine where her father works and camps there. Returning after ten days she discovers that most of their neighbours died.

(98 words)

Your turn

Source of inspiration for your plot:

Theme:

Synopsis of a linear (no sub-plots) story:

B   Add a sub-plot

Model

Theme: Greed and envy

Draft synopsis of your sub-plot story:

Maggie's father George didn't go to a family funeral, but had left the family to marry a well-off widow, the landlady of a public house who lived in a nearby village. He was aware of the epidemic, but had hoped that his whole family would be wiped out by the time he brought his new wife back to meet them, as he'd always seen them as a burden and an obstacle that prevented him from having fun and enjoying life to the full. He'd only married his children's mother because he'd been forced to by combined pressure from the local vicar and the mine manager.

(100 words)

Your turn

Using the story line above create a sub-plot of no more than 100 words

5.6 To add in a twist and double twist

(see **Chapter 20** for examples)

Objective   To add in a twist to the plot.

Your task   Using the synopsis that you've created above add in a twist.

Model

Blanche, George's new wife is delighted to become the adoptive mother of Maggie, John and Ann and insists that they all move into her popular public house, but soon discovers that George is a bully and an alcoholic. George disappears one night shortly after, and is found near the dock area of the town with his throat slit and the money he was delivering to an associate of Blanche's missing.

Blanche tries to comfort the children by buying them new clothes and treats. They grow to love her and to see her as their saviour.

(92 words)

Your turn to write a twist to the plot that you started above in no more than 100 words.

The double twist:

Blanche organises an auction. The children are healthy, pretty and pliant. She is looking forward to selling them to the highest bidder and getting them out of the way, or as she will tell her customers "sending the sweethearts to the seaside for the benefit of their health".

(48 words)

Now try to write a double twist for the plot that you wrote above in no more than 100 words.

5.7 Outlines

Objective   To create a method that you are comfortable with to enable you to keep track of the progress of your plot.

Your task   'Scene by scene', 'problem by problem', 'action by action' write down the key action etc. that will take place in each 'scene' or 'chapter' of the novel you imagine that you'd like to write. Use bullet point style notes, or even a mind map style breakdown. Then transform each of these into a brief (c.200-300 word) outline of the content of each chapter of your novel, or the whole of your short story. You can use this when writing a synopsis of your novel or story.

Synopsis (and Flash Fiction)

The word 'synopsis' may open the floodgates to negative memories associated with schools and exams. Don't let these echoes of the past overwhelm you. Think instead that you are writing a 'story-line profile' and that this profile is a vital ingredient in helping you to achieve your writing ambitions. If that doesn't help you then try to imagine that you are writing a review of your story and have to provide the readers with an outline of the content. Short stories in general do not require a synopsis, but you may be asked to provide a few lines about the content, setting etc. The next activity is aimed at those who would like to write a novel, or longer piece of fiction.

ACTIVITY

5.8 Short, but sweet

Your synopsis should be as exciting and engaging as your novel for the reader. It is like a malt whisky that has been distilled to bring out its flavour. You are aiming at distilling the essence of your plot into a few captivating sentences. It is the 'bait' to catch an agent or a publisher.

Objective   To write a working synopsis.

Your tasks   **A**   Read two recent 'best selling' historical novels.

B   Make a synopsis of each chapter (no more than 200 words for each chapter). Then condense these into a 500 word summary of the whole novel.

Tip: Use the blurb at the back of the novel to keep you on track with writing your summary.

C   Trawl the internet for summaries, reviews and press releases of your chosen novels and compare what you've written with what you've discovered. Then add in any key points that you've missed to tighten up your summaries.

D   Repeat the process of writing chapter summaries and a novel synopsis for the novel that you'd like to write. Do remember that even if you don't want to give away the ending of your story you must do this when writing a summary or synopsis to submit to a prospective agent or publisher. They need to know the end, whereas if you are writing a blurb to go with your novel, or a press release, you don't have to give away the ending. The aim of a press release is to inform bookshops, newspapers, the media etc, about the existence of your forthcoming novel and how exciting it is. A blurb, which is found on the back of your novel, is aimed at attracting a reader to buy your novel in a bookshop etc. even if they've never heard of you as an author before, and so it acts as a taster. You shouldn't give away too much about your plot, but just a few captivating details.

5.9 Flash Fiction

Flash fiction stories are mini short stories. They are very much in vogue at the moment and by scanning the web you should be able to find a range of them on different themes and for varying lengths. Flash fiction can be as short as 10 words and up to 250, but the majority are somewhere between 50 and 100 words. The longer flash fiction may involve twists, and double or even triple twists. Flash fiction might be defined as 'compacted stories' and therefore are similar to a story synopsis that you may have written for a longer story or a novel. They are also an excellent way of using up all those story ideas for plots that you don't want to turn into a novel.

Objective   To write a flash fiction story in fewer than 30 words, which is based on one of the plots that you've already outlined above, or if you prefer a different idea or theme.

Model
Blanche trafficked in children, but Maggie wasn't any ordinary cargo. One laudanum laced bowl of soup, and Blanche was on her way to a souk.

Your task   Below write a flash fiction historical story in no more than 30 words.

Tips

1. **The Gamble –** Remember that your reader is gambling when they embark on reading your novel, because they are investing their time and money and in return they are hoping to gain something from your story such as entertainment, escapism and a sense of satisfaction. Your role as a writer is to make certain that their gamble pays off, by ensuring that they gain at least 'something' that they want from your story.

   Your main characters will need to 'solve' or 'overcome' a series of problems or resolve a challenge such as how to stay alive, survive, protect their family or win a battle for their particular cause. They will also have to resolve their own internal battles with their own personality such as generosity over miserliness, courage over fear, tolerance over intolerance love over hate etc.

2. Above all it is important to remember the plot you create must take your reader on a journey. It may not be a comfortable one, but it has to be satisfying and grip your readers' attention to the very last sentence.

Lillian Harry

"The trick is to determine your own theme and concentrate on that. Once you have that clear, you can also look at other areas, which will be useful for the wider picture, but don't allow yourself to be sidetracked. Anything that is particularly interesting but not relevant may well be used in a future project, but don't allow it to muddy the waters of the current one."

www.lillianharry.co.uk

Chapter 6 – Settings

Settings can be as important as characters and period, in capturing the imagination of your reader. Places that people can identify with because they live there, have visited them or which are well-known to them through films, books or other sources are like friends. Settings could be defined as where the action in your narrative takes place. In a short story this might be only one place, or even a room in a house, but in a novel there may be many different scenes set in different locations.

The settings for these scenes if they are specific, have to be as accurate as possible. If they aren't then someone will pick you up on your inaccuracies. You can avoid this by always checking with all the visual and historical sources available to you, and consulting with local history societies and historians, and of course always acknowledging them for their help.

Landscapes change, buildings change and even if a place is marked on an early map the position of the dwellings can move. A Devon longhouse can be transformed into a medieval farmhouse and then be modernized during the Victorian period. The 'rule of thumb' that you should always apply is never assume that the place you are writing about is the same as it was. An example is the Tamar Valley (**www.tamarvalley.org.uk**) on the border between Devon and Cornwall in England. Today it looks at first glance as if it has always been lush, green and rural, until your eye is caught by the remains of chimney stacks, Kit Hill chimney stack built in 1858 being the most eye-catching. The chimney replaced a windmill that had stood there in the 1830s and was used for steam engines which pumped water out of the mine. Silver Mining began in the Tamar Valley in the medieval period to be replaced by mining for tin, copper and arsenic, which reached 'boom' proportions by the mid-19th century. After the decline of mining, a radical transformation took place. The valley was then transformed into a rich market gardening area, famed for its daffodils and strawberries. Traces of the former market gardens are still visible, but nature is reclaiming them. Changes in the landscape and in cities can be found world-wide. The significance for the writer is that you must always question what you can see or what you read about a particular location.

Physical setting: the role of places and landscape in historical fiction writing by Andrew Thompson

In his introduction to Malory's *Morte d'Arthur*, published in 1485 the printer William Caxton addressed readers who were sceptical about King Arthur's historical existence. Caxton listed 'divers places of England [where] many remembrances be yet of him', including Winchester's Great Hall where the round table was displayed and Glastonbury Abbey where the king was buried, before confidently asserting: 'all these things considered there can be no man reasonably gainsay but there was a king of this land named Arthur.' The logic of Caxton's argument, that the existence of places claiming Arthurian heritage proved the monarch's existence, continues to be used by many of those who argue that Arthur was a real historical figure. It is a powerful example of the way in which places assume identities and become imbued with meanings and how settings lend authenticity to stories, irrespective of whether or not we believe them to be true.

This chapter differs from the others in this book in that it is not written by a practitioner of historical fiction but by someone with expertise in landscape history and archaeology who also enjoys reading historical fiction. It is more theoretical than many other sections of this book. But it has the very practical aim of helping and encouraging writers to understand and think about how they identify, research and describe the settings for their stories.

What follows reflects two areas of interest. One is a fascination with how places are perceived and represented in art, literature (including historical fiction) and wider social and cultural discourses. Here the aim is to explore different ways in which writers of historical fiction describe the settings and create a sense of the places in which their stories are located. The second area to be addressed is the relationship between historical fiction, history/archaeology and landscapes/places. Writers of historical fiction are constantly being exhorted to produce work which is historically accurate and 'true to the period'. Yet among historians and archaeologists there has never been a consensus about what constitutes 'the truth' since conflicting interpretations of the same event or place have been influenced by competing ideologies and agendas. In the past it was felt that, having allowed for such biases, it was possible to arrive at some approximation of the objective truth. But in the last few decades, under the influence of postmodernism, many historians have abandoned the search for unifying 'truthful' narratives and focus instead on analysing or deconstructing contemporaries' perspectives or discourses of the period being studied. For example, recent books on King Arthur by professional historians deny he existed and concentrate on how he has been variously represented as Celtic Christian war leader, symbol of medieval chivalry and icon of English, Welsh or Cornish national identity in changing cultural, political social contexts since the early middle ages (1). This trend is also evident in landscape history and archaeology. Recent studies of Stonehenge explore how the monument has been continuously reworked and reinterpreted by Neolithic and Bronze Age peoples, the Romans, medieval writers who ascribed its origins to Merlin and giants, assorted druid and new age groups, the tourist industry, English Heritage and the National Trust.

Critics often deride historical fiction for not being 'real' history. They ignore the fact that it does not claim to be. There may, however, be a case for arguing that historical fiction would be 'more historical' if it sometimes reflected a greater awareness of recent trends in history and archaeology. Moreover, recent approaches to history and archaeology often have an imaginative flair and creativity which can sometimes narrow the gap between fiction and non-fiction and could provide inspiration for fiction writers.

Identifying and researching the setting

Setting in historical fiction is, of course, both temporal and spatial. Other contributors to this book have stressed the importance of producing a story which is appropriate to the particular historical period and based on thorough research. The most believable historical fiction, whether short story or novel, occurring in one location as small as a cottage or ranging across a continent, is created when similar care has been devoted to establishing physical setting(s) suitable for the action and the period.

There are several reasons why a particular setting might be chosen:

- A storyline might relate to or be suggested by a specific place where documented events are known to have occurred. For example Peter Tremayne's Sister Fidelma novel *Absolution by Murder* takes place during the Synod of Whitby.
- A place may be especially appropriate for exploring a chosen theme. Frank Tallis's crime novels about the young psychologist Max Liebermann have been described as 'almost like taking a university refresher course' on the cultural and scientific world of Vienna at the turn of the 20th century (2). Places with which the author is familiar might suggest a story or at least provide a context. Many successful writers attest to being inspired by places they have visited, or by where they live.

- In some novels, such as Michener's epic *Poland* or Rutherford's *Sarum*, the evolution of the country or place is central to the plot, impacting on the protagonists who, in turn, play their parts in transforming the places in which they live.

The description of places needs to be as accurate for the period chosen as any other element of historical fiction writing. For places, as with other things which could change within the course of a decade, such as clothing fashion, choosing a very precise historical period provides both constraints and opportunities to make the story more believable. Although there is considerable scope for imaginative latitude, especially for lesser known places and earlier periods, thorough research is essential to avoid errors which can damage the story's credibility.

Historical sources are covered in a separate chapter but it should be noted that some are particularly relevant to establishing an authentic sense of place. For early periods accessible accounts of archaeological research, rather than highly technical reports, are now increasingly available. Generalised stories about primitive prehistoric barbarians, 'Celts' living in vaguely described huts, or hillforts or medieval monasteries with no reference to architecture, dates or orders should be avoided. There is a wealth of archaeological material available to inspire detailed and plausible fiction about prehistory and the middle ages. For later periods maps, pictures and photographs are particularly important for filling in detail and avoiding errors as they document how the layout of towns and villages, roads and railways, street names and doors and windows on individual buildings changed. Care is needed, however, particularly with pictures. The works of 18th and 19th century artists influenced by fashions such as landscape painting were not aiming to produce photographic accuracy but a picturesque or perfected representation of what they saw.

Bernard Knight's Exeter and Devon, Ellis Peters' Shrewsbury and Candace Robb's York are just three examples of how successfully careful attention to detail develops a sense of medieval place. As well as detailed description, all three help the reader by including maps. This is a particularly useful tool when characters' whereabouts or journeys are important to the plot, as they frequently are in the Brother Cadfael series. Indeed, the novels were so successful in creating a sense of place that 'Cadfael Country' has become a brand used by Shropshire Tourism.

In addition to research, the most effective depictions of places are usually based on firsthand knowledge and experience of them. This may be helpful for individual buildings but is especially important for representing townscapes and landscapes through which characters move.

Exploring a place on foot or even by car should, although it often does not, provide an antidote to a still widespread popular contagion, which unfortunately is still often spread through fiction: the idea that large parts of the English countryside and even some towns and villages are 'timeless'. This imaginative construct owes much to 19th century writers who sought to establish rural idylls like the Cotswolds and attendant virtues such as deference and social stability as key components in English national identity or who like Thomas Hardy feared the impact of urbanisation and social change on an idealised and unchanging Wessex. This misconception or deliberate creation of the myth of the unchanging countryside has proved remarkably durable.

Yet several generations of landscape historians and archaeologists have established that the components of the English countryside such as lanes and trackways, field boundaries and hedgerows, parish churches, the shape and size of villages and the regional variations across the country are the products of centuries of human activity stretching back to prehistory. The landscape is a palimpsest[*] on which each historical period has left its mark, obliterating some of what existed before but also often preserving and incorporating some of it. Richard Muir's *The New Reading the Landscape* is an excellent introduction to this way of approaching a wide variety of landscapes. The way parts of Stonehenge were reconstructed by the Romans or Bronze Age and Roman territorial banks and ditches were incorporated into Saxon estate and later medieval parish boundaries which still survive indicate that our ancestors knew they were not living in a timeless environment. Good historical fiction reflects this as, for example, when the outlaws in Bernard Knight's *The Noble Outlaw* know their shelter at Bronze Age Grimspound on Dartmoor is centuries old. Similarly accurate descriptions of Georgian houses should reflect the fact that in many parts of the country newly fashionable classical stone facades were simply added to the front of medieval timber framed structures.

If the landscape, places and even individual buildings are seen as palimpsests with their own histories they can be presented as the background or context within which peoples' lives unfold. This is how they are usually represented in historical fiction and how they were approached by historians and archaeologists. In the last two decades, however, there has been an increasing appreciation that landscapes communicate and determine what people think as well as influence or reflect what their

---

[*] **Palimpsest**: a manuscript page on which successive texts have been written. The oldest texts were erased to make room for new ones. The origin of the word is Greek and meant 'to scrape clean and then re-use'

work. Muir's book has chapter titles such as 'landscapes of belief', which includes megalithic monuments, holy wells and monasteries, and 'status, power and authority' which covers parklands and rabbit warrens. In the 17th and 18th century garden design and the architecture of stately homes transmitted wealthy landowners' territorial claims, attitudes towards natural order and political affiliations.

Representations of landscape in Arthurian fiction

The impact that different approaches to place and landscape can have on historical fiction can be demonstrated by looking at how one genre, Arthurian fiction, has changed in the last sixty years. Arthurian literature also provides a good example of the way in which fiction, scholarship and place can be interconnected. For Arthur has been claimed for particular places by Celtic patriots, English nationalists, British imperialists and local champions from folklorists to tourist boards. But, as we have seen, place and landscape are not just settings where dramas unfold; they are imaginative constructs which over time acquire histories and meanings. As Simon Schama observes, 'nature and human perception...are...indivisible. Before it can ever be a repose for the senses, landscape is the work of the mind. Its scenery is built up as much from strata of memory, as from layers of rock.(3)' Similarly, some archaeologists refer to cultural landscapes as having biographies (4). From this perspective writers are not simply inspired by places because of the scenery or historical association. They themselves become part of the story and play a vital role in defining places, shaping their identities and 'putting them on the map.'

At Tintagel this process has been literal as well as metaphorical. Tintagel first became associated with Arthurian myth in the 12th century when Geoffrey of Monmouth's *History of the Kings of Britain* introduced many new places and events including the famous story of Arthur's conception. To seduce Igraine Uther is given her husband's appearance by Merlin's magic so he can enter Tintagel which 'is situated upon the sea, and on every side surrounded by it; and there is but one entrance into it, and that through a straight rock, which three men shall be able to defend against the whole power of the kingdom. (5)' In Geoffrey's time the castle had not yet been built. The place name Tintagel, which derives from the Cornish *Din Tagell* meaning the fortress of the narrow entrance, may have helped to preserve folk memories of a post Roman stronghold whose existence was not confirmed until the 20th century. When a medieval castle was built in the early thirteenth century it was probably designed to cement the Earl of Cornwall's association with the Arthurian tradition which Geoffrey had invented or publicised. Mass interest in Tintagel's medieval heritage was stimulated in the Victorian era by Tennyson's *Idylls of the King* when the name applied, as it had always done, only to the castle and not to the neighbouring village of Trevenna. This changed in 1900 when the enterprising inhabitants sought to exploit the economic potential of Arthurian tourism by engaging in what today would be called a rebranding exercise (6).

Since the mid 20th century much Arthurian fiction has been set in the post-Roman 5th and 6th centuries which are still popularly known as the Dark Ages. This period's popularity was inspired initially by major developments in scholarship (7). These included Collingwood and Myres' pre-war classic *Roman Britain and the English* (1936) which asserted that Arthur had been a Romano-British military commander fighting the Saxons, renewed post war interest in early Welsh literature and excavations in the 1960s demonstrating post Roman occupation at Glastonbury Tor and nearby South Cadbury hillfort which tradition had long identified as Camelot. South Cadbury, where a rare and brief alliance between academics and popular historians generated media excitement and culminated in the publication of the hugely influential *The Quest for Arthur's Britain* (1968) edited by Arthur Ashe, revealed substantial 5th century fortifications and what was interpreted as a large feasting hall although not the eagerly anticipated proof of Arthur's existence.

Fiction influenced by these developments includes Rosemary Sutcliff's pioneering *Sword at Sunset* published in 1957, four works by Mary Stewart and Bernard Cornwell's *Warlord Trilogy*. All contain historical notes stating that Arthur probably existed while emphasising that due to the paucity of evidence most of the story, including the central character, is fiction. They are characterised by thoughtful attention to detail based on the authors' conscientious reading of the literary and scholarly sources they select for research. Arthur is portrayed as a Romanised Christian British king or warlord fighting against both pagan Saxon invaders and native rebels across a Britain devastated by war. Cornwell, for example, makes places like Isca Dumnoniorum (Exeter) the backdrop for action: 'Culhwch…led his spears in a swift campaign across the great moor, then south into the wild land on the coast. He ravaged Cadwy's heartland, and then stormed the rebellious Prince in the old Roman stronghold of Isca. The walls had decayed and the veterans of Lugg Vale swarmed over the town's ramparts to hunt the rebels through the streets. Prince Cadwy was caught in the Roman shrine and there dismembered.(8)'

For Mary Stewart 'research is most useful when dealing with place rather than action.(9)' The topographical detail which distinguishes her writing is based on close study of maps and extensive field work employing acute observation. She describes Tintagel castle as 'built on a promontory of rock which is joined to the cliffs of the mainland only by a narrow causeway. To either side of this causeway the cliffs drop away sheer to small bays of rock and shingle tucked in under the cliff. From one of these a path, narrow and precarious, and passable only on a receding tide, leads up the face of the cliff to a small gate let into the roots of the castle walls. This is the postern, the secret entrance to the castle. Inside is a narrow stairway of stone leading up to the private door of the royal apartments.(10)'

Trezise suggests that the 'best place-conscious fictional texts are too subtle and detailed to take the form of a travel brochure' and 'have a special role linking imagination and landscape, deriving energy from both sources.(11)' In *The Crystal Cave* Uther's men enter Tintagel through the postern having climbed the path while the waves 'came roaring up like towers and drenched us with salt fully sixty feet above the beach...we fought our way along, faces in to the soaking, slimy cliff, then a jutting buttress gave shelter, and we were tumbling suddenly on a treacherous slope cushiony with sea pink, and there ahead of us, recessed deep in the rock below the castle wall, and hidden from the rampart above by the sharp overhang, was Tintagel's emergency door.(12)' Stewart sweeps the reader along so effectively it is easy to overlook the fact that the postern she describes does not exist and is more reminiscent of a medieval castle than a 5th century promontory fort. The postern is a dramatic device which bridges the gap between her plot which is based on Geoffrey of Monmouth, Tintagel's visible medieval fortifications and the state of knowledge when *The Crystal Cave* was published in 1970. Since the 1930s archaeologists had believed that Tintagel's post Roman remains were evidence of a Celtic monastery although not all commentators were convinced. It was only in the 1980s and 1990s, after a fire burned off much of the topsoil on the headland to reveal an extensive settlement with over 150 buildings, that further investigation resulted in Tintagel being reinterpreted as a 5th and 6th century secular stronghold(13).

A very different type of fiction has been inspired by Glastonbury which since the 12th century has often been identified as the Isle of Avalon, 'the island of apples.(14)' Glastonbury is, in fact, on a peninsula rising above what are now the reclaimed wetlands of the Somerset Levels. Local archaeology includes Romano-British pagan shrines, possible early Christian chapels and the abbey. The medieval abbots, eager to boost the abbey's income and prestige, energetically promoted Glastonbury's claims to links with both King Arthur and Joseph of Arimathea. Since the late 19th century the area has stimulated various counter cultures that have produced their own alternative histories. In the late 20th century some radical feminists embraced earlier theories that Glastonbury had been a centre of pagan worship suggesting that the Isle of Avalon's geography was shaped like the Great Goddess whose religion had been central to a matriarchal prehistoric society.

Such ideas inspired Marion Zimmer Bradleys' 1980s cult novel *The Mists of Avalon* which reinvents Morgan le Fay, who is conventionally viewed as an evil sorceress, as the heroine Morgaine a priestess of the Mother Goddess who struggles against patriarchal Christianity. The setting is the Summer Country, a land with ill defined contours yet steeped in mysticism which 'lay mostly under water, bog and salt marsh' although the sea was retreating so that 'one day this would all be rich farmland...but not in Avalon [which] now lay eternally surrounded in the mists, hidden from all but the faithful'(15). Rosalind Miles' recent Guinevere trilogy presents the queen as the defender of the Summer Country's ancient religion against the machinations of the Christian church. Instead of topographical detail Miles uses flora and fauna to establish a sense of place: 'In the water-meadows, king-cups and lady's smocks dotted the long grass as Guinevere made her way to the riverside... Along the bank, clusters of willows hung weeping over the water, their long green fingers rippling the slow-moving stream.(16)' Returning to Avalon 'black waters pulsed steadily, bearing them along. Here and there an owl lamented, and she heard a heron cry...The faint air of spring, the pink-and-white scent of apple blossom reached her from far away...Avalon, Avalon, mystic island, home.(17)'

Sarah Zettel's novels rework tales of Sir Gawain and his three brothers in a post Roman context. *Camelot's Sword* is Gareth's story set in Cornwall shortly after the deaths of Tristan and Iseult in a period of political instability. The picture of an impotent King Mark ruling from Tintagel and owing allegiance to the High King based at Camelot is reminiscent of the fragmented kingdoms analysed by recent historians such as Christopher Snyder(18). Zettel's story is rooted in evocative images of the Cornish landscape derived from a powerful imagination and a flying visit to the county. At fictional Cambryn 'paths between the stone and thatch houses with their little courtyards spread out like old roots. They delved into earth and stone to reach the cellars and storage chambers that were hiding places in times of war or great storm. Then they pushed up to met the great timbered hall with its central tower, second storey and roof of pale slate.(19)' The non-fictional Bodmin Moor confronts Gareth's party with 'mile after mile of rolling, open country with ragged, lonely heights and deep bowl-like valleys' where 'in foul weather...A traveller could wander lost in the openness until they died of cold and exhaustion, or the hidden bogs dragged them down.(20)' The power of Zettel's descriptions derives from the fact that for a day and half she experienced Tintagel and the moor on a flying visit to England. Her diary entry for Tintagel vividly records her awestruck excitement: 'it was the land itself, the stone and sea and sky that caught me the most. It was them that made me understand how this place became a land of legend.(21)' This brings us back to the importance of experiencing landscapes first hand before or when writing. But it also in no way detracts from the authenticity of her writing to say that it also demonstrates Schama's point about how our perceptions of place draw on the collective memories and impressions of those who have preceded us there.

Since the 1970s the academics have generally denied Arthur's existence. Now the conventional view that the 5th and 6th centuries were a period of Saxon invasion, chaos and war is being challenged by claims that archaeology, DNA analysis, landscape studies and literary texts point instead to processes of peaceful assimilation and gradual cultural change(22). There has been a growing divide between the academics and the wider population who continue to visit sites like Tintagel and Glastonbury which are, often because of the influence of historical fiction, perceived as Arthurian. Academics are, however, increasingly interested in how perceptions of Arthur and the characters associated with him have evolved and what this reveals about changing cultural, political and social attitudes. From this perspective, irrespective of whether it is ultimately derived from any historical truth, Arthurian and, indeed historical fiction more generally, and those of us who read it contribute to the next chapter in the story of the people and the places it represents.

Notes

1. Higham, Nicholas. King Arthur: Myth-Making and History London: Routledge (2002)
2. Jewish Chronicle online, 3 October 2010, **http://www.thejc.com/arts/ books/murder-most-freudian**
3. Schama, S. *Landscape and* Memory, London: FontanaPress (1995), p.6-7.
4. E.g. Pollard, Josh & Reynolds, Andrew. *Avebury: the biography of a Landscape*, Stroud: Tempus (2002).
5. **http://www.lib.rochester.edu/Camelot/geofhkb.htm** - Giles, J.A. ed. & trans. *Geoffrey of Monmouth's History of the Kings of* Britain.
6. Thomas, Charles. *Tintagel: Arthur and Archaeology*, London: English Heritage/Batsford (1993).
7. For a detailed account of what follows see Higham, Nicholas *King Arthur: Myth-Making and History* London: Routledge (2002), p.1-37; Hutton, Ronald. *Witches, Druids and King Arthur*, London: Hambledon and London (2003) p.39-58.
8. Cornwell, Bernard. *Enemy of* God, London: Michael Joseph (1996), p.64.
9. **http://www.lib.rochester.edu/camelot/intrvws/stewart.htm** - interview with Raymond H. Thompson.

10. Stewart, Mary. *The Hollow* Hills, London: Book Club Associates (1974), p.109.
11. Trezise, Simon. *The West Country as a Literary Invention,* Exeter: University of Exeter Press (2000), p.x.
12. Stewart, Mary. *The Crystal Cave*, London: Coronet (1971) p.435.
13. Thomas, Tintagel.
14. For detailed accounts of Glastonbury's history and archaeology see Rahtz, Philip and Watts, Lorna, *Glastonbury: Myth and Archaeology*, Stroud: Tempus (2003); Hutton, Donald *Witches, Druids and King Arthur* p.59-85.
15. Bradley, Marion Zimmer. *The Mists of Avalon*, London: Michael Joseph (1982), p.112-113.
16. Miles, Rosalind. *The Child of the Holy Grail*, London: Simon & Schuster (2000), p.24-25.
17. ibid, p.437-439.
18. Snyder, Christopher. *An Age of Tyrants: Britain and the Britons, AD400-600*, Pennsylvania: Penn State University Press (1998)
19. Zettel, Sarah. *Camelot's Sword*, London: Harper Collins (2006), p.7.
20. ibid, p.303.
21. **http://www.sff.net/people/sarah-zettel/Site/Cornwall.html**
22. E.g. Pryor, Francis. *Britain AD*: A Quest for Arthur, England and the Anglo-Saxons, London: HarperCollins (2004)

Andrew Thompson has designed and led history and archaeology courses, and study tours for universities and adult education organisations including the Workers' Education Association and Elderhostel.

andrew@landscapes.eclipse.co.uk

ACTIVITIES

6.1 The hidden landscape

Objective Think of a place or landscape you know well and try to write about it from different perspectives

Your task
* In a notebook try to write descriptions based on the following different viewpoints using no more than 500 words for each description;
* A straightforward description of the physical place as a palimpsest;
* As it might be viewed by a local person who has known it all their life ;
* A tourist who has never been there before;
* As different characters in a story might perceive and experience it.

6.2 Exterior landscapes

Objective To find a rural or urban landscape that has visibly changed over the centuries

Your task To pick a rural or urban landscape that you are fascinated by and research its exterior appearance. Then write a description of how it looks today and compare it with how it might have looked according to the sources that you have discovered. You can write your descriptions in your notebooks. If you haven't got any specific sites in mind a few examples have been listed below.

Examples:
* In the 19th century the area around St. Austell (Cornwall) was noted for being a centre for the china clay industry. The spoils from the clay pits created a surreal landscape of giant conical ice cream-shaped white mounds known as the 'Cornish Alps'. These were considered as a fixed feature of the landscape even 10 years ago, but now have almost all been levelled or grassed over.
* In 1967 Coal Harbour was the last whaling station to close in British Columbia see **www.vancouverisland.com** for details.
* Coolgradie (**www.coolgardie.wa.gov.au/ tourism/coolgardie_tourism**) and Kalgoorlie (see **www.kalbould.wa.gov.au)** in Western Australia were

once 19th century 'gold rush' towns, but their appearance has changed as mines closed and new deposits were discovered.

Tips

+ Don't assume the weather followed the same pattern as today and it can dramatically alter the appearance of a landscape e.g. In certain parts of Berkshire (U.K), you will find that the mist can look as if it is a blanket suspended just above ground level. The result is that you can only see your feet and the ground. Whereas in Glastonbury (U.K.) the effect that the mist causes on the ancient pilgrimage site of St. Michael's tower on Glastonbury Tor, which is over 500 ft high makes it look as if it is an island in the middle of a sea of mist.
+ Don't forget that you can use dialogue as a vehicle for providing your reader with descriptions of settings.

6.3 A sense of place

Objective A house (home), flat or building (e.g. and inn, pub, hospital or even a museum) as a setting

Your task Dame Daphne du Maurier's novel (www.dumaurier.org) *House on the Strand* (1969), focuses on Dick's ability to travel back to the 14th century, and his mental ability to experience historical events without being able to change them, and is set near Tywardreath, which means "House on the Strand". Du Maurier describes the places she mentions with the depth of detail that shows she knows the places that she writes about, both through historical research and from visiting the places that she describes.

   This is particularly noticeable in earlier novels *The Loving* Spirit (1931) and *The King's General* (1946). Her novels often describe with passion and well-researched historical detail, the houses that were important to her such as Menabilly. Your task is to research the history of a building that exists today and trace back its history. Note down the changes that have occurred to it since it was first built. Then pick one of the periods that you have been able to uncover information about and write a description from the point of view of someone who lives, visits, or worked there during that period.

6.4 Interior landscapes

Objective   Describe a room

Your task   To describe in as much detail as possible a room that one of your characters might have lived in or visited during the period that you are writing about including the view from the window (if there was a window). Describe the room as if you were an 'audio describer'* and try to create a picture in words to be told or read aloud to someone who was blind or partially sighted.

* see **www.skillset.org**

Tips

If you were describing a character you would try to avoid the over use of 'seemed to'. Remember that you can 'show and not tell' your reader about settings in the same way that you would describe characters.

A   Using comparisons and analogies e.g.

For characters:

X was as nervous as a thoroughbred horse.

Y was as bad tempered as a baited badger.

For settings:

The inn reminded X of a country cattle market. It smelt of ripe dung and all the drinkers were standing. The slated floor slabs were mud-coated and even the sprinkling of sawdust was manure brown.

B By describing feelings through dialogue e.g. a character can explain to another one how they are feeling e.g.

> "Well, my dear, as you've been so kind as to ask me my joints are playing up, but it is my heart I'm more worried about. It's the strain of worrying about my grandson fighting them Boers that I fear may take me off before the war is over. His mother is so caught up with the four girls that she doesn't appear to have considered that he may never come back, but I have. The thought he'll die out there is always scratching away at the back of my mind like mites in a cat's ear.

This device can be used to inform your reader of the importance and role of a setting as well. For example:

> "I love this room, Mrs Jones. It reminds me of when I was a child. Did you make the quilt? My mother used to use scraps from anything that could be no longer worn. She had a brown rag rug that she'd made from sacking. It wasn't as pretty as your blue one, but it was made with love. The bed is similar too, although we didn't have an oak bed head carved with ships and sea monsters..."

Write your description of a room in no more than 500 words.

Chapter 7 – Characters

At the 'beating' heart of every novel or short story is the main character or characters. Memorable characters stay with us long after we've finished reading. We may on the surface have nothing in common with them at all, but we identify with them and their ultimate fate. In a novel minor characters can linger in our minds as well. We don't necessarily have to like the characters, but we do have to be interested in what happens to them.

You may decide that you want to base your main character on the 'life' of a real person such as a King's mistress, a famous admiral or a revolutionary leader etc. If this is the case then the chronology of their lives will already be well documented, and there will also be insights into their motivation and personality, often in the form of primary sources, including diaries of the period or letters. Selecting a 'real' person as your central character automatically means that you will not be able to change their name or title unless, of course you are writing historical fantasy fiction. You might be able to invent a 'familiar' 'pet' or 'a nick name'[*], which is a secret one that is only used by their closest friends. You could also invent a derisory one that is used by their enemies. However, your challenge when writing about someone whose life has been meticulously documented in works of non-fiction, is that the names of all the other people who have played a key role in their lives are fixed as well. Hence your main character might have been intimate friends with three women all with the same first name e.g. Catherine. One way to overcome this is to give these characters different pet names if they haven't already got one, and to address them whenever possible by this familiar name.

The advantage of using 'well-known', or noteworthy people from the past, is that you don't have to create a family or surnames for them, and you will not have to create an historical timeline for them, because it will have already been done for you. All you have to do is to put flesh onto the bones of their life which you already have at your finger tips, through primary and secondary sources. You have to transform the facts about the person you've selected into a three dimensional character.

You may wish to introduce characters that you have created as 'extras' into your narrative. In order to do this and to create a sense of historical 'verisimilitude'[†], and similarly if you are creating your own characters whose drama is acted out within the time frame that you've selected

---

[*] **Nickname** is a word that first appeared in the English language in c. 15th century
[†] **Verisimilitude**: the appearance of being real or true

picking a suitable and memorable name is important. For instance Chris Humphrey's character Jack Absolute, who is a character in Sheridan's play *The Rivals*, and is now an officer, warrior, lover and spy in his own series of novels. Search plays, letters, poetry, stories, and newspapers for suitable names that were popular in the period you have chosen to write about. Ask any friends that you have who are interested in family history, or go along to your local library and scan back through families to see how far first names go back, also look at Parish registers, censuses etc. and see if they are transferred from father to son e.g. Thomas, Arthur, Nathaniel, Elizabeth, Ann(e) etc.

A writer's life often becomes a sedentary one, and so don't forget that whenever you are visiting a new town or even your own, to check out every war memorial that you come across. This will often tell you a lot about local surnames. Tragically, you will often find clusters of men from the same family who all died in the Boer War and the First World War. However, from the historical novelist's point of view this can provide you with family names that are appropriate for the place and the period that you are writing about. Another way to find the perfect name for your character is to go on a graveyard hunt.

Selecting names for your characters which match their personalities and role in your narrative is important, but even more so is making certain that the name of your main character is going to be both appropriate and memorable. The name of a character becomes an identification tag for the reader e.g. Cadfael, Verity Brown, Kydd, Crowner John, Ivanhoe, Rhett Butler and Scarlett O'Hara. Somehow if Rhett Butler in 'Gone with the Wind' had been called Henry Butler generations of readers might not have found him so attractive. Margaret Mitchell originally wanted to call Scarlett Pansy, which was also the original working title for *Gone with the Wind*, but Macmillan the publisher thankfully persuaded Margaret to change both the name and the title. The name Pansy certainly doesn't match the wayward Scarlett's character, and had she remained Pansy would the novel have become a world-wide best seller?

ACTIVITIES

7.1 Graveyard Hide and Seek

Objectives To find suitable names for your characters to suit their personalities and also the period that they inhabited.

To discover a new character.

Your tasks **A** Visit a cemetery or graveyard that has headstones that date back to the period that you are writing about. Clearly this will not be possible if you are writing a novel that is in a place or time that is too distant for you to investigate. The older the church the more likely you are to find old gravestones surrounding it. A lot of the larger public cemeteries date from the Victorian period onwards.

Not only will graveyards provide you with details of both first and family names, but also give you a host of background information about how old the people were, and often what they died of. They may tell you if their children predeceased them, and according to the grandeur or simplicity of the stone and its carving, if they came from a well to do family. Always look for the unexpected such as a memorial stone to a loved one who died on the *Titanic*, or in a famous battle such as the Charge of the Light Brigade. Some stones will have sentiments from the bereaved about their lost ones, others will have quotes from the scriptures, and some will have statements about their lives, left by the departed. These will sometimes be witty and sometimes poignant. For instance in Lydford (Devon, UK) one of the tomb-stones is of a watch-maker, George Routleigh. The epitaph on the lid of the tomb, which is now to be found inside the church, is in the form of a poem that he wrote about his own life and profession, and ends with equating his profession with his life, and it ends:

"In hopes of being taken in hand
By his Maker
And of being thoroughly cleaned, repaired

And set-going
In the world to come."

While in the tiny Cornish village of Werrington, on the north west exterior wall of St. Martin's church is a memorial to one of the many black slaves who came to England in the 18th century. Philip Scipio died at the age of c.18-20, and was buried on the 10th of September 1734. He was brought to England by the Duke of Wharton and became Lady Lucy Morice's servant.

For more information about Philip Scipio, and other black slaves such as Everisto Mucheovela (d. 1868) who originally came from Mozambique, but was bought by Mr. Thomas Johns, a Cornish mining engineer, and is buried in Wendron, Cornwall , UK,(**www.londoncornish.co.uk,** The winter, 2007 issue).

Obviously, one drawback about carrying out this activity in the UK is the weather. If it rains too much then the interior of a church should also be full of interesting memorials and tombs. Don't forget to cast your eye over the list of previous vicars, priests etc. of the parish as they often have wonderful biblical names to conjure up characters from.

B Seek out and find three interesting tomb stones or memorial plaques (from the same century) and jot down all the information on them in the table below, and write a description of the stone itself e.g. is it carved in granite, slate, marble etc. Has it got cherubs on it or a skull with crossed bones? Is the letter 's' carved to look like the letter shape 'f'? Are the dates used carved using Roman numerals? You may want to take a photograph and fill in the information that you've collected at home. You could make a collection of interesting headstones to use at a later date.

C Find another three in a different cemetery or graveyard (from the same century) and jot down all the information on the headstone and also write a description of it.

Graveyard Hide and Seek Table

Location of cemetery etc. and the name of the headstone or memorial	All the information that is written on the stone or Plaque	Describe the stone, plaque etc.
1)		
2)		
3)		
4)		
5)		
6)		

Once you have completed this task take a first name from one of the headstones in one cemetery and one from another, and create a selection of names for your character. The reason for suggesting that you take a name from different cemeteries is that you always have to remember that it is best to avoid 'real' names if possible, particularly for 'villains'. Even if you write a disclaimer in the front of your novel to the effect that the characters are not based on 'real' people, you still need to think carefully about your choice of name, especially if you are writing time-slip or historical fantasy fiction.

For anyone writing about the past, selecting a character's name that is appropriate for a period, is as important as is checking to see if what we consider to have been a popular name in the period actually was. The name Myfanwy is an excellent example. It sounds as if it is a name that dates back to Arthurian times, but although it would be nice to imagine that it was a name around at the time that the stories were gathered together in the *Mabinogion*, it is unlikely. Myfanwy, unfortunately, is more likely to be a 19th century variant of an earlier name.

However, if you were writing time-slip or historical fantasy fiction today's popular names would be acceptable, and so Brie, Jordan and India could be used for female characters.

Write your list of composite names below:

7.2 A quick character sketch

Objective   To write a snapshot portrait of a character

Your task   Select one of the names and write a description of your character. Try to do this without thinking about it. Just write a brief descriptive portrait of them below of no more than 200 words. Write this description using whole sentences.

You may not have access to a cemetery, church, abbey or graveyard or prefer not to visit them, and so below is a selection of other tasks that you might like to try:

1   Visit an art gallery and select a portrait from an historical period that you would like to write about. Note down any information that you can find out about the person, and then write a description of what they looked liked, and what you think they were like as a person. If you aren't able to visit a gallery then you might like to use a book on art borrowed from a library or an on-line site such as **www.npg.org.uk** (National Portrait Gallery, London).

2   Search back through old family photographs until you find a face that you don't recognise, perhaps in an Edwardian wedding or an early engagement portrait. Give this unknown person a name and write a thumbnail sketch of who they were, including their 'imaginary' relationship to anyone else in the photograph. If you have haven't any of your own family photographs then ask your friends if they have, or carry out a quick search on the web.

3   Football clubs, old school clubs, Army regiments etc. These all have extensive photographic and picture archives. Just pick any subject and pick a nameless 'face' that appeals to you, and write about them. Most public libraries will have non-fiction books that you can use to pick a face from a specific period. If you want to do this activity using the web then search for pictures of 'Ellis Island immigrants' for instance, and select a face to write about.

4 Pick a ship, an aeroplane or a train and a period, and then describe an imaginary seaman, ship builder, pilot, engine driver or passenger. Don't forget to give them a name that you have made up! For inspiration check out sites such as the ones listed below. The web site details were correct at the time of publication, but may have changed subsequently.

Ships:

www.vikingeskibsmuseet.dk (Viking long boats)
www.plimoth.org (for the Mayflower)
www.hms-victory.com (Nelson's HMS Victory)
hmsbelfast.iwm.org.uk (HMS Belfast, launched in 1938)
www.lategreatliners.com (the Normandy and other liners)
www.maritimemuseum.co.nz (New Zealand)

Fishing and whaling:

www.whaleworld.org (Australia)
www.scotfishmuseum.org (Scotland)

Aircraft:

www.aviationmuseumguide.co.uk
yellowairplane.com/Museums (general)
htmwww.aarg.com.au (Australia)
www.aviation.technomuses.ca (Canada)
www.warbirdalley.com/museum.htm (general)

Trains:

www.nrm.org.uk (UK)
ukhrail.uel.ac.uk (UK)
www.indiasite.com/delhi/museums/rail.htm (India)
www.nevsky-prospect.com/warsaw.html (Russian)
www.railsusa.com/links/Railroad_Museums (Canada and the USA)

5 Skim through a book on the history of fashion, or visit a fashion or costume museum and select an outfit. Then write an outline character profile based on the outfit including background information about what the outfit was bought for e.g. a ball, an outing to the theatre for work etc. Did the wearer make the outfit themselves, or was it made for them? You could also create a character profile for the seamstress or factory worker who made the clothes. How about writing a short story based on one item of clothing such as a bonnet, an item of hosiery, a pair of hunting boots, or a pelisse (a fur trimmed and often high-waisted coat worn by women c. early 19th century), and what role this item played both in the life of the person who made it, and in that of the person who wore it.

Alternately, you might like to create a character for a piece of jewellery, which could become an heirloom, passing through a series of characters that you might like to write sketches for.

6   Watch an opera, ballet or a play and choose a character. Describe this character's life and personality in detail, transforming them into more than just a two-dimensional character e.g. Carmen in Bizet's opera - What was her life like as a child? How did Carmen end up working in a cigarette factory? In Mozart's opera *The Magic Flute* how did Papageno learn his craft as a bird-catcher, and would he have preferred to have learnt another trade? You might even like to extend this activity and try to create a character who might have listened to a piece of music when it was first performed e.g. Sir Edward Elgar's *Pomp and Circumstance* marches played first in 1901 including *Land of Hope and Glory* , George Gershwin's *Rhapsody in Blue* (1924), Vivaldi's *The Four Seasons* (1723), or a piece by Ludwig van Beethoven. Alternately, you could listen to a piece of music and describe the composer, conductor or musicians' characters at the time the piece was first performed.

7   Visit a famous historic garden and then draw up a series of character profiles, one for the person who owned them, another for the landscape gardener who designed them or the gardeners who planted them, and then another for the person who supplied the plants and seeds. Select two of the characters that you've created and use their interest in gardens as the starting point for a short story, based on the relationship between them and their love of plants, or each other

8   Attend a re-enactment of a battle, visit a museum that specialises in arms and armoury and pick a weapon. Create a character that might have owned or used the weapon in combat in an appropriate military campaign e.g. The English Civil War, The Boer War, The American War of Independence etc.

You may like to check out the following sites for inspiration:

> www.royalarmouries.org
> www.nares.org.uk
> www.histrenact.co.uk
> www.eventplan.co.uk
> www.thesealedknot.org.uk
> www.nps.gov/spar
> www.aaftankmuseum.com
> www.tankmuseum.org

9   If you have an historic home or place nearby, you can use a visit to create a gallery of characters who might have lived and worked there at a particular period, from the scullery maid upwards.

For examples of possible sites to visit:

> www.nationaltrust.org.uk
> www.nationaltrust.org.au (Australia)
> www.english-heritage.org.uk
> www.historic.org.nz (New Zealand)
> www.heritagecanada.org (Canada)
> www.vpa.org/museumsus.html (USA)
> www.castlesgardensireland.com
> www.scotland.com/castles

10   Just take a walk around you own town, city or district and find a family house that 'appears' to be from a period that you might be interested in writing about, and invent a character who might have lived in it. Write down a detailed description not only of your character, but the role the house, farm, flat or apartment played in their lives e.g. They were born and lived there as a child.

If you prefer to do your walking with your fingers on the keyboard, then you can check out sites such as **www.museumwales.ac.uk** (St.Fagans National History Museum of Wales)

www.greenough-pioneer-museum.com

www.collectionsaustralia.net

www.heritagepark.ca

www.oldhouses.com

11   Pop into a second hand or antiquarian bookshop. Find a book with a name plate, and then remember or jot down both the title of the book and the owners name, and any other details such as an inscription that commemorates an event like a birthday or a prize giving. Write a description of the person who received the book and also a portrait of the person who gave it to them. What significance did the choice of book and title have to both parties? You might even like to go one step further by writing down some notes about the printer or type setter of the book you've chosen, and if they enjoyed their work?

12   If you are fortunate enough to live near a museum or religious establishment such as a cathedral that display illuminated manuscripts go along and select a rare book or manuscript and think about possible characters that could have had an involvement with the item from the illustrator, the person who commissioned it to the benefactor who gave it to the museum, church etc. If you are interested in maps then you could build up a collection of character sketches related to a well-known map such as the Mappa Mundi (**www.herefordwebpages.co.uk**) including the cartographer who drew the map. See also: **www.britishmuseum.org**

Tip

By writing a cluster of portrait profiles you are also creating the basis for a possible short story or a novel. You just need to select a topic, for example education, and then focus on a school or university etc. Starting from the professor or head teacher you can work downwards to the humble student. When creating these groups of profiles it is useful to note down the relationship of the characters to each other e.g. school cook – mother of student and mistress of the headmaster.

7.4 Building up a portfolio of character profiles

Objective   To put flesh on the bones of characters, and to give them personalities that match the role that you want them to play in your story.

Your tasks
- Add any extra questions that you think might be useful to the list below. We suggest that initially you just jot down notes rather than use whole sentences. You can photocopy the list below and use it as a template if you wish. Write down your answers on a separate sheet of paper.

- To create a composite name from the list that you have created in the 'Graveyard hide and seek', or any of the other activities above that might be appropriate for a main character, and another that might be appropriate for a secondary character. Then fill in the questionnaire about them (see **pp. 97-98**) to create a character profile.

7.5 Portraits versus profiles

Objective   To investigate how you prefer to build up character profiles and what are the advantages and disadvantages of both methods.

Your task   Compare your 'quick sketch portrait' to your questionnaires. Which method did you prefer and why?

Character Questionnaire
Interview with your Main Character

Name:

Age:

1. Family details (brother, sister, wife, parents etc.).
2. **External characteristics** (Physical description) - What do they look like?
3. Have they got any habits? (e.g. drumming their fingers on the table, comfort eating?)
4. What do they do? (e.g. work as a blacksmith, soldier, gold miner, governess, maid, artist, duchess or duke)
5. Where do they live? (e.g. town, country, city, village, or wilderness)
6. What makes them happy? What makes them sad? (e.g. watching a vaudeville show, hunting deer with friends, or visiting their family on their day off)
7. What, if any, are their ambitions?
8. What is the area of their life that upsets them the most at this particular moment?
9. What is their favourite colour and why? What is their favourite food and why?
10. What do they smell like? (e.g. of roses, freshly baked bread etc.)
11. Is their eye sight good? Have they got hearing difficulties?
12. What do they feel like when you touch their skin (e.g. rough, silky)
13. What is their first language? Is it English? French? Have they got a regional accent e.g. Scottish? How does this affect the way that they speak? For example do they confuse common idioms when they use them, and as a consequence raining 'cats and dogs' might become raining 'bats and dogs'. Do they have a stammer or speech impediment? Is there one word that they use frequently e.g. addressing all children as 'pet'.
14. What does their voice sound like e.g. deep and sensual?
15. **Internal characteristics (psychological and personality profile):** Are they risk takers? Are they prone to melancholy? What sort of sense of humour have they got?
16. Anything else?

Character Questionnaire
Interview with a Secondary Character

Name:

Age:

1   Relationship to your main character:

2   External characteristics (Physical description) - What do they look like?

3   Have they got any habits? (e.g. chewing their bottom lip when worried, gambling)

4   What do they do? (e.g. carpenter, seamstress, lawyer, bishop, pirate, fisherman, milliner, opera singer)

5   Where do they live? (e.g. by the sea, on a canal, or on the Prairies)

6   What makes them happy? What makes them sad? (e.g. buying a new ribbon for their bonnet makes them happy)

7   What, if any, are their ambitions?

8   What is the area of their life that upsets them the most at this particular moment? (e.g. they can't earn enough money to feed their family. They've got too much money and they are worried that no one likes them for who they are, but only for what they can get out of it)

9   What is their favourite colour and why? What is their favourite food and why?

10   What do they smell like?

11   What do they feel like when you touch their skin (e.g. rough, silky)

12   Internal characteristics (psychological and personality profile):

13   Anything else?

7.6 Personality Plus

Objective   Creating a character profile is one skill, but bringing them 'alive' is another. Your aim is for your reader not just to be 'interested' in your main characters, but 'passionate' about them. In order to achieve this, the writer has to not just empathise with their characters, but feel passionate about them in order to portray them as strong characters, worthy of the readers investing their time to read about them.

How can you achieve this 'personality plus' factor for your characters? If you are a person who tends to view most people as 'nice' and doesn't have particularly strong emotional responses to people, then this next activity is going to be difficult for you.

The 'anger' and 'love' that you hopefully will have felt while writing these cameos, is the raw emotion that if you are able to hold on to when you describe your characters, will help you to give them the 'personality plus' factor.

Your task

A   **Creating a strong personality for your 'villain' or 'anti-heroes'.**

1   Think back to your school days and try to remember someone that you 'hated'. If you can't handle the concept of 'hate' then think about someone you 'disliked', and why. Was it because they were a bully and pinched your chocolate biscuit at lunchtime, or because they came top in every examination. Now describe in no more than 500 words what it was that you hated, or disliked them for. Don't write down their names, but refer to them as X.

> **Model** (This is a fictitious model):
>
> X never lost her hair ribbons. Her hair was always tidy and she could do up her school tie without any help. She always came top in the spelling tests even though she never learnt them, and was the teacher's pet. Worse still she was always

> telling tales about the other children. It was a total nightmare for me, because I was always having to rub things out and we weren't supposed to do that, but I just couldn't get the hang of spelling even some common words, and her squeaky voice would always pipe up with, 'Miss, Y is rubbing out her work *again.*" I loathed her and had a great desire to make her some special 'rubber' sandwiches and make her eat them.[*]
>
> [*] **rubber**: eraser (American English)

Write your example in your notebook

2   Think about your life today or your adult life including work. Try to think about someone that you 'hated'. If you can't handle the concept of 'hate' then think about someone you 'disliked', and why. Was, or is it because they always pretend that your ideas are theirs and get the praise for them instead of you? Now describe what it was, or is, that you hate or dislike about their behaviour towards you or others. Don't write down their names, but refer to them as X.

> **Model** (This is a fictitious model):
>
> X was the chairperson of a committee who were organising a special event. I'd been delegated to carry out certain tasks. I completed these to the letter, but X was not satisfied and accused me of not doing them as instructed, even though X had sent me the instructions in writing. If I hadn't needed the job I would have left, but over a period of six moths everything that I did was 'wrong' according to this person. The fact that the event was a great success due to my hard work and endeavour, only brought forth further scorn from the person, who was able to detail every marquee tent peg that was out of line, or so it appeared to me. X was a big time bully and only got away with it because of their position of

> power gained by riding rough shod over anyone that got in their way. This included X's children who were nervous, quivering wrecks.

Write your description below in no more than 500 words in your notebook

B   **Creating a strong personality for your 'hero', 'heroine', or 'good guys'.**

1   Most of us have special people in our lives who have helped us out or whom we admire. Describe this person and why you admire them. Do not write down their name, but refer to them as **X**.

> **Model** (This is a fictitious model):
>
> X rescued me after my husband (wife) had an affair. I didn't know her very well at that time, but she stepped in and gave me both practical help such as looking after the children, or picking them up from school. She also gave me moral support and encouraged me to grieve, but not to wallow in it. She gave me time and made me feel loved and valuable at a time when I was at my most vulnerable.

2   Describe a 'famous' person from the past that you admire and why.

3   Describe someone that you loved and why. Just refer to them as X.

4   Make a list of all the characteristics that you value most in your friends and relations: e.g. loyalty, honesty etc.

5   Try mixing and matching all the positive traits that you've listed above to create a 'super' hero/ heroine, but do remember to give them at least one personality trait that isn't positive, otherwise they would be unbelievable.

6   Write a description of your 'super 'character with personality plus in no more than 500 words.

7.7 Something borrowed and something new

Objective   To create a character by' borrowing' some of the personality traits of a famous person from the past, and then use these characteristics to create a new character, by transferring them into a different body.

Your task   To select a well-known person from the past and list the traits that you 'assume' they might have had, and then create a new character that might have lived in a period that you would like to write about.

Model

Name of famous person: Marilyn Monroe

'Assumed' personality traits and characteristics:
Vulnerable, obsessed with aging, attractive to men from all social classes etc.

Write a short scene for your new character that enables you to describe something about their personality incorporating some of the traits from your list:

Lady Howarth Grey was upset. She was certain that the female staff of her London house were laughing at her new hair style. If only they knew that it was she who ran her husband's estates and kept them in employment. Her husband could never be prized away from his library, except if some philosopher or wit was invited to dine.

Her ability to manage her husband's finances would never be believed as her face and figure marked her out as a great beauty. No man had ever complimented her on her mind. Her tiny waist and ample bosom were enshrined in poems, but not her skill in adding up columns of figures.

She knew that she was aging by the minute and that even by candle light fine wrinkles had started to appear on her forehead. Her waist appeared tiny, but that was due to the exceptional design of her corset, rather than nature. Her charming curls were now piled high in what could only be a described as 'abandoned bird's nest style', and so she could understand the maids' giggles, even if they made her want to cry. Fortunately, for the moment men from the boot boy upwards found her attractive, but for how long she wondered...

Write your description below:

Name of famous person: e.g. Marilyn Monroe

'Assumed' personality traits and characteristics: e.g. vulnerable, obsessed with aging, attractive to men from all social classes

Write a short scene for your new character that enables you to describe something about their personality incorporating some of the traits from your list:

7.8 Dressing up or sniffing out your character?

Selecting appropriate clothes suited to your character, adding in touches about the etiquette and manners of the period can all make your characters more memorable, but so can a characteristic scent or smell that we associate with them. Remember that today the range of perfumes, colognes and fragrancies is vast, but in the past the range of scents would have been far more limited.

Objective	To find a scent or smell that you associate with a particular character.
Your task	To add extra scents and smells to the table below.

Attractive and gentle scents	Pungent and lingering
Devon Violets (scent/perfume brand name),Eau de Cologne (brand name), lavender, rose water, musk, orange blossom	hay, rosemary, cinnamon, cloves, mint, fish, garlic, bad breath, silage, dung (cow, sheep)

7.9 Less a blemish more a trade mark

Objective   To create a list of small or annoying physical blemishes that you might be able to use to help your reader to identify more closely with them.

Your task   To create a list of blemishes

Examples to start your list off:

Baldness, split ends (hair), spots, stained teeth, flaky nails, freckles...

7.10 Laughter and characters

Everyone laughs in a different way. They also use different laughs for different situations. When building up character portraits it may help to think about matching your characters with a particular laugh or even creating a character to go with a laugh. The way someone laughs can endear them to you, but other laughs can become so annoying and grating that they might provide a motive for murder.

Objective   To create characters just from the way they laugh.

Your task   To create characters to match each of the following words and phrases that describe different ways of laughing or expressions of amusement.

cackle, chortle, smirk, roar, smile, grin, guffaw, chuckle, screech, bellow, to shake with laughter

Can you think of any others e.g. to hoot with laughter?

Model

Brother Stephen, who was in charge of the wine cellar, was the shape as the barrels he stored there. He was in his seventies, but when someone made him laugh he would chuckle like a school boy and his whole body would wobble from side to side with delight.

Write your description in your notebook

Tips

Michael Jecks
"There is so much to consider when thinking about writing a book. Personally I'd always concentrate on the characters, with a careful eye to make sure that they're consistent. I've found that the best way to do this is to have a whiteboard on which the characters are depicted briefly – their key features (nothing too extensive, just guidelines to remind me what they're like), so: big nose, scarred cheek, blue eyes, etc. Before I used the whiteboard, I discovered the wonderful merits of Post-It Notes. No, not the small ones: they make enormous "Table Top" pads, which are about A1 size. You can write on them, pull off the page and stick it to a wall, shelf – anywhere. I used to have one for each main character, with description and motives in front of me so I could refer to them whenever I needed to."
www.michaeljecks.co.uk

Richard Lee
"What draws me to historical fiction is not the history, but the fiction. People underestimate the joy and the challenge of this. The goal of all fiction is to convey a truth about people. Writers seek for moments when characters suddenly reveal themselves, reacting to another character or a situation. They reveal themselves, and we say 'yes, that's what they are; that's what people are like'. In historical fiction when they do this they also tear a hole in time. They reveal where they are related to us and where they are not: the thrill is 'Ah - so that is what they were like.' It isn't the history that counts - these moments are usually the most purely fictional, the things that history cannot show us - but they are the moments that bring history to life."
Richard Lee is publisher and founder of the Historical Novel Society **www.historical novelsociety.org**

Stephanie Grace Whitson

"A historical fiction author as obsessive about accuracy as I am can't feed, dress, or move her characters before she researches. She can't have them talk or think, either, because women in the 19th century did not eat what I eat, dress like I dress, or move through the world the way I do. They didn't think or talk the way I do, either. I begin with a blank slate.

That being said, the problems that people face are basic to humanity. People in every age worry about the meaning of life. They wonder how a loving God can 'let that happen.' They wonder about their own place in the universe and wonder what's worth dying for. So, while the 'big picture' for my characters doesn't vary all that much for this morning's news, everything else does."

www.stephaniewhitson.com

Chapter 8 – Voice and Viewpoint

From whose point of view are you going to tell the story? Whose perspective are you going to choose to narrate the story? Will you use the first, second or third person's **narrative voice** to communicate with your audience? Who is the **narrator**, the person telling your story, going to be?

Is it going to be your main character or characters in which case you could use "I" or "we" (the first person), or is it going to be he/she or they (the third person)? It is possible to use the second person "you", but the obstacle to using this viewpoint is that the narrator is speaking to the protagonist or treating the reader as the main protagonist. Fortunately for the aspiring writer this viewpoint is rarely used and then usually only for short works.

Do you want your narrator to be an all-knowing and **omniscient** narrator? A narrator who does not alter the course of the narrative, or one that can reverse the outcome of the narrative in a god-like manner. This was a popular device with 19th century novelists such as Edward George Earle Lytton Bulwer-Lytton, 1st Baron Lytton in *The Last Days of Pompeii* (1834), Charles Dickens and Nathaniel Hawthorne in *The Scarlet Letter* (1850) set in 17th century Boston. However, authors like Bulwer Lytton and Dickens used a mixture of viewpoints in their novels.

An omniscient narrator can comment on the action of the story from one or many characters' viewpoints, or simply describe the action without comment, or evaluate the importance and impact of the actions on their characters as they occur. The choice is yours, but be careful if you elect to use the point of view outlined above using an omniscient third person narrator. It is also useful to remember that using the third person viewpoint means that you, as the author, can make asides and comments as the story progresses, but it requires the author to beware of not turning their novel into a lecture. The result may be that your readers become bored with a story that requires no effort on their part to solve the clues and to predict what happens next. The third person narrative is very popular, but recently there has been a swing in some sub-genres of historical fiction writing towards using the first person as a narrator to tell the story.

At this point your mind may be reaching technical jargon overload. What is important for you to decide, is who is going to be your narrator or narrators. In order to help you with your decision it will help if you carry out two simple experimental activities.

N.B. For definitions of the words highlighted in bold see the **Glossary** at the back of the book.

ACTIVITY

8.1 Which viewpoint and narrative voice do you feel the most comfortable writing ?

Objective   To experiment with using different narrative voices.

Your task   Below are a selection of narrative voices that are used in writing fiction and historical fiction. The explanations of the different narrative voices given below have been distilled in order to make them easy to access. They are to provide you with a starting point and after you have tried the activities you may wish to explore the subject further. However, always keep it firmly fixed in your mind that your object is to write your novel, and do not let any interesting diversions take away precious "writing time" that you may have carved out of your busy everyday life.

Your task is to pick a famous historical character or personage from any period, and to write the same scene using the different viewpoints below. You will need to adapt the scenes and for some, to introduce extra characters. You will have a model for each one to act as an example.

First person narrative.

Main points to remember:

* The first person narrator is referred to using either I (singular for one person), or we (if it is plural) for character/characters within their own story.
* The benefits to a writer of using the first person are that the main character's ideas, thoughts and emotions, can be explained more directly to the reader. They are first hand and 'from the horse's mouth' e.g. I was in love for the first time. This sentence conveys more intimacy than 'He/she was in love for the first time." Your character may or may not be aware that he/she is sharing their secrets with you as a reader. You might, as a reader just be 'eavesdropping' on their thoughts. They give your reader an insight into the 'unspoken' world of the character. You can use the first person narrative to tell a story within a story.

- It is possible for the first person narrator not to be the main character. This narrative voice is not often used. An example of how this might be used is if your main character (protagonist) was for instance Princess Alexandra, the wife of Edward VII, and you told the Alexandra's story through the eyes of her lady's maid, or Queen Victoria (her mother-in-law).

- For those of you who are interested in trying to write 'autobiographical fiction' where the first person narrator is the character of the author, but behaves as if they are a character within the story, then you might be wise to read Umberto Eco's *The Name of the Rose* (First published in Italian in 1980 as *Il nome della rosa*) before embarking on your own novel using this **narrative mode** or **mode of narration** (the skills and devices that an author uses to write his/her plot). In Eco's story the main characters are William of Baskerville, a Franciscan friar, and Adso of Melk who is a novice accompanying Baskerville, but who acts as the narrator.

Model

Setting: Twelve year old Marie-Antoinette was the only eligible bride for the fourteen year old Louis Auguste, later to become Louis the XVI of France. One of the obstacles to their betrothal was her teeth, which were crooked. This resulted in a French doctor performing oral surgery on Marie-Antoinette without anaesthesia over a three month period, to achieve a beautiful straight smile that would satisfy the French nation.

Character: Marie-Antoinette

I was so cross. Cross was not a strong enough word. Why should I have to have my teeth straightened? It wasn't my fault that my sisters and mother caught smallpox. If only Maria Johanna hadn't died then I wouldn't have to be betrothed to Louis Auguste, and I don't want to be Marie Antoinette, Dauphine of France.

I don't want to marry my doltish second cousin once removed, but above all I don't want to have a surgeon, especially a Frenchman, touching my teeth. It's disgusting and inhuman!

Second person narrator

It is very uncommon to find a novel written using the second person point of view, because it means that your reader becomes, or feel as if they are a character in the story.

Model

(The reader becomes Marie-Antoinette and is addressed by the narrator as being Marie-Anoinette)

You must be cross? I am certain that you could come up with a better one. Why should you have your teeth straightened? If only Maria Johanna hadn't died then you wouldn't have to be betrothed to Louis Auguste, and I know the last thing you want is to become Dauphine of France.

You must understand that I don't want you marry your doltish second cousin once removed, but above all I don't want you to have a surgeon, especially a Frenchman, touching your teeth.

You can write your example in your notebook

Third person viewpoints

Considering this from a literary perspective, there are three possible different ways of using the third-person narrative as storyteller.

The first is subjective and was used in 20th century fiction, to give a behind the scenes glimpse of the emotions of the characters through the eyes of the narrator.

Model – Third person subjective

I as the narrator always know what Louis Auguste, Marie Antoinette's second cousin once removed must be thinking. Why should she have to have her teeth straightened? He must understand that it wasn't her fault that her sisters and mother caught smallpox. If only he would say what he wants, which is that he couldn't care less about her teeth being crooked or straight,

> because he doesn't want her to become Marie
> Antoinette, Dauphine of France. He doesn't want to have
> to marry anyone.

You can write your example in your notebook

The second is the objective view-point, which is popular
because in theory you are trying not to be biased when
describing your characters thoughts and actions and you
only describe what can be seen through their actions.

Model – Third person objective

Marie Antoinette ran to her bed chamber and picked up
a small vase with a posy of spring flowers in it, and
hurled it at the door. The French doctor had arrived. He
would operate on her teeth in the afternoon without an
anaesthetic. The French people wanted a bride with a
perfect smile for Louis Auguste, her cousin. She did not
have straight teeth. She had crooked ones and so
whether Marie Antoinette wanted to or not, her teeth
would be straightened.

Write your example in your notebook

Third person omniscient

This means that the story is told from the standpoint of
the story teller who knows all the facts, and was often
used in the 19th century and can add an extra sense of
realism and truthfulness to the story.

Model – Third Person Omniscient

We have all been children. We should all know what it
feels like to be forced to do something that we have no
wish to do, especially if the consequence of that action
will inflict pain on us.

"I won't have that French doctor operating on my
teeth. I just won't. Louis Auguste definitely won't care if
my teeth are straight or not. Anyway, I'm sure that he
doesn't want to marry me and I certainly don't want to
marry him," Marie Antoinette shouted and then flounced

> out into the garden leaving everyone in the room to discuss ways in which she might be coerced into doing her duty.

Write your example in your notebook

Epistolary voice

This uses a fictional series of letters or documents to reveal your story or plot.

Model – Epistolary voice

My esteemed wife,

I am writing this to inform you that my return to France will be delayed. Our future Dauphine, Marie Antoinette is refusing to let me operate on her crooked teeth. It is true that at the moment the teeth that are crowded into her mouth and that they overlap in a most unfashionable way. The result gives her a rather charming smile, but one that is only appealing on the face of some roguish peasant child or mischievous street urchin. It would not do for Versailles or for the people of France...

Write your example in your notebook

Other Viewpoints

Other viewpoints that you might like to investigate are ones where there are multiple narrators, using alternating character viewpoints, untrustworthy narrators and character voices.

Please note: Do not feel that you have to adhere to any one narrative style or mode. Many writers use a combination of different ones. What is paramount is that you are comfortable with the narrator or narrative mode that you decide to use to tell your story and that you are aware of which viewpoint you have chosen to use.

Composite model

"I won't have by teeth operated on just to please Louis Auguste. I'm certain that he wouldn't do the same for me." Marie Antoinette took a deep breath and tried not to cry, she wanted to, but her ability to cover up her true

---

> emotions, which had been acquired as a very young child, stopped her. She was determined not to let anyone know that it wasn't just that she didn't want to become the Dauphine of France, but rather that she was afraid to have surgery performed on her by a French doctor.
>
> Maria Theresa glared at her daughter and wondered what on earth the child was thinking about. She had schooled Marie Antoinette to accept her role as a member of a distinguished royal family. She was twelve years of age, which was old enough to accept her responsibilities as her sisters had been willing to do.

Write your own narrative style in your notebook

8.2 Which viewpoint do you prefer as a reader?

Objectives To help you to discover which viewpoint is currently used the most.

To assist you in identifying with which narrator voice appeals to you as a reader the most and why.

Your tasks 1 Pick a genre e.g. romantic historical fiction, historical military fiction and go to your local library or book shop and browse through as many novels as you can find in the genre.

2 Keep a tally in the table below of which authors use which narrative voice in which novels (try to find at least five different authors in your chosen genre or sub-genre).

3 Try to decide why this viewpoint appeals to you. Is it because using the first person 'I' makes the association between you and the main character closer, more personal and therefore you are more involved with what happens to the main protagonist? Is it because the use of the third person he/she gives you a greater insight into the interaction of all the characters?

Narrative Voice Tally Table

Name of author	Title of novels and the narrative viewpoints that they use in each novel e.g. I (first person)

Tips

If you still aren't clear about which voice, viewpoint, narrator and who to use to tell your own story, then you have two options. The first is further detailed research about the use of different narrative voices and modes, and the second is to watch a film! The film is "Stranger than Fiction." It was released in 2006 and stars Will Ferrell, Emma Thompson (as the novelist) and a wrist watch that becomes a 'character' it its own right. It demonstrates in a highly entertaining way the use of a particular narrative voice and its possible consequences.

Narrators in Historical Fiction by Elizabeth Maslen

The narrator, the 'voice' who is telling the story, is always crucial in fiction. We rely on the narrative voice to set the scene, to introduce characters, to use the right language for the situation, and, above all, the 'voice' has to be the driving force that makes us want to read on. So the narrator has a particularly important role in historical fiction: for we have to believe in what at first will be an alien setting, in the way that setting affects the characters and the development of plot and, importantly, we have to feel comfortable with the narrator's language, evoking the period but not alienating us by being too period-based in vocabulary or sentence construction.

In works like Pat Barker's trilogy based in the First World War (*Regeneration, The Eye in the Door, The Ghost Road*), researching the period would not have been enough to sustain the reader's interest in this story about the futility and tragedy of war; the reader has to be drawn into an older world and situation which are so described that we are persuaded we know this world from the inside, not as remote spectators. The author has various ways of luring the reader into this frame of mind. Barker does this by using a narrative 'voice' which is not one of the characters, but which takes us inside the head of her protagonist, to share his point of view, his prejudices, his suffering – and very importantly, to accept what is part of his familiar world, and what he himself finds unfamiliar.

This is a technique that William Golding uses in his novel *The Inheritors*, but with a clever twist: his narrative 'voice' describes the world, a prehistoric world of cave and danger, through the eyes of Lok. But at the same time the narrator is giving us clues about Lok that are unusual, telling, for instance, that the child on his back has 'one hand clutched in the chestnut curls that lay on his neck and down his spine': only some time later are we given sufficient clues to realize that we are seeing life through the eyes and thoughts of a Neanderthal man, his world about to be destroyed by our own species, *homo sapiens*.

So the timing of the release of information by the voice of the narrator can be a skilful tool in manipulating the reader's involvement with a world and characters far removed from his/her own experience. Mary Renault uses this gradual release of information in her novels *The King Must Die* and *The Bull from the Sea,* two works based on the life of Theseus. But she also uses another narrative technique: her narrator does not, as Barker and Golding do, refer to the main character as 'he'; her narrator speaks with the voice of the main character, the Theseus of Greek legend. So legend becomes the real-life experience of the man at the centre of the tale, pondered on by the man himself. The narrator's musings on the implications of his own story seem to mirror ways the reader may think about his own experiences and the behaviour of others; they are not the ponderings of a narrator who is observing from the outside.

Yet this first-person narrator, the 'I' who is having the experiences in the story, has been used quite differently in Salman Rushdie's *Midnight's Children*: for here the narrator is not exactly a 'real' person, but speaks, as it were, for the Indian continent as it emerged after Independence and Partition. The child has a personality but strangely fantastic attributes, so that the reader is never allowed to settle into a sense of familiarity and normality; for this child and its friends of the same age represent all that India went through as it emerged from Imperial domination into the shaky beginnings of democracy. Furthermore, we cannot be sure of the reliability of the narrator, as he too is groping, through images of strangeness, for the underlying meaning of what he is experiencing. The human fallibility behind the great events of history is vividly played out; the narrator's foregrounding of fantasy images being Rushdie's way of portraying India's stepping into the unknown.

The narrative 'voice' is clearly, then, very important in the way the reader responds to any tale; but nowhere is this voice more important than in detective and thriller fiction, and particularly when such works are set in other periods than the reader's own. For in such works, the reader expects to be looking for clues alongside the character in the tale who is doing the investigating; and this means that we have to feel at home in an unfamiliar landscape. We face the challenge of having to assess not only the action but each narrative 'voice' that controls the tale and the release of information: are they reliable or unreliable? (In most instances, in this genre, readers like to feel they are being given all the clues, if deftly hidden, and are irritated if the investigator produces proof like a rabbit out of a hat, relying on evidence we haven't been given). Is the 'voice' that of an observer or of someone who will emerge as closely involved in the plot? If, chapter by chapter, the reader confronts more than one narrator, more than one version of what is going on, who is to be believed? And how far is the investigator on the side of law or, more subversively, on the side of justice, a critic of law in the period being evoked as impersonally applicable in every case?

Clearly, as in all historical fiction, the narrative voice must establish the setting in such a way as to draw the reader in. Ellis Peters' medieval world is skilfully evoked through the eyes of her monk investigator, Cadfael, who, having lived much of his earlier life as soldier, is both part of his monastic community and able to see the limited viewpoint of those who have never lived in the outside world. The narrative 'voice' is not his, but enters into his thinking, so that we both observe and to a point partake of his way of dealing with too narrow church convictions or too draconian a civil law.

C.J. Sansom, in novels that are both thrillers and detective tales set in Henry VIII's reign, employs a first-person narrator, the investigator Shardlake, who is both at the heart of the escalating conspiracies on Henry's reign, and an outsider: he is burdened with physical deformity, and increasingly uncomfortable in the Reformation world. Sansom's research of the period is meticulous but, importantly, the world that has been researched is brought alive through Shardlake's familiarity with it, and by his own shock at fresh, unexpected revelations within it. Lindsey Davis, setting her detective-thriller works in the Roman Empire, also uses a first-person narrator but with a very different 'voice': her investigator, Falco, narrates his own stories, using the quick-fire, quipping language familiar to those who read Raymond Chandler's works. Yet at the same time his way of taking the reader with him into his ancient setting is both to paint lively word-pictures and invite us to believe our viewpoint is his. The easy familiarity of his tone, as if he is confiding to like-minded friends who, like him, look quizzically at authority, is alluring.

Stephen Saylor also uses a first-person narrator in his novels set at the end of republican Rome, as Caesar is about to come to power. But Saylor's narrator, the investigator Gordianus, uses the meditative tone of a diarist, pondering the psychology of the great figures of his day, the motivation driving a Cicero, a Pompey or a Caesar. He does not rely on wit to draw us in, but on his homely honesty, and his 'take' on the power politics of his day, which at times mirror our own modern world very disturbingly. This mirroring is a marked feature of Ariana Franklin's narrative 'voice'. Her narrator observes, from the outside, a medieval England where prejudices and hostility to anyone not belonging to the community are all too easily roused. Such a world could alienate us, but the narrator, while not the voice of a character, homes in on an unexpected protagonist, Adelia, a foreign, woman pathologist trained in a far more civilized, sophisticated South Italy, drawn into this backward England against her will, and having to come to terms with its prejudices against women and its superstitions about medicine, and especially corpses. So we are enticed into the mind of a highly intelligent, skilled woman in an unfamiliar world where women are more commonly seen as mere possessions; and Franklin's vivid, colloquial language gives the narrative 'voice' a familiarity that manipulates us into sympathies with those battling against hostility and injustice.

The sheer range of narrative techniques in this sample of historical fiction gives some idea of the role of the 'voice' of a narrator. At its best, as in the examples above, this 'voice' is simply something we accept, without consciously submitting to its powers of persuasion. But the books we lay aside after a few pages are the ones whose authors have not paid sufficient attention to the crucial underpinning the 'voice' gives to the story.

Elizabeth Maslen is Senior Research Fellow at the Institute of English Studies, University of London

www.ies.sas.ac.uk
www.women.qmul.ac.uk/virtual/women/atoz/maslen.htm

Chapter 9 – Dialogue

Pick up any historical novel that has been written recently and flick through the pages. You may be surprised to see how many of them consist of dialogue interspersed with short bursts of prose. This should immediately tell you as an aspiring writer that dialogue is very important. It is a means by which you can convey information to your reader. It enables you to let your reader eavesdrop on your characters and what is happening in their lives and their secrets, without having to directly tell them what is happening.

Writing effective dialogue that flows is the hallmark of professional writers. Some writers have a natural ability to write dialogue, whilst for others it can initially be a real struggle.

What will make writing dialogue easier for you is if you are a 'listener'. If you enjoy going into a café, pub, theatre, bus, or anywhere there are people and simply listening to what the people around you are discussing, and how they are discussing it then you are a listener. Do they use rich descriptive language, or are their verbal exchanges littered with four letter words? What are they discussing and does the language they use give us a clear picture of the event, problem or person they are talking about? Try not to look at the people you are listening to. Close your eyes briefly and try to imagine the people who are talking before you look at them. Then compare the picture that you have created of the speakers in your own mind with the real ones. Ask yourself questions such as did I match the speaker to the right social class? Was the character I'd imagined appropriate for the conversation that was taking place and the language that was being used? Did the conversation result in you creating stereotype characters for the speakers? Write the words **stereotype**[*] and **dialogue** on a piece of card or in your notebook to remind yourself when you start writing, that certain patterns of speech in dialogue will automatically conjure up character and situation stereotypes for your reader e.g. police station and a murder suspect.

At workshops a substantial percentage of novice writers find writing dialogue the most daunting of activities. It is usually because they aren't

---

[*] **Stereotype:** a standardized image, convention, concept or idea that is shared by a group of people

confident about the technical aspects of writing dialogue and the punctuation that is required when writing **direct speech**[*] (conversations).

The 'need-to-know' rules of punctuation for writing conversation (direct speech) and dialogue are:

1   Every time the speaker changes start a new paragraph.

2   Dialogue should be indented. Decide if you are going to indent your speech with two or three spaces before you start writing and keep the same pattern throughout your short story or novel.

3   Any words that are spoken and the punctuation that goes with them, are enclosed in inverted commas (speech marks). These can be either single or double. Currently, a lot of the major publishers appear to favour single inverted commas e.g.:
    'Any last words?' asked the executioner.

4   Even if the words that are spoken form a sentence, they are not followed by a full stop, but by a comma when the verb of saying[†] (e.g. said, call, bellow) comes afterwards, for instance:
    'I love the new milliner's[‡] shop in Milsom Street. They've so many captivating styles to tempt your purse, 'she said.
    'Don't you mean your husband's purse, or is it your current besotted admirer's?' Arabella asked.

5   If the subject (the person who is speaking) and the verb of saying start the sentence, the first word spoken has a capital letter and the verb of saying is followed by a comma, as in the examples below:
    Arabella said, 'I suspect that it will be your current besotted admirer who will be paying for your new hat and not your husband?'

---

[*] **Direct speech** (sometimes referred to as quoted speech): Saying exactly what someone (e.g. your character) has said

[†] **Saying verbs:** These verbs are used to show that someone is speaking. They are commonly used when writers want to use a different or more expressive word than 'said' for their direct speech tags. They are useful for the writer, because they can provide additional information about the speaker's tone of voice and as a result add both pace and depth of meaning to your dialogue e.g
    'Fire!' she *screamed*.
    'Get everyone out, now,' he *shouted*.

[‡] **Milliner:** a person who sells or makes hats for women. The origin of this work is thought to date from the 16th century when Milan was famous for such goods and fancy ornamentation for clothes.

6   This last 'rule' is the one that often causes writers who are just starting out the most difficulty. If you interrupt your spoken sentence and insert a verb of saying and its subject (the speaker) one comma is needed when breaking off the speech and another before you continue it. Please note that the first word that follows after the inverted commas and when your sentence continues should start with a lower case letter. Example:

> 'I would not be the talk of society,' Charlotte replied, 'if I hadn't my flock of admirers to buy me trinkets, would I my dearest Arabella?'

7   Compare the use of the comma, full stop and lower and upper case letter with the example below where you are not breaking a sentence, but using two separate ones. Example:

> 'Undoubtedly, I am the talk of society,' said Arabella. 'The main advantage of this is that my devoted flock of admirers feel beholden to shower me with the all the trinkets that I desire.'

Do remember that inverted commas (speech marks) aren't just used to show direct speech, but also for quotations, titles of books, plays and foreign words etc. This means that if you mention any of these in direct speech you need to make it clear what they are by using double inverted commas or single. Today some publishers use italics or underline them to highlight house names, newspapers, names of ships, unusual words etc.
Example:

> "I borrowed a book from the subscription library last week my dear Arabella. It was a light romantic satire and fun, but not in the least bit true to life. It was called 'Emma'. Have you had chance to read it yet?" Charlotte asked.

You will notice in this chapter that sometimes single inverted commas have been used for the examples of dialogue with double inverted commas inside to show quotes etc. and on other occasions double inverted commas have been used with single inverted commas to highlight quotes etc. This has been done intentionally to enable you to evaluate which style you prefer to work with. Don't do this when you are writing your own novel or story. You need to decide, which style you prefer and stick to it.

Lastly, but most importantly for your confidence's sake, always have at least one novel in the historical genre that you intend to write in, near you at all times. When in doubt open it at random to a page with dialogue on it, and then compare the punctuation and layout to your own.

What functions does dialogue serve?

- Dialogue provides a vehicle to help readers create a picture of the characters through the words that they use and how they use them. They may speak in an informal way, or a formal way. If they are using a formal register then the vocabulary that they use will reflect this e.g. they might not use first names or colloquial (slang words, or idioms) expressions. They might address the person that they are talking to as 'Sir' or 'Royal Highness' etc.

- Using dialogue ensures that the reader is given a pattern that they are familiar with in their everyday lives and that they can identify with. This gives novels a sense of verisimilitude (realism).

- It is a means to feed the reader with information that moves the plot forward.

- To create a sensation of tension and emotional relationships between characters. They can share words of love, exchange secrets and anxieties through their own words without the author being omnipotent and describing their emotions at a distance. Using dialogue effectively enables your characters to speak for themselves.

ACTIVITIES

9.1 Comparing our everyday conversations with conversations in novels

Objective   To be able to identify the differences between everyday conversations and those that characters have in novels and short stories.

Your task   **A**   To eavesdrop on three different conversations in three different places for example:
- Any form of public transport (including bus stops, train stations, airport lounges etc.);
- In a café (in a shopping, centre, market, service station etc.), a bar, pub or restaurant;
- At a sporting event of any kind;
- At a concert or performance (rock, folk, circus skills, a play, opera etc.).

It doesn't matter how mundane the conversations appear, your task is to concentrate on listening to three conversations (short bursts rather than lengthy interchanges) in different places and to commit to memory the gist and main subject of these conversations, and also any hesitation devices that the speaker uses). Then write down what you overheard.

Model

Venue: A bus

Subject and gist of the conversation: Pig racing. The couple were discussing how the local council had no idea how to organise a pig race, because as any farmer knew pigs didn't run in straight lines, but circles.

Hestitation devices: um, er, well,
Hesitation devices (we often use these when we are speaking in order to give us a chance to think before we speak or answer a question.) We often use more of them when we are nervous. They are a delaying tactic that we apply automatically when we are talking.

B Pick a historical novel that you enjoy reading and see if you can notice any difference, apart from the subject of conversations. Look carefully to see how many, if any, hesitation devices the author uses. What conclusion can you draw from this experiment? Is it that although the dialogue in the novel you chose appears to be real, in fact it is only written to give a semblance of being real. Why don't authors include the small hesitation devices that we use almost all the time? When they do use them is it for a specific purpose e.g. to show that a character is trying to cover something up or that they are nervous?

9.2 Eavesdropping

Objective   To use snippets of conversations that you've overheard to convey humour, anger, pathos* and information.

Your task   It may take you a few weeks to collect together enough snippets of conversations to complete this activity, but as you overhear suitable conversations then you can try to write an appropriate dialogue on one of the themes above that might be suitable for the historical period that you are interested in writing about. Please note that in the dialogues below some models have used single inverted commas and others double. You might like to experiment with both to see what difference they make to the appearance of your dialogues on the page.

---

* **Pathos**: a quality in speech, or a written communication that arouses feelings of pity, sorrow or sympathy

Dialogue Type: Humorous

Model

Subject and gist of the eavesdropped conversation: Pig racing. The couple were discussing how the local council had no idea how to organise a pig race, because as any farmer knew pigs didn't run in straight lines, but circles.

Period: Medieval

'Well, John did you hear what that daft half-wit, the new Abbot Aelfric has gone and done for the Michaelmas fair?' Richard asked.

John took a slow, and long sip of ale before he answered.

'No, what's the half baked idiot done now?'

'He's decided that the pigs are going to run in straight lines. I mean anyone should know that pigs won't run in straight lines. They only runs in circles.'

John's eyes widened in horror.

'He's not just got a face like a trout then he's also got a mind like one as well. That's what going to a University and learning to read and write does for you. I reckon that it saps away the common sense you'm born with.'

Write your dialogue below:

Dialogue Type: Anger

Model

Subject and gist of the eavesdropped conversation: Two young women in a hairdresser's describing a friend whose boyfriend they'd seen with another girl.

Period: Second World War

'Lizzie, it was awful. I just couldn't believe my eyes. There Will was in the back row of the Gaumont cuddling up to Pat, that awful girl from the fish and chippie near the barracks. I mean we all know the reputation of the Americans over here, but Will just had the most perfect manners. Meg's going to be devastated. First Bert is killed at Dunkirk and now this. Frankly, I'd love to strangle Will with the silk stockings he gave Meg.'

'I can think of worse things we could do to him. Meg's so kind. Men like Will make me so cross, they are bastards,' said Lizzie.

Write your dialogue in your notebook

Dialogue Type: Pathos

Model

Subject and gist of the eavesdropped conversation: A conversation overheard in a post office between two pensioners about the recent death of a younger friend.

Period: End of the nineteenth century

"What are you supposed to say, Emily? Everyone knew when they sent her off to the seaside that she wouldn't be coming back. It's very sad for her children of course, but consumption just carries people off. Life just isn't fair."

"No, it certainly wasn't fair to Maggie. Her husband has always been sickly, she looked after her parents and then to have five children one after the other. It would be enough to kill anyone. It's a miracle that she lasted as long as she did, but I do agree with you it is a tragedy for the children. Particularly for Gwyneth as she's the oldest sister and will end up having to look after them all, even though she's only just ten."

Write your dialogue in your notebook

Dialogue Type: Information

Model

Subject and gist of the eavesdropped conversation: An art class where the demonstrator was explaining how to paint sky.

Period: Renaissance

'So, my dear Michelangelo tell me your secret. How did you make the sky look as if it was part of a summer day here in Rome?'

'I had to lie on my back with my nose almost pressed against the Sistine chapel ceiling for an eternity, or so it seemed. I think God should redeem my sins for my efforts, don't you my charming young pupil? No, don't answer, I know what you really want is my secret recipe for mixing the colours I used for creating the blue of heaven on earth. Well, listen closer as I whisper the secret into your shell like ear. First of all you grind dry powdered pigments into a medium, such as egg. The pigments I used are ...'

Write your dialogue below:

9.3 Verbs of saying

Objective Verbs of saying (e.g. said, shout and answer) are powerful tools that by careful selection authors can use to conjure up the tone of the scene.

Your task Compare the two examples below and decide, which gives an impression of urgency and why?

1 "Be careful! It could be dangerous," he said.

2 "Be careful! It could be dangerous," he shouted.

3 "Be careful! It could be dangerous," he yelled.

4 "Be careful! It could be dangerous," he called.

9.4 Making a collection of verbs of saying

Objective To save you time when writing it is useful to have a checklist of verbs of saying that you can use sparingly to add impact to your dialogue and story.

Your task To compile a checklist of verbs of saying in the table below. This has been divided into two columns, the first **Mild Verbs of Saying** and the second **Strong/Powerful Verbs of Saying.** There is no right or wrong in this activity, which can become compulsive. You may find that every time you open a book you are scanning it to find different verbs of saying. We would be very interested to find out how many you can uncover. Please do contact us through the web site **www.myfanwycook.com** and let us know your final total.

Mild Verbs of Saying		Strong/Powerful Verbs of Saying	
said		shout	
comment		yell	
state		declaim	
remark		interrogate	
add		regale	
agree		tease	
interject		banter	
question		cry	
call		enthuse	
impart		demand	
		argue	
		implore	
		roar	
		bellow	
		sneer	
		snap	
		snort	
		meow	
		snarl	
		grumble	
		laugh	
		chuckle	
		yell	
		scream	
		bark out	

Beware: Using a wide range of saying verbs can signify an accomplished writer, but they can also indicate an inexperienced writer who is trying too hard to avoid using the saying verb 'said'. The writing that results from just trying to replace 'said' with other saying verbs can be stilted, and then it becomes a disadvantage rather than an advantage. Beware the overuse of interesting and powerful verbs of saying.

A sense of period

Ensuring that the dialogue you write is easy for your reader to identify with, but also reinforces the sense of time and place that you are writing about, takes skill. It is almost like adding the smallest details to a miniature painting and requires you to think in the same way as a painter adding the final, tiny brush stokes that bring their work alive.

One way of achieving this is to occasionally replace the verbs that we would use today with verbs that were commonly used and understood in the period. You can use the same procedure with idiomatic expressions or names of objects. Using vocabulary that was in common usage at the period has its dangers. Using the occasional one is fine, but just as when you take tablets prescribed by a doctor who states clearly that you should not take more than X tablets in a day, the same warning could equally apply to introducing words that aren't in current usage today into your dialogue.

Where can you easily access the authentic vocabulary of the time? Newspapers, transcripts of old court cases, advertisements, broadsheets and plays rather than novels, because plays were written to entertain a target audience and therefore are likely to contain all the language that was in vogue at the time. Letters particularly the kind that were sent back home from young men on the grand tour of Europe, because such letters were often designed to be read aloud to the families at home. Letters, and diaries from prisoners, soldiers and of course love letters. Collections of letters such as Jane Austen's correspondence with her sister Cassandra of which only c.160 out of c.3, 000 have been discovered. Poetry and novels on the other hand can be misleading as far as vocabulary and the use of language is concerned. They might tell the reader about themes and subjects that were popular during the period and the literary conventions of the period, but not necessarily anything about the spoken language. Such sources as letters and plays also provide us with authentic information about how people addressed each other e.g. Jane Austen addresses her sister often as, 'My Dear Cassandra' (see **www.pemberley.com** for further information). Do remember that this approach to writing dialogue may not suit your style of writing, and for certain periods in the past this kind of information is just not available in English translation, or at all.

ACTIVITIES

9.5 Pish! Using verbs appropriate to your chosen period

Objective   Unearthing verbs that you might be able to use in writing dialogues

Your task   Using primary sources should they exist from a period that you are interested in, make a list of verbs that were in common usage and try to incorporate a few of them in a mini-dialogue, between two characters of your own choosing. For example the verb 'belie', which Shakespeare used and means 'to misrepresent or to show to be untrue'. You will also find interjections of period such as 'pish' used in Shakespeare's plays. 'Pish' is an exclamation of contempt or impatience. Other examples of words that might have been in common usage from the 16th century onwards are 'afford', which originally meant to give, supply or yield. 'Peruse', was introduced into English in the 15th century and means now, as it did then, to examine with care, or to browse and read through in a leisurely way.

Try to find ten verbs and then write them below:

Model

Period: c.1800-1820

'Pish! Elizabeth why should I care what Sir James Martineau cares about me. He may afford you the politeness of acknowledging you when our paths cross, but he ignores me.'

'Charlotte, that is your own doing, is it not? You give the impression that you've never even perused the most popular of novels let alone read anything of any consequence.'

Write your mini-dialogue in your notebook.

9.6 Whispering sweet nothings

Objective To write a mini-romantic dialogue.

Your task To write two mini-dialogues that might suit a romantic-style historical novel. Try to make one of these more suggestive than the other.

---

1 | **Model**

Period: 1920s

'I know I'm not much good at dancing, but would you like to dance Evelyn? I just love, the way you dance, but then that's not all I love about you, but you do know that don't you?' asked Arthur.

'Thank you, I like dancing, and I would love to dance with you even if you do step on my toes,' said Evelyn, and gave him a smile that made him forget for one brief instant the ghosts of his friends who had died in the trenches, and who usually never left his side.

Write your dialogue in your notebook.

---

2 | **Model (more suggestive)**

Period: c.1860s

'Madame, your gown is spectacular, but not I suspect as splendid as the body that lies beneath it if the portion of it that is visible is a sample of the rest.'

'I am glad that you are able to take pleasure in the view that Monsieur Henri's creation allows you. The décolleté neckline only gives you a glimpse of what I may I assure you Sir are not the best of my attributes. They Sir, are hidden from your view for the present time, at least.'

Write a mini-dialogue below:

9.7 To swear or use dialect?

You may intend to write a hard hitting novel set around a military campaign or sea battles. This may entail your characters using expletives[*], which means that you will have to decide how often and what type. It may be that you decide that one of your characters habitually uses idioms or dialect. Sparing use of both may help you to build a sense of time, place and character. For example if you decide to set your novel at the end of the Second World War, then if your character had been fighting in the desert he might well have used colloquial phrases such as 'to take a shufti (or shufty)' at something meaning 'to take a quick look'. The word 'shufti' having been borrowed from the Arabic verb 'shufti'. Its origin may date back as far as the RAF c. 1925.

If you decide to use dialect it is much more difficult to pinpoint periods. For example in 1960s Devon in the UK, the use of dialect was still common in the rural areas and even amongst children in schools. The dialect included its own grammatical structures, vocabulary, intonation and idiomatic expression. Fifty years later except amongst the older members of the community the only traces that remain are in the intonation and also a few words such as 'mazed' (crazy) and 'dreckley/dreckly' (I will do it directly). Fortunately many parts of the UK have managed to hold on to more of their traditional dialect and idiomatic expressions.

Objective	To use idioms and dialect effectively to enhance your dialogue writing skills. It is particularly useful in distinguishing between social classes, but also for introducing humour.
Your task	To create a character and write a scene set in any past period where your character could have used both idioms and dialect.

> **Situation:** Office of the housemaster of a major English public school c.1910. On the recommendation of a Devonshire vicar a farm worker's son, Tom Conibere, has been awarded a bursary to study mathematics and science. He has just arrived and Mr. Smythe-Smallhampton is asking him about his interests and previous schooling.
>
> **Dialect:** Devonshire

[*] **Expletives:** (swearwords or a sounds that express an emotional reaction and need not have any meaning)

> **Dialogue Model**
>
> Tom didn't dare look at the housemaster's face and so he stared at his shoes instead.
>
> "Right, Conibere just tell me something about your interests and the sports you've played. And do look at me, as you aren't in church now and it's most disconcerting to have someone contemplating their feet."
>
> "Well, Sir you'm knows what it's like. Us played cricket, but my best sport was shooting. I'd go out and shoot them darnd big blackbirds. Beautiful it was in the dimpsey* waiting to get the buggers."
>
> *__Dimpsey__: twilight

Your turn

Situation:

Dialect:

Dialogue:

9.8 Subject related idioms

If your narrative takes place against a specialist setting or background, to add an atmosphere of authenticity you may wish to include selected idiomatic expressions in your dialogue. In order to achieve this you can save time by creating files of idiomatic expressions on subjects and themes. Remember not to overuse them in your dialogue. Certain subjects such as sport, horse racing and farming are a rich source for idioms.

Objective	To become aware of the range, origin and variety of idioms that have been, and are used in speech, and to start to compile lists of idioms on specific topics.
Your task	To find at least five idiomatic expressions for the subjects below and to complete the table overleaf.

Idiom	Meaning	Origin
Naval and Maritime		
Example: *two* (or three) *sheets to the wind*	Someone who has had too much to drink and is staggering about	Originally it was three sheets to the wind. The first usage was c. 1821. It refers to the ropes, which secured the sheets (or sails) and which in high winds would cause sailing ships to stagger about like a person who was drunk.
Your examples		
Gardening		
Example: *to nip in the bud*	To stop or prevent something when it is just beginning	It is derived from allusion to the de-budding of plants. The earlier idiomatic form was 'nip in the bloom': see Henry Chettle's romance *Piers Plainnes Seaven Yeres Prentiship* (1595).
Your examples		

Tips

- If you don't feel confident about writing dialogue then you might like to consider writing a short story before embarking on writing a novel. It will provide you with an opportunity to experiment.
- It may be tempting if you are working to a specific word count to use 'dialogue' as an easy way to fill out your novel or story. Your readers are likely to spot that you have included dialogue that doesn't serve any purpose, and so make certain that the verbal exchanges between your characters are there for a reason.

Barbara Cleverly

"Conversation can be tricky. How did they speak in the past? You'll know because you'll have immersed yourself in contemporary texts. The trouble is – you risk losing your readers if you stick faithfully to the phrases you've collected. Avoid jarring neologisms and keep it simple. Good, straightforward English will always be pleasing and convincing. Use a few historically appropriate phrases for impact but be sparing. Ellis Peters always judges it perfectly as does Mary Renault. Read other good historical writers and deconstruct their sentences. How do they achieve their effect?"

www.barbaracleverly.com

Useful Sources

www.phrases.org.uk
wwww.idioms.thefreedictionary.com
www.sportsidioms.com

Chapter 10 – Description and Mood

When we want to create a mood or write a description, it is useful to try to engage all the reader's exterior senses e.g. visual (what they can see), sounds, smell, taste, touch and also their interior ones as well, such as the emotional responses that they may have to particular places, scents, fear etc. Description is a tool used to serve a purpose such as creating a sense of place in your story or for characterisation. It is also used to give explanations etc., but is rarely used just for its own sake.

The skill that the aspiring writer needs to acquire is to decide which of the senses you want to stimulate in your reader. It may be all of them, but at other times you may just want to concentrate on visual imagery, your aim being to try to coax and persuade your readers that what you are writing is 'real', and so enabling them to experience the scene that you've written. Using sensory descriptions that create an image in your reader's mind is one way of provoking an emotional response from your reader. Imagery can be created through using similes and metaphors, but can also be strengthened by the use of a wide range of appropriate vocabulary.

Unfortunately, the overuse of descriptive imagery can have the opposite effect. Your aim is to achieve a balance of vivid descriptions that are appropriate to the subject you are writing about, without falling into the trap of using lots of descriptive adjectives and adverbs when a few carefully chosen ones would have more impact.

The power of original detail in descriptions

Using original detail in descriptive writing is a powerful tool as it helps to make your writing more believable. It's the details that capture our imagination, a beautiful sunset, a birthday present wrapped in sumptuous gold paper with a matching ribbon. These details are 'real' and we can use them to draw readers into the period of history and the story that we create. Using specific detail will help your reader to identify with the period and setting that you are writing about. If you mention a drinking vessel then you need to be specific. Is it a chalice, a porcelain cup or a pewter tankard? If it is a chalice then what sort of chalice is it? Is it made from gold, silver or pottery? Is it a 6th century Etruscan *bucchero* chalice or a plain Scottish Presbyterian Communion Cup of the 18th century? Details make objects, places and the lives that your characters are leading come alive.

Your choice is which items and scenes to describe. A rule of thumb that successful writers of short stories often apply ruthlessly, is that if the item or place isn't significant to a story then you have to leave it out. Places and items aren't simply descriptions and a background for your characters to play out their story. They have their own 'role' to play and you don't want the important details to be swamped by other less significant passages of descriptive writing.

Break it up

When writing your short story or novel try to remember that pages and pages of descriptive writing are hard for a reader to concentrate on, and boredom may set in. Don't forget to intersperse description with dialogue or at least vary the type of description e.g. background and character.

The basic tools

When writing descriptions we use a range of technical tools. We will often do this automatically. We often use these devices without knowing what the technical term is. Below are listed a few of the common ones and examples of how they can be used.

Alliteration: the use in a phrase or sentence of words that begin with the same letter as in 'Silvia's sumptuous silk sash'. However, the term alliteration can also be used to refer to the repetition of a letter within a word, or a combination of initial and medial repetition 'Alison always allowing'. It can also be used to describe the repetition of the same sound as in 'fierce phantoms fought Francis'.

Your mini-task is to pick up any novel, magazine or newspaper and find three examples of the use of alliteration and write them in your notebook.

Personification: the origin of this word comes from the Latin verb *persona* meaning an actor's mask, and *facere*, to make. It means to make (an object, animal or emotion) into a person. In everyday speech we use this form all the time when we refer to a ship as 'she' or we call our cars 'him' or her' or when we use expressions such as 'Fate walked in.'

Your mini-task is to find three other examples of personification from any source and write them down.

Simile and metaphor: a simile clearly compares or likens two different things in one or more of their properties or features; for example 'clever as a river rat' or 'white as a freshly laundered sheet'. Metaphors have been defined as compressed similes, because a phrase, word, idea or object is used to suggest a likeness or comparison between them for instance 'Mr. Cutty-Smythe sailed into the church stately as a galleon under full sail' or 'He fired a volley of questions at the speaker.'

Your mini-task is to find an example of both a metaphor and a simile from any written source and to write them down.

ACTIVITIES

10.1 Colouring in

Like any artist, as a writer you need to have a palate of colours available for you to write vibrant and captivating description of places, people and the periods in which they live. It may also help as a writer of fiction set in the past, to be aware of the symbolic meaning of colours.

Objectives	◆ To keep a colour diary
	◆ To write a descriptive scene that focuses on using the imagery of colours to create vivid and vibrant descriptions
Your task	To keep a colour diary for a minimum of three weeks. For this activity you may find it simplest to buy a small notebook that you can slip into your pocket, unless you have a Netbook that you carry around with you most of the time. You will need to divide your notebook up with separate headings for all the colours (and non-colours black and white). You will also need two sub-section headings: 'Expressions, Idioms and phrases' and 'My own colour creations' for each colour. Remember that just as characters' personalities are usually neither 'black' nor white' colours come in shades, hues and different tones.

Example

Colour: Green

> pea green, acid green, apple green, sea green, lime green, emerald, peridot, ice green, pale green, mint green, peppermint green, sage green

---

Expressions, Idioms and phrases

green with envy
green as grass
to give someone the green light
green stuff (money)
to be green (inexperienced)
a greenhorn (inexperienced or naive)
the green-eyed monster (jealousy)
green belt (e.g. protected area of countryside around
    a city
green around the gills
the grass is always greener on the other side
to give someone the green light
to have green fingers (or a green thumb)
The Green room*

* **Green room**: A room where actors met before and after a performance. Early English theatre had several graded according to the salary of the actor. The first reference is in Thomas Shadwell's play *A True Widow* (1678). Possibly the last remaining 'Green Room' is now at Drury Lane in London.

My own colour creations

greengage green, mould green, spinach green, green
and wholesome as a cabbage, green as wet slate,
green as Hurdwick stone, mushy-pea green, spring-
green, green as a frog, green as the Greenman

Write your examples in your notebook.

Colour:

Expressions, Idioms and phrases:

My own colour creations:

10.2 The white feather[*] and the green dress[†]

Objective   Using idioms or expressions to enhance your descriptive writing.

Your task   Using one of the idioms or expressions that you've uncovered write a scene (no more than 500 words) in which the idiom could be included.

Example

"Alice you can't possibly be married in green, even if it is a very pale green you know it's supposed to bring bad luck, and your mother will have apoplexy. It may be 1921, but it's just not done. Lady Beckington is one of the generation who believes that old rhyme, 'Married in green, ashamed to be seen'. "

"Well, Clarice you may be my best friend, but whatever you say I'm wearing green. When I married James in 1918 I wore white and he was blown up in the trenches two weeks later. So this time I'm wearing green silk and that is that."

---

[*] **White Feather**: Since the 18th century the white feather has often been associated with cowardice. To give a white feather to a person being considered a symbolic sign of cowardice. It is thought that the origin was the belief that gamecocks with white tail feather were poor fighters.

[†] **Green dress**: A green wedding dress is traditionally considered to be unlucky in England unless worn by Irish women.

10.3 That smells nice!

Marcel Proust (1871–1922) was a French novelist, and although not a historical novelist, his ability to use descriptions of taste and smell about his childhood memories, dramatically changed the way that writers from different genres have written descriptions. *A la recherche du temps perdu* (*In Search of Lost Time*, which was first translated under the title of *Remembrance of Things Past*) and was published in seven parts. Proust argued that smell and taste were senses that although fragile, left an enduring impression on our minds. This is a concept which aspiring historical writers need to be aware of, and to use in their descriptive writing. It means that you need to be able to describe the smell of blocked drains, your favourite cake being cooked, bleach or pungent cheeses, and if you are a vegetarian and don't eat meat or buy it and you are writing about a butcher's shop, then it means going inside one just to smell it, however much it may revolt you.

Objective	To isolate different types of pleasant scents or smells and then describe them.
Your task	Select three different things that have a fragrant and enticing scent and describe each one in fewer than 300 words. This descriptive writing activity is not an imaginative one, and so you will need to smell the place or thing that you are describing. You might want to think about scents that will have been around in the period that you are considering writing about e.g. lavender. It's recorded that the ancient Greeks used lavender as a perfume, but referred to the herb as *nardus*, after Naarda, a city in Syria. Lavender has been in constant use ever since as a perfume and medicine. You might also like to carry out some background research to discover how long the smell has been around.

You can check out places and sites such as:
- **www.perfumesguide.com**
- **www.farina1709.com** 50667Cologne, Germany
- **www.parispass.com**
  - Fragonard Parfumeur - Le Musée du Parfum, 9 rue Scribe, 75009 Paris
  - Fragonard Parfumeur - Le Théatre-Musée des Capucines, 39 Bld des Capucines, 75002 Paris

Giovanni Maria Farina was the first perfume house to create the fragrance Eau de Cologne in 1709 and is the world's oldest perfume company. Farina's perfume was patronised by most Royal families in Europe (for example Queen Victoria and King Edward the Seventh) and by many famous people including Mozart, Napoleon Bonaparte, Benjamin Disraeli, Marc Twain, and Oscar Wilde. Equally as famous are the names of those who have created perfume bottles for the company. The company have their own perfume museum in Cologne and have original records of all their transactions dating back to 1709. The bottles carry a label with a small red tulip, which has been used as a trademark to signify its rarity and value.

If you are interested in the history of perfume then you might like to visit one of the old established perfume shops in London such as *Floris** (**www.florislondon.com**) or *Penhaligon's* (**www.penhaligons.com**), which will give you an insight into which fragrances were popular and when.

---

* **Floris** have been 'purveyors' of perfumes to the Court of St James since 1730.

Write your descriptions in your notebooks or somewhere that you'll be able to access them if you want to use them in your novel or short story.

10.4 Yuck! What a disgusting smell!

Objective   To isolate different types of unpleasant or disgusting smells and then describe them.

Your task   Select three different things that have a disgusting, pungent or horrible smell and describe each one in less than 300 words. This descriptive writing activity is not an imaginative one and so you will need to smell the place or thing that you are describing.

Certain smells will have been around since before records began, such as the smell of rotting food and manure. You might like to carry out some background research to discover how long the smell has been around that you are thinking of describing e.g. if you are writing about leather tanning then if possible it would enable you to add in extra detail if you had experienced what it smelt like. Every place that you visit will have and have had its own distinctive smell. Details do count and so if you are trying to write a story set in Sarawak or Brunei, you might want to describe the durian. It's a particularly tasty fruit, but its smell is considered so unpleasant that it has been banned from some hotels and on public transport. It has been known for over 600 years to travellers from Europe and pictures of the almond flavoured fruit are easily accessible, but a photograph doesn't convey its smell. In cases such as this then clearly you will have to rely on the descriptions of those who have eaten it to assist you in writing about the durian, unless you have the opportunity to visit Malaysia and taste it yourself.

However for this activity try to select odours that the ordinary reader will be able to identify with, such as fish that has gone off, or milk that has been spilt and not cleaned up. Cheeses are a wonderful source of inspiration if you intend write about 'vomit-inducing smells'. Go into a cheesemongers or a specialist cheese shop and ask to smell 'Stinking Bishop'[*] or something equally as pungent, and then describe it. Goats cheeses can also be particularly devastating smell-wise. Alternatively, you could visit some of the world's smelliest museums e.g. the Musée du Camembert[†].

[*] **www.teddingtoncheese.co.uk**
[†] **www.camembert-country.com**

Write your descriptions in your notebooks or somewhere that you'll be able to access them if you want to use them in your novel or short story.

Tip

Don't forget the air. Try to describe the difference between the air in a city and in the country or inside a flat or house and outside in the garden. Also don't forget that if you are writing about the air it will smell different, depending on the season that you are writing about. This is particularly true when writing about the past. In cities in the past the air in the summer would have been less polluted because people wouldn't have had fires roaring away to keep them warm.

Similarly transport smells have changed dramatically and if you are writing about steam trains you must try to experience the hot air, and smell and feel the soot that went along with it. Railway preservation societies exist all around the world and in the UK it is relatively easy to still experience the smell of travelling by steam train (see **ukhrail.uel.ac.uk, www.nrm.org.uk, www.swindon.gov.uk/steam, www.talyllyn.co.uk, www.didcotrailwaycentre.org.uk, www.southdevonrailway.org, www.firstgreatwestern.co.uk,** and for India **www.nationalrailmuseum.org**)

10.5 That feels like silk!

Objective   To describe fabrics and materials

Your tasks   **A**   To select three different types of material, if possible ones that would have been available during the period that you would like to write about, and then describe each one in no more than 300 words. You might select a precious metal such as gold or silver, or a particular type of wood such as oak or rosewood. Perhaps you are interested in fabrics such as satin, silk or wool, or perhaps you'd like to write about wrought iron or paper. Remember the objective of this activity is not to describe the object, but the material from which it is made.

Example

The black soapstone is as sheer as silk. Gleaming like polished jet or coal it fleetingly captures passing reflections on its surface. It's heavy, but not icy cold to touch.

N.B. The description above is written in the present tense.

Write your descriptions somewhere that you'll be able to access them if you want to use them in your novel or short story.

B To describe in detail three objects and the materials which they are made from. If possible select an object from the period that you are keen to write about, and also what it was used for e.g. anything from a prehistoric flint axe to a Kewpie (Cupie) doll, which were manufactured from 1913 onwards, and originally made in bisque or celluloid.

Write your descriptions somewhere that you'll be able to access them if you want to use them in your novel or short story.

10.6 If 'music be the food of love'?

Objective To write descriptions about music of the period that you are writing about. This will be a difficult task for aspiring writers who would like to write about the far distant past, but whistling, humming, singing and drumming are possible examples of early music that you could include.

Your tasks Write all your descriptions somewhere that you'll be able to access them if you want to use them in your novel or short story.

A Listen to a piece of music, song or an instrument from the period that you are interested in writing about, and describe how it sounds, but not how it makes you feel.

B Describe how you think the piece would have made your character feel.

C Make a list of phrases and expressions that we use about objects or actions that mention music or songs e.g. a kettle whistling, dawn chorus (of birds) etc.

D Try to make up some phrases of your own e.g. her voice was as shrill as a flute's top note, drumming out a letter on the Hanson Ball writing machine etc.

10.7 Yummy! Lip smackingly delicious!

Food, yummy, scrummy and glorious, but sometimes bland and tasteless. As an aspiring writer you will need to convey all these to your readers to help build up a picture of the period you've chosen to write about.

Objective   To create pictures in words that conjure up the taste, aroma, texture, visual appearance and emotional reactions to food.

Your tasks   Write all your descriptions somewhere that you'll be able to access them if you want to use them in your novel or short story.

A   Write a description (in no more than 300 words) of your favourite food, make certain that you describe what it looks like, smells like, tastes like, feels like (in your mouth) and why you like it.

B   Carry out some research into any period in the past and pick a meal to describe. It could be a meal that comprises toast and sardines, alternatively it might be a royal banquet. Then write a scene in which one character describes the meal and their reactions to it.

C   Write a description (in no more than 300 words) of a food that you dislike eating. Make certain that you describe what it looks like, smells like, tastes like, feels like (in your mouth) and why you dislike it.

D   Carry out some research into any period in the past and pick a meal to describe what you imagine would have tasted disgusting to you. It could be just one dish or item of food, or a full meal. Then write a scene in which one character describes the meal and their reactions to it.

10.8 Spiders scare me half to death!

Objective   To write descriptions of things that frighten people and why.

Your tasks   Write all your descriptions somewhere that you'll be able to access them if you want to use them in your novel or short story

A   What frightens you? Make a list of things and places that you are frightened of e.g. rats, snakes, being shut up in confined spaces.

B   Make up an imaginary list of what one of your characters might be frightened of e.g. being burnt for witchcraft, being enslaved or transported to Australia, spiders etc.

C   Pick one fear from the list that you've compiled for your character, and write a snapshot scene (no more than 500 words) in which they come face to face with their 'fear,' although it doesn't necessarily have to be them who is experiencing it directly e.g. they might be watching prisoners boarding a ship to be transported etc.

10.9 That 'X' always reminds me of...

Objective   Often when we visit a place, see a picture, catch a glimpse of an unknown face on a street or hear a tune it reminds us of somewhere or someone else.

Your task   Write all your descriptions somewhere that you'll be able to access them if you want to use them in your novel or short story

To write a scene in which a character sees something that reminds them of a significant previous event in their life.

Model

Gerard walked through the silent village. In one cobbled courtyard his eye was caught by a small hand carved wooden horse on wheels. It reminded him of Dobbin, the grey and white spotted toy horse that his father had carved for him. He mustn't look back. He

---

> could never look back as he didn't want to face the past again, and yet he wanted to rescue the abandoned wooden horse. The desire contradicted his logic, but he had to save it from the coming bombardment. It was as if all his future happiness depended on it.

Your turn

10.10 In the name of the rose

We may see an object, but we may not be aware of what it symbolised to a particular community or group of people in the past. Flowers, superstitions and rituals all played a part in the lives of our ancestors, and it can add an extra dimension to your story if you are aware of their significance.

Objective   To practise incorporating superstitions and symbols that had meaning to individuals, communities or societies during past times.

Your task   Your task is to find three 'symbolic' items and to write a short descriptive scene (no more than 500 words) in which they are mentioned along with clues to your reader about their significance.

Background - The Rose

Roses have always been prized for their beauty, but they are also symbols of love and beauty. We often associate it with St. Valentine's Day and also with the nursery rhyme *Roses are red, Violets are blue*, which can be found in collections as early as *Gammer Gurton's Garland* of 1784.

The rose was considered as sacred to such goddesses as Aphrodite and Isis, but also the Virgin Mary in Christianity. The phrase *sub rosa*, which means 'under the rose' means to keep a secret, and its origin may be the Ancient Roman practice of placing a wild rose on the door of rooms where secret meetings were taking place.

Model

Darkness cloaked the small Cornish fishing village. The moon and stars were hidden behind thick clouds. It was too cold to rain, but Jacob's years in the Navy told him that sleet or snow would fall before dawn arrived. The salt air might stop it settling, but it was not a night to venture out. He would have preferred to be indoors by a fire instead of shivering outside on a night when only ghosts should be prowling the streets. However, wreckers he knew wouldn't be put off by the foul conditions that December evening. In fact it would be ideal weather for them to lure any unfortunate vessel that had strayed off course to its fate.

His mission from the Duchy of Cornwall was to track them down to their secret meeting place. He'd prowled the narrow streets on many nights over the past months eying every cottage with suspicion, but tonight his luck was in. One well-maintained fisherman's cottage had a tiny white silk rose entwined on the top of its door knocker. Seagulls screeched from time to time above his head. Jacob waited.

Your turn

Write your descriptions and background notes somewhere that you'll be able to access them if you want to use them in your novel or short story.

10.11 Blink!

Objective   To introduce you to the impact of light when writing descriptions. *Chiaroscuro* —the importance of light in art descriptive writing.

Your tasks   **A**   Pick a room in your own home and over a period of a week write four mini-descriptions of no more than 300 words about the effect the time of day has on the light in that room. If you decide to use your bedroom then before you switch on the light in the morning, try to write down what the room looks like. Is the furniture clearly visible? etc. Then last thing at night describe it with the lights switched on.

B   Pick a place outside, and over a period of a week write four mini-descriptions at different times of day, to show the impact that light or the absence of light has on the place you are writing about.

10.12 Soundscapes

Objective   To practise using 'sound effects' to add extra 'colour' and 'depth' to your descriptions.

Your tasks   Write all your descriptions somewhere that you'll be able to access them if you want to use them in your novel or short story

A   Write a scene (maximum 500 words) that is set at night during the period that you are interested in writing about.

Model

The stillness frightened him. He was used to carts rumbling over cobble stones and the banter of men whose voices were raised after an evening in their favourite tavern. He looked up at the crystal clear night sky and the stars that twinkled down like candles. He remained motionless with his back against the roughly hewn granite wall of a sheep pen. At first all he could hear were faint snuffling and grunting sounds which got louder. He peered out through a hole in the wall. All he could see were the black silhouettes of stunted windblown trees. He wondered if the stories of the beasts of the moor

---

could be true. If so it was an invisible beast, because the sound was getting louder and louder, but he couldn't see anything close by. The screech of an owl cut into the silence. The snorting was getting closer. He was tempted to stand up, but didn't. A rustling close by made him look down. Near his feet two long nosed creatures with spikes appeared to be looking for food, munching and sniffling as they went foraging. Nathaniel had never seen one of these creatures, but knew it to be a hedgehog. He wanted to touch it, but knew better. Hedgehogs like rats carried fleas. Then he heard the sound he'd been waiting for, the muffled sound of a horse and rider as it galloped through the grass. A rider carrying stolen documents that he knew it was his task to watch. A shot exploded through the night air like a flash of summer lightning. The sound reverberated around the tors like an echo in a cave. The rider's horse whinnied in fear. Another shot rang with the piercing clarity of a church bell. Nathaniel had failed. The shot he feared had been the death knell of the rider and his own aspirations to climb up the rope ladder and become a master spy.

B If you have chosen to write a city 'soundscape' then write another one that is set in a rural area. You might like to try writing it set in a different period than the one that you are interested in.

Mood

We can ensure that our descriptions are richer and more interesting by making certain that we try to engage all the readers' senses. We also use the same writing skills to create mood. In addition there are technical skills such as the length of the sentences that we choose to use that can help to create the mood.

ACTIVITIES

10.13 Using sounds to change mood

Objective   To use sounds to intensify the mood of your writing.

Your task   Write a scene that you would like to include in a story.

> **Then:**
>
> 1   Rewrite it introducing as many sounds as possible that would show that the action was taking place on a summery day e.g. bees buzzing.
>
> 2   Rewrite it using only long sentences introducing sounds that you would only notice at night e.g. floorboards creaking, owls hooting etc.
>
> 3   Rewrite it as if it takes place during a storm and include all the sound effects that you can think of e.g. rain like musket shot hitting the roof tiles, thunder claps like discordant applause etc.
>
> 4   Take the original piece that you wrote and include any sound effects that you think might be appropriate to the mood that you would like to create.

10.14 Using pace to change mood

Objective   To experiment with different sentence lengths to see how it affects the mood of your writing.

Your task   Write a scene that you would like to include a story.

> **Then:**
>
> 1   Rewrite it using only short sentences.
>
> 2   Rewrite it using only long sentences.
>
> 3   Rewrite it using a mixture of sentence lengths.

10.15 I blame it on the weather

Objective   To observe how varying the weather conditions that your action takes place in, can change the mood of your descriptive writing.

Your task   To write three mini-descriptions (in no more than 500 words) that include a character in an appropriate setting, each one demonstrating the impact of different weather conditions on the character's mood.

Model

1   Florence was looking forward to the garden party that Lady Huntson was organising to celebrate Charlotte's birthday. Under normal circumstances she might not have been invited, but Charlotte had insisted that Lady Hunston invite her. Insisting that it wasn't Florence's fault that her father had gambled all their money away and then shot himself nor had Flo any control over her mother dying of grief as a consequence. The weather had been perfect for the past week and Florence's dress and hat were ready. The material had been rescued from several of her mother's old formal dresses and hats. Florence had transformed them into something less ostentatious, but which would enhance her figure and fair hair to their best advantage. She wanted to look like a perfect English rose, because she had to find a husband. The Huntsons had a whole gaggle of eligible Americans staying with them and there had to be one who was rich enough to marry her and to look after her younger brother and sister as part of the bargain. It was all weather dependent, because sunny weather would show both her and her dress to the best advantage.

   Looking out of the window she smiled. The birds in the Dower house garden sang a welcome chorus to the dawn of a hot August day. A light early morning breeze carried all the scent of dew, lavender and mock orange blossom, and Florence knew that today for once, everything would be perfect.

---

2 Florence was looking forward to the garden party that Lady Huntson was organising to celebrate Charlotte's birthday. Under normal circumstances she might not have been invited, but Charlotte had insisted that Lady Hunston invite her. Insisting that it wasn't Florence's fault that her father had gambled all their money away and then shot himself nor had Flo any control over her mother dying of grief as a consequence. The weather had been perfect for the past week and Florence's dress and hat were ready. The material had been rescued from several of her mother's old formal dresses and hats. Florence had transformed them into something less ostentatious, but which would enhance her figure and fair hair to their best advantage. She wanted to look like a perfect English rose, because she had to find a husband. The Huntsons had a whole gaggle of eligible Americans staying with them and there had to be one who was rich enough to marry her and to look after her younger brother and sister as part of the bargain. It was all weather dependent, because sunny weather would show both her and her dress to the best advantage.

Lying in bed in the early morning her body refused to move. She heard rain beating against the window. Fate couldn't be so cruel, but when she looked out of the window she started to cry. The previous day's cloudless sky was now charcoal grey. The lawn in front of the Dower House was already sodden. The party would be postponed, the Americans would go, and she knew that she wouldn't be able to find any English man of substance to marry her.

3 Florence was looking forward to the garden party that Lady Huntson was organising to celebrate Charlotte's birthday. Under normal circumstances she might not have been invited, but Charlotte had insisted that Lady Hunston invite her. Insisting that it wasn't Florence's fault that her father had gambled all their money away and then shot himself nor had Flo any control over her mother dying of grief as a consequence. The weather had been perfect for the past week and Florence's dress and hat were ready. The material had been rescued from several of her mother's old formal dresses and hats. Florence had transformed them into something less ostentatious, but which would enhance her figure and fair hair to their best advantage. She wanted to look like a perfect English rose, because she had to find a husband. The Huntsons had a whole gaggle of eligible Americans staying with them and there had to be one who was rich enough to marry her and to look after her younger brother and sister as part of the bargain. It was all weather dependent, because sunny weather would show both her and her dress to the best advantage.

Lying in bed in the early morning her body she wondered if fate had been kind to her. She hardly dared draw back the curtains, but she did. The sky wasn't a sheet of blue as it had been for the previous days. Small blue and grey clouds were scudding by at an alarming rate. She opened her bedroom window and noticed that there was a stronger breeze that on previous days, and dampness in the air, but at least it wasn't raining. She had to believe that the rain would hold off until after the start of the garden party. If they had even one single shower in the morning then they might postpone the garden party, but she couldn't allow that to happen she would just have to will it to remain dry.

Tip

Remember if you are writing about a particular day, month or season and are including descriptions that involve the weather do try to check the records of the period to see if it mentions floods or snow or even hot dry summers. The seasons were not often as we'd like to imagine them. While researching the background to Princetown War Prison from 1809-1816 it became clear through the letters of an American prisoner that they had rain every day throughout the August he was imprisoned there. Without research I would have assumed that they'd have had a few dry days on Dartmoor during the summer at least!

10.16 Blowing in the wind

Watch the effect of the wind on the behaviour of a group of young school children and it will leave you in doubt as to the power of the wind on affecting human behaviour.

Objective   To demonstrate the impact of wind on either a setting or a character that you would like to include.

Your task   To write a scene in which you set the tone and mood of the piece simply by focusing on the impact of the wind.

> **Model**
>
> The force of the wind made it almost impossible for Nasredinne to move forwards. He knew that if he could reach the cluster of palm trees ahead he might be able to survive. It wasn't the force of the wind that was his only enemy, it was the sand. He'd covered his mouth and nose, but his hands felt as if they were being slashed by a constant stream of windborne sand grains. He'd always been stubborn, but he should have listened to the warnings they'd given him and not tried to finish his painting. Trying to capture the Sirocco as it swept across the desert in paint was one thing, but being subject to its full force was an experience he realised he was unlikely to survive.

10.17 Ouch - that hurts!

Objective   To describe a physical sensation or pain

Your task   To write two very short descriptions c.100 words in which one of your characters is in physical discomfort e.g. ill or in pain. Try to describe the pain (show).

> **Model**
>
> 1   Elspeth's stomach was empty, but she retched again. Her mouth burnt inside. The bile rose in her throat again. She was so weak that she had difficulty in raising her head from the pillow.
>
> 2   Peter's finger ached. The knuckle was painful to touch. It wasn't agony, but a dull throb that became a sharper pain every time he tried to move it.

Tip

Zola believed that when you write you have to be able to be all your characters. It may be as important to be able play the role of your readers as well. To try to understand what makes them tick as well as your characters and ensure that the descriptions that you write create vivid pictures in their minds of the mood that you wish to create.

Ariana Franklin
"First rule. Not too many adjectives. I don't say eschew them completely, like Ernest Hemingway did, but if the writing doesn't get over the fact that something is 'scary', 'exciting', 'beautiful', 'horrifying' etc., then adjectives are just a waste of space and seem amateur."
Ariana Franklin is author of the *Mistress of the Art of Death* Series
www.arianafranklin.com

Chapter 11 – Love, Romance, Passion and Sex

What is romantic fiction? Today we often think of romantic fiction as being similar to fairy tales. It is considered to be the happy ever after 'Cinderella' genre of story, exemplified by such authors as Barbara Cartland and Georgette Heyer. However, what about the tragic love found in the novels of Thomas Hardy or Emily Brontë's' *Wuthering Heights*, or Margaret Munnerlyn Mitchell's *Gone with the Wind*? Romantic fiction embraces the courtly and idealised love of the medieval knight, infatuation, romantic romps in the 'chick lit' style, and even the currently popular love between vampires, and also between couples of the same sex. Although the romantic fiction purist would argue that these do not fit the true definition of a romantic novel or story, because often the friends and family of the main character are of as much importance as the main relationship between the heroines and the hero. Historical romantic fiction has the extra ingredient of being a romantic story, which is set in the past. Regency romances are one example of a sub-genre, which we often associate romantic fiction with, but it is also often an integral part of many other genres.

What ingredients do you need when writing historical romantic fiction?

Who are you writing for? Who is your target market, or audience? These are the questions that you will need to answer before you start writing. Why? Because it will help you to clarify the type of novel that you would like to write, and also help you to decide how much and what sort of detail to include, when writing the romantic or passion-filled scenes in your story. Quite often readers and writers will 'raise an eyebrow' if the publishing houses of Mills and Boon (**www.millsandboon.co.uk**) or Harlequin (**www.eharlequin.com**) are mentioned. However, the significance of these two imprints is that they are successful and in the UK alone they have at least 3 million regular readers annually. Mills and Boon was founded in 1908 and have been focusing on romantic fiction since the 1930s. In 1971 they became part of the Harlequin Enterprises of Canada. Whatever one's personal reading preferences are, these two publishing houses know their business and their market. They both carry interesting tips on how to write the type of fiction that they are looking for on their websites. Even if you have no intention of ever writing the type of historical romantic fiction that they produce, you should look at their sites and glean any tips that you can from them. Similarly, Severn House (**www.severnhouse.com**) and Robert Hale (**www.halebooks.com**) in the UK are two smaller independent publishing houses that have championed the cause of romantic historical fiction successfully. The majority of their readers borrow novels from public libraries rather than buy them, but the quality of the writing and writers who write for them again merits the attention of any aspiring writer of romantic historical fiction.

"Bodice rippers" is often applied in a negative sense to a sub-genre of historical romantic fiction. These novels are usually sexually explicit romantic novel and the plot involves the seduction of the heroine. They usually follow a template where a vulnerable female character meets a more powerful character, who is usually wealthy and whom she dislikes intensely at the outset of the story. Lust steps in and changes her attitude to the main character. They commonly use seduction scenes as a plot device at regular intervals to ensure that they are 'page turners'[*]. The first time the term was seen in print is debated, but its origin appears to date to 1980 when it appeared in both *The New York Times* and *The Wall Street Journal*.

For an aspiring writer of historical romantic fiction whether you are aiming to write for the mass paperback market or are hoping to see your novel in hardcover, the one thing to remember is that authentic historical detail does count and so if you decide to write a 'corset' or 'bodice ripper' style story, then check to make certain that the bodice you are describing existed in the period you are writing about.

[*]The expression dates from the 1970s.

Tip: Check out the following web sites
- www.archive.org
- www.museumofcostume.co.uk
- www.fashion-era.com

ACTIVITIES

11.1 Reading historical romantic fiction

What sort of historical romantic fiction do you enjoy reading? Why do you like it? What other kinds of romantic historical fiction writing are there, and what can you learn from them?

Objective   For you to read at least three romantic fiction novels and to analyse what you can learn from them.

Your tasks   (Write your list and answers in a notebook or appropriate computer file/document.)

A   Select and read three historical romantic novels including one Mills and Boon or Harlequin style novel and if you are not familiar with the work of enduringly popular novelists such as Georgette Heyer, include one of their novels in your three. The advantage of historical romantic fiction is that usually it is both non-taxing and quick to read.

   If you aren't certain who are popular authors in this genre then ask in your local library or local bookshop, or skim through the online pages of **www.thebookseller.com**.

B   Make notes about the style they are written in, any devices that they use that you think might be useful and a list of expressions that they use which might come under the heading of the vocabulary of love.

C   Decide which one you liked the best and why? Then consider which one might appeal to the mass-market reader of romantic fiction, and from their point of view select the most engrossing novel. Finally consider which audience you would like to write for. Remember that it can be a good idea to keep at least one novel of the style that you admire close at hand while you write, just so that you can flip through the pages occasionally to remind yourself of how much graphic detail your genre of romantic fiction can tolerate or expect.

If you find it embarrassing to read 'full frontal' sex scenes in any of the novels that you read then you might like to consider writing a gentler form of romantic fiction where you can use euphemisms*instead.

> *
> **Euphemism**: a mild or indirect way of describing something which embarrasses or shocks us. This is done by substituting words and expressions that we feel are more acceptable and less offensive e.g. 'to sleep with' is milder than 'to have a f... or s....'.

11.2   They lived happily ever after

The traditionally accepted definitions of romantic fiction for both novels and short stories are that the central narrative or plot should revolve around the two central characters as they build a romantic relationship together. The theme of how they develop this relationship can include sub plots that don't relate to their growing love for each other and can involve conflict, but it is their 'romantic' love that needs to remain at the 'heart' of the story. You should also aim to end your story in an optimistic or satisfying way, because you are celebrating love, emotional commitment and many readers still expect the story to end in marriage. Adultery, even today, is not acceptable for many romantic fiction fans, but might be palatable if the theme embraces unconditional love.

Useful web sites:
   + **www.rwanational.org** (Romance Writers of America)
   + **www.rna-uk.org** (Romantic Novelist's Association, UK)

Please note that every year the Romantic Novelist's Association in the UK runs competitions for new writers, the Joan Hessay New Writers' Scheme Award, the Katie Fforde Bursary and the Elizabeth Goudge Trophy and the RNA is associated with the Harry Bowling Prize for New Writers.

Objective	To create a simple linear story line that involves two characters and their quest for romantic love which could be set in the period that you are interested in writing about.
Your task	To write an outline plot for a romantic story in no more than 500 words.

> **Model**
>
> 1277 and in Ross-on-Wye (Herefordshire) Agnes Syuur's niece Christine is staying with her in Brookend. Christine visits the triangular shaped market place at the junction of two roads and meets Adam, a nephew of Walter of the Mill. Adam's family are wealthy burgesses from Hereford, but Christine has nothing except her youth, striking looks and her ability to craft small items of jewellery. They are immediately attracted to each other, but because of Christine's background marriage appears impossible as Adam's parents are opposed to it. Adam swears that if he can't marry Christine he will enter the church and never marry. The situation is saved because 1277 is the year when the rent rolls were compiled for the Bishop of Hereford, and one of the small items that Christine has crafted finds its way into the Bishop's possession. He commissions Christine to make tokens and favours for him to give as gifts, and in return convinces Adam's parents that she will make an ideal bride for Adam, their eldest son.

Write your plot in your notebook

11.3   The Vocabulary of love

What vocabulary (words or phrases) might we use if we wanted to portray a tender, passionate or romantic moment? Examples:

Kiss, touch, caress, stroke, touch fingers, kiss palm of hand, brush lips against his/her cheek, a stolen kiss, fondle, cuddle ...

Objective	To create a vocabulary of love check list.
Your task	Below are a series of lists in the form of a table, which you can add to whenever you come across an interesting word or phrase that conveys, affection, love, lust or passion.
	In **Activity 11.1** you should have already compiled a list of words about love that you may wish to add in the tables below.

Table 1 – Romantic Love - Vocabulary

Physical vocabulary (mild and romantic)	kiss, fondle, touch, stroke, hug, cuddle, tickle, caress, hold, hold hands, hold close
Related to animals and hunting etc.	bite, paw, grab, preen, stalk, rut, lick, steal
Emotions that we feel	delight, cherish, languish, desire, longing (for), devotion, admiration, frustration, adoration, affection, care (for), appreciation, longing, hankering, hanker (for), cosy, friendship, passion, contentment, exhilaration, happiness, physical satisfaction, devotion, excitement, anticipation
Emotions that love creates	illusion, reassurance, comfort, peace, security, jealously, anger, guilt, obsession, anxiety, paranoia, ecstasy, delight, a sense of longing

Table 2 – Romantic Love – Useful expressions and idioms

Useful Expressions
eyes glistening/ dancing with expectation/excitement, an inviting glance

Idioms
love is blind, love makes the world go round, to fall head over heels in love

Tip

Try to avoid clichés e.g. "her kiss was sweeter than wine"," lips like ripe cherries" etc. Instead of "lips like ripe cherries" you might try replacing the analogy with a different fruit e.g. "like damson plums". In the first example if you were setting your story in the 1950s you could replace "wine" with "Cherryade", which would then read: "Her kiss was sweeter than Cherryade".

11.4   Just one kiss and then...

Objectives   To write a series of scenes that involve physical contact between your main character e.g. kissing, courtship[*], making love or having sex.

To find out if you are comfortable with writing scenes that aren't just romantic, but which involve describing sex, passion, desire and lust.

[*] **Courtship**: The 'wooing' or period during which the wooing of one person by another takes place. It was first used in this sense in c. 1580-90. 'Woo' is an Old English verb that dates from before 1050 that means to seek affection traditionally with desire to marry.

Your task   Please keep your answers short (no more than 300 words). Keep the descriptions that you write somewhere accessible in case you decide to use them in your story or novel. Think carefully about the background that you pick as a backdrop for the scene. Sometimes contrasting instead of complementing the setting and the kiss, will make the scene more memorable e.g. a sweet kiss contrasted with the ripe odours wafting from a Venetian canal in the middle of August.

A   To write a scene c.500 words in which your main protagonists kiss for the first time and where it took place. This could be anything from a peck on the cheek to a lingering and sensual kiss.

B   To write a scene c.500 words in which your characters get more physical, but are interrupted by a third character before they can make love.

C   To write in c. 500 words 'the bedroom scene', which doesn't have to take place in a bedroom, but anywhere that might be physically possible e.g. balanced on a slippery roof in the middle of the night while trying to escape the clutches of a rake* of a guardian, may not ring true to the reader; while in the carriage that is whisking them away would work, but would undoubtedly leave both characters with bruises caused by the bumping carriage as it sped on its journey. This is where many writers become squeamish. The ability to describe murder is one thing, but sex scenes can make even experienced writers quake in trepidation at the prospect. Some aspiring authors have a natural gift for writing the more intimate and erotic side of consummating a romantic relationship. If you are contemplating writing erotic fiction by trying to force yourself to write 'touch by touch' descriptions, then you should consider sticking to less raunchy romantic fiction writing. Physical lust and passion may be a step too far for you as an aspiring writer. Try it and see, you may surprise yourself!

> * **Rake**: The word has been used with great effect in Regency fiction. It is a shortened form of 'rake-hell or rakehell'' which was popular in the late 16th century to describe a dissolute or profligate man. The shortened form 'rake' has been in common usage since the 17th century.

D The voyeur[*] or the passing stranger
Imagine that you are a person who is watching the romantic moment either as a voyeur or a passing stranger and describe it from their viewpoint (in no more than 500 words).

> * **Voyeur**: a 20th century French word in origin that refers to person who obtains pleasure and excitement from observing others romantic and intimate acts.

Tip
Beware of too much intimate detail as it can become boring and a real 'turn off' to your reader.

Tips from a professional writer of romantic fiction

Jane Jackson

Tips for writing historical romance

Choose a period that fascinates you and a theme about which you care deeply. (A theme I enjoy exploring is a woman's place in a man's world) You are going to be working on this story for up to a year, so it's important that you are captivated and absorbed by it. If you aren't, how can you expect the reader to be?!

   With historical romance the love story takes precedence. But the world in which the story takes place needs to be as authentic as possible. You will come across books that purport to be "historical" but they are simply modern stories in fancy dress. This is a shame because the authors of such stories are missing a fantastic opportunity to bring the past to vivid life for today's readers.

   So, how to make it "real"? Research thoroughly. Study books of etiquette and social customs relating to the period. Class was far more sharply defined in the past than it is now, and it was far harder – in most cases impossible – to cross the class barrier until the mid 1860s when, as a result of the Industrial Revolution, there was a rapidly expanding middle class who had made their money, not simply inherited it.

   Ensuring your background is real and believable will give you a solid base for your love story. To make your story stand out, to make it unique, try to ensure that it could only have happened to these two people in this place at this time. How to achieve this?

   I have one character already established in the location, and the other arrives as a stranger. The reason for the incomer's presence is a threat to the status quo. These two are forced into each other's company for good solid reasons (hence the necessity for accurate research to achieve realism and believability) and the threat or change the incomer represents sets up a powerful conflict deepened and complicated by the fact that this man and woman are strongly attracted to each other.

...continued

Your detailed biographies for each of your main characters will have helped you understand who they are, where they are coming from, what they want, what they are (or are not) prepared to do to achieve it, and what they are risking by pursuing this course of action. In other words, what might it cost them?

Yet though social customs, etiquette, and men's and women's ambitions may have changed over the centuries, at heart human beings have always been driven by the same needs: Security - a place where they feel safe; food; to love and be loved, to belong to a family/community/tribe/class. For women: to marry well and have a family; for men: to make their mark in the world through achievement.

By setting these universal needs against a background and situation specific to the period you have chosen, and by ensuring your writing invokes all the senses, you will create a story that draws the reader into another world, one as real and vivid to them as this one.

Nine of Jane Jackson's novels are currently available including *Heart of Stone* (Severn House, 2009), *Bonded Heart, The Chain Garden, Dangerous Waters, Tides of Fortune* and *Eyes of the Wind*.

www.janejackson.net

Chapter 12 – Style

The style that an author uses to tell the story of their characters, consists of the distinctive skills and devices that an author uses to write their plot (mode of narration). These characteristic devices that authors use on a regular basis, become their trade mark which distinguishes them from other writers. It could be that they always use the first person singular 'I' to narrate their story. It might be that they use very short sentences systematically, or that they start sentences with 'and' or 'but' more frequently than other authors.

If you were a student of literary criticism, then you would investigate these patterns that writers use which can almost hypnotize their readers and make it almost impossible for the reader to put one of their books down. The kind of novel that makes you oblivious to everything including housework, going to bed at a reasonable time in order to be fresh for work the next morning and even going to work at all!

A selection of stylistic devices that different authors have used to hallmark all their novels includes:
+ Using a chapter for each character;
+ Writing a prologue;
+ Incorporating flash back;
+ Flash forwards;
+ Short sharp sentences to increase the pace or long descriptive ones to slow it down;
+ Strong verbs to increase the pace and tension e.g. 'hurled' himself at instead of 'threw' himself at (someone);
+ Abandoning the use of 'he/she said' when writing dialogue;
+ Stressing certain key words by highlighting them in italics to emphasise their importance e.g. I *know* she is innocent ;
+ Telling a story from the end forwards;
+ Mastery of the art of 'back story' telling for a series of novels. This consists of filling your reader in on what has happened in previous novels so that they are able to enjoy the current one without having had to read all the previous novels in sequence;
+ Giving a main protagonist a characteristic word or way of speaking, for example he or she might habitually stutter over a particular word or might use a word that is specific to a particular region e.g. in Devon and Cornwall 'mazed' means 'mad or crazy';

- ♦ Never using certain forms of punctuation e.g. semi-colons and writing shorter sentences;
- ♦ Writing longer and more complex sentences and using semi-colons regularly.

N.B. What is different about the list above compared with the other lists that you have read in this book so far? The answer is that grammatically it is correct to use semi-colons, but how did you react to this change in pattern? Did it annoy you or did you prefer it? Which style of punctuation is more to your taste? The reason for introducing the use of semi-colons in the list above was to encourage you to think about 'style', and how a style of writing is dependent not simply on the order of words or the words themselves, but also on such things as punctuation and layout e.g. Is each chapter going to have a title or will you start it with a quotation from a poem[*] for instance?

The author's style of writing is dependent partly on the transitions that they make when writing. A transition is a device that an author uses to indicate that a change is about to take place in a story by using sentences, phrases, words and punctuation. This change might be the location, mood, time or pace of their story.

Style is one of the most difficult ingredients to provide structured guidance about for the aspiring writer. We all write from our own perspective and bring with us our own experiences of life. If you give a group of participants at a workshop a theme to write about, they will usually all interpret it differently. Not only will their personal experience leave its mark on their narrative, but also on the style in which they write it.

Reading is one of the most important things you can do to improve the quality of the style that you write in. Read historical novels, but also the classics and contemporary novels of any genre that become best sellers, and as you are reading try to pick out any devices they use repetitively, which may appeal to their readers. Try to identify and note down what appeals to you about the style they have used to write their novel e.g. a chapter per character etc.

---

[*] Don't forget if you are quoting from anyone else's creative work you will need to check out the copyright law of the UK or whichever country your author published the work that you are quoting from. These are very strict. Check out: **www.opsi.gov.uk/acts** including Copyright, Designs and Patents Act 1988, CHAPTER 48.

12.1 Is style important to readers?

Objective   To carry out a mini survey to discover if it is the way an author writes (his/her style) that appeals to readers, or if it is the subject or characters that are the deciding factor.

Your task   If you are a member of a reading group then ask the members of the group if it is the style a writer uses that attracts them to that particular author, as well as the genre e.g. Is it the way they use one chapter for each character? Is it that they use a lot of detailed descriptions to enrich their novels? Is it that they use a lot of dialogue? If you aren't a member of a reading group just ask your friends who enjoy reading, and don't forget to ask any children that you know as well. You may be intending to write for an adult audience, but children often have a direct and informative way of identifying what does and doesn't work in terms of style and content. Try to ask at least 10 people for their opinion. Jot down your findings in the table below.

Is style important to readers?

Which authors use which styles and why do readers like them?	
Author	Stylistic Devices
1	
2	
3	
4	
5	
6	
7	
8	
9	
10	

12.2 Developing your own style

Experimenting with different writing styles is one of the ways that may help you to identify and enhance your own style. It may assist you in creating a personal style that your readers will be able to identify as a hallmark of your writing.

Objective
To try to write in a similar style to 'best-selling' novelists. Your aim is to experience how using the devices that they have used changes the impact of your writing and to broaden your appreciation of different styles. It may be tempting to transfer the style of a successful author and apply it to your own writing. Copying someone else's 'successful' stylistic devices directly can be a form of plagiarism[*]. What you are aiming to do is translate or transform the devices that you uncover to suit your own way of writing to give it more texture and depth and to make it more interesting for your reader. Your objective is to create your own consistent, distinctive pattern of words etc. and not to copy someone else's, unless you are writing a parody[†] for humorous purposes.

[*] **Plagiarism**: the act of taking the ideas or work of another person and using them as if they were your own. Curiously the origin of the verb plagiarise is from Latin, and combines two words, one that originally meant plunder, and the other to kidnap.

[†] **Parody**: a piece of writing that imitates or mimics the style of another writer for humorous purposes. For example you might have a character who is an Elizabethan playwright in your novel, who imagines that he is a better playwright than Shakespeare. This character then might use Shakespeare's style in writing his own adaptations of the bard's successful plays.

Your task
To try to write in the style of bestselling[*] authors of the past and present. You can select either writers of historical fiction or general fiction. In an ideal world where time was elastic and you had as much time to read as you would like, it would be great to be able to read three or four novels written by each of your selected authors, but that isn't the case. Avoid novels that have been translated, because sometimes it is difficult to separate the style of the author from the style imposed by translating from one language to another. So pick two novels written by the two novelists that you select, and read five whole pages of text at random from

each of the novels. Try to isolate their characteristic style, and then try to write a whole page either by hand or on the computer on a theme that you are interested in, but incorporating their style. Try to make it read as if they had written it, even if isn't on a subject or period that they have written about.

* **Best-selling** (or bestselling): Best-selling novelists and novels are often considered to be those who have sold a particular number of novels as defined by the current book trade figures, but for the purposes of this task 'best-selling' means 'popular'.

A   Pick an author whose novels are still popular even though they are dead e.g. Georgette Heyer, Agatha Christie, Daphne du Maurier, C.S. Forrester, Rudyard Kipling. Then complete the task outlined above.

B   Select an author writing today, who has more than two novels on display in your local bookshop or library. Next complete the task explained above.

Tip

Do remember that part of the craft of a professional writer is to write in a style that is comprehensible, clear, interesting and entertaining for their readers. Entertaining does not mean that it has to be funny or humorous, but that it keeps the reader on their toes and engrossed as they turn the pages of the story, novel or E-book.

Chapter 13 – Nuts and Bolts

This guide and tool-kit is designed to introduce you to the ingredients you need to write an historical novel or short story. Unfortunately, it can't transform any difficulties that you may have with grammar, spelling and punctuation, but there are certain practical steps you can take that may help you if you do have difficulties in these areas. It may benefit you to find out exactly where your problem areas are, so a) you become aware of them and b) you can fill in any gaps in your knowledge.

Spelling

1   Every time you run a spell check, write down on a piece of paper the words that it highlights as being misspelt. Over a period of two weeks you will most probably notice a pattern of errors. Common words that people misspell or confuse with others are: received, their, separately, practice (or practise*). Once you have a list you will be able to see the words that you misspell regularly. Highlight these words and keep them near your computer, so that you can predict where you are likely to make a spelling mistake.

2   If you are writing in English, make certain that your computer isn't set to American spellings. If it keeps changing 'colour' (English spelling) to 'color' (American spelling) then re-set your spell check.

3   Lack of consistency in the way that you spell things may give the appearance that you can't spell. Therefore you need to decide before you start if you are going to end words such as realised, revitalised, maximised with 'ised' or 'ized' and then stick to the ending you've selected throughout your manuscript.

4   Simple mistakes of capitalization of words that we often get wrong through habit e.g. the seasons winter, summer, autumn, spring do not start with capital letters unless they are used to start a sentence. This is because they are not 'proper' nouns, but 'common' ones. If however, you decided to call a character Spring then it would start with a capital letter, because you have transformed it into a 'proper' noun. We use 'proper' nouns for names of people, countries, days of the week and the months etc.

---

* Check the definition of these two words in a dictionary to find out how they differ in meaning.

5   Spelling problems caused by 'inflection', which means that the spelling of words change to match, or express different grammatical functions e.g. beg, begging, begged. Once again don't trust the spell check on your computer as it will often give you an American spelling instead of an English one particularly for verbs such as 'got'.

6   Hyphenated words – unless you have a linguistic bent or a proofreaders[*] mind then this can be a nightmare, but don't panic you just need to buy or borrow a book. It is:
    - *New Hart's Rules*, Oxford University Press, The Handbook of Style for Writers and Editors. The first edition was published in 2005 and the ISBN is 978-0-19-861041-0.

The title of this book has been highlighted, because if you intend to take writing of any kind seriously then it is a must. Another excellent book, but much more expensive is *The Oxford Style Manual*, Oxford University Press, Robert Ritter, ISBN, 978-0-19-860564-5

7   Another essential tool for an historical novelist is a dictionary. Spell checks on computers are very useful, but a good dictionary (hard copy or on-line) should provide you with additional information such as if the word is or was used **colloquially** (in informal conversation) or as **slang** and something about the origin of the word and when it was first introduced into the English language. Using words and phrases that were current at the period you are writing about can be effective. However, what the writer needs to be aware of is how to avoid words (verbs, nouns, adjectives and adverbs) that just didn't exist in the period that you are writing about. If you were writing a novel set in the Elizabethan period and wrote a scene where a character was having her hair shampooed it wouldn't ring true to the avid reader of historical fiction. This is because the verb 'shampoo' came into common usage in the English language in the 18th century, and is taken from a Hindi word meaning 'to knead'. Similarly 'pyjamas' (U.S. 'pajama') were adopted into the English language in the 20th century via the Persian or Urdu languages. Hence Queen Elizabeth the First, even if she wore a garment that looked like pyjamas, wouldn't have called them that.

---

[*] 'Proofread' and 'proofreader' are not generally hyphenated words in English, but they can be! This is why a handbook such as *New Hart's Rules* is an 'essential' tool for the fiction writer.

Please note that the on-line versions of these dictionaries are constantly updated and so they will contain more words and definitions than the hard copy versions.

If you intend to invest in a dictionary, you have a wide range to choose from, but do look at them first and see if they contain the kind of information that you need, for example:

* **www.collinslanguage.com** (Collins Unabridged English Dictionary, containing c. 500,000 English words)
* **ukcatalogue.oup.com** (The Oxford English Dictionary, containing c. 600,000 entries)
* The 'ultimate' dictionary for writers of historical fiction who are interested in the origin meaning and usage of words in the English language, is OUP's *The Historical Thesaurus of the Oxford Dictionary*, which is "the largest thesaurus in the world" of its kind. At the moment this two volume historical thesaurus, which contains almost every word in English from Old English to the present day, is only available in a two volume hard copy edition. The organisation of this thesaurus is described by the publishers as following: "A unique thematic system of classification, with entries arranged in a comprehensive semantic hierarchy according to their meanings. Each individual synonym is presented in chronological order according to the first recorded date of the word's use in English, as listed in the *Oxford English Dictionary* with earliest synonyms given first. There are three major sections in the THTOED, reflecting the main activities and preoccupations of users of the language..." (see **ukcatalogue.oup.com**).

If you are looking for an American dictionary see *Webster's 3rd New International Dictionary of the English Language*: **www.merriam-webster.com**

Grammar

Do not feel guilty, if as a consequence of the teaching of English in UK schools over the past three decades, you aren't confident about the differences between adjectives, adverbs, conjunctions, different types of nouns etc. Grammar is a collection of structural rules that we follow when composing sentences and phrases, and also words and how they relate to each other. The rules of grammar, like punctuation, can be acquired on a need to know basis. The most important task for you is to find out what you do need to know and where the gaps in your practical knowledge are.

Punctuation

Do you know the correct usage of full stops, capitalization (or capitalisation), question marks, commas, inverted commas, dashes, brackets, apostrophes, hyphens, colons and semi-colons? If not then you need to keep a simple book explaining their use close to your computer or work station for reference purposes i.e. A children's guide to punctuation such as *Improve Your Punctuation* published by Usborne Children's Books (see **www.usborne.com**).

Please note that the use of semi-colons appears to be less frequent in novels than in the past, and is often being replaced by commas or shorter sentences.

Tips

There are two straightforward ways of finding out where you have problems:

1   There are certain common grammatical and punctuation pitfalls that you might need to check for:
    - Changing tenses in the middle of a sentence, paragraph or chapter for example:
      He was trying very hard not to showing his emotions. (Incorrect)
      He was trying very hard not to show his emotions. (Correct)
    - The incorrect use and writing of should **of**, would **of**, could **of** instead of the correct use should **have**, would **have**, could **have**
    - Using the word 'less' instead of 'fewer'
    - Misusing bullet points
    - Problems caused by using singular and plural forms in the same sentence (agreement)
    - Apostrophes:
      "I bought lots of **vegetable's**." This isn't correct, because apostrophes are not used to show that a noun - in this case vegetable - is plural. They are used to show possession e.g. "Their **vegetables'** taste was delicious." Apostrophes are also used to replace a letter as in the sentence: "The vegetables **aren't** here." The sentence if written in full would read: "The vegetables **are not** here." The apostrophe has been used to replace the letter 'o' in the word not.
    - For a list of common pitfalls see *Grammar Book*, Michael Temple, ISBN 1853779865 **http://bookshop.blackwell.co.uk/jsp/id/ Grammar_Book/9781853779862**

2 Try a practice test for one of the main TESOL or TEFL examinations to identify where your problems lie. You will find some free tests on-line or you can borrow (from a library) or buy a copy of the tests with answers. You need to try a test that is at CAE level (see below). These tests are designed for non-native English speakers, but be warned the grammar sections are challenging for many native English speakers as well.

www.examenglish.com (IELTS, TOEFL, TOEIC) grammar and writing

ACTIVITY

13.1 Create a checklist

Objective   To identify and be aware of the common slips that you regularly make in grammar and punctuation.

Your task   Keep a list of the mistakes that you make as you identify them, and then look at this list before you check your own work through at the end of every writing session.

The remedies:

1 Buy a basic grammar book that is small, compact, and contains almost everything that you will need to know and that won't overwhelm you:

Suggestions:
- Invest in the £1 pocket guide published by Blackwell, which covers both grammar and punctuation: *Grammar Book*, Michael Temple, ISBN 1853779865 **bookshop.blackwell.co.uk/jsp/id /Grammar_Book/9781853779862**
- If you are really interested in the subject and would like more detailed information we can recommend:
  - *The Good Grammar Book* by Michael Swan and Catherine Walter (English level: Elementary to Lower-Intermediate)
  - *A Practical English Grammar* by A. J. Thomson and A. V. Martinet English level: Intermediate to Advanced

For information about these grammar books look at the following web site: **ukcatalogue.oup.com**

2 Pay someone to check you work.

Even if you have a friend whose grasp of English grammar is excellent, offer to pay them as you may need them to help you another time. Also you need to ensure that the person who is checking is just going to check the spelling, grammar, punctuation etc. and not try to edit or change your style or the content. You could pay a professional proofreader that you find through a professional body such as SFEP — the Society of Freelance Editors and proofreaders (**www.sfep.org.uk**). If you are thinking of having it checked by an English teacher then you might be well advised to find a TESOL or TEFL teacher.

The reason being is that they are more likely just to stick to your request to check it from a technical perspective and not from a literary one and also because it is their job to teach the nuts and bolts of English to students who have to pass exams that require a high standard of grammatical competency. If you decide on asking a TESOL or TEFL teacher to proofread your work for grammatical errors etc. then check to see if they have the higher TESOL or TEFL qualification, or the equivalent degree. This means that they will have either DELTA (Diploma in English Language Teaching to Adults) validated by Cambridge ESOL or the Trinity College London Licentiate Diploma to TESOL.

Sentence structure and length

If you are not certain about what constitutes a sentence, then you may wish to find out more about sentence structure by delving in to one of the grammar books mentioned above. However, what is important to know is that in broad terms there are two types of sentences. There are simple sentences which contain a verb and a subject, and complex sentences. Complex sentences will contain a subordinate clause. There are different types of subordinate clauses a) Adjective clauses, b) Adverb clauses (various types) and c) Noun clauses. The impact of simple sentences on your writing is that they can add pace to your writing whereas complex sentences can slow the action down. A complex sentence can be used to enhance your descriptions and to slow the pace of your writing down.

ACTIVITY

13.2 Simple or complex sentences?

Objective To experiment with simple and complex sentences and to observe what impact using these has on your style of writing.

Your task To write a series of short sentences that contain a subject (e.g. he/she) and a verb (e.g.) talk, but no conjunctions (e.g. and, but and no comparisons using forms such as like, as etc.) and no subordinate clauses (this acts like a phrase added on to the main clause). There are various kinds of subordinate clauses for example:

- He hid **where** no one could find him. (The use of **where** tells you that this is an adverbial 'place' clause)
- She won the baking competition **because** she was a far better cook than Mrs. Drake-Baring. (Using **because** makes this an adverbial clause showing 'reason')

1 **Simple sentences**

> **Model**
>
> Bonnie Prince Charlie stopped running. He listened. He waited. His heart was beating loudly. He couldn't hear the soldiers. He crept forward.

Write your example in your notebook.

2 **Complex sentences**

> **Model**
>
> Bonnie Prince Charlie wasn't feeling at all bonnie. He hadn't had to run since he was a child and he was exhausted. He stopped and listened to see if he could hear any sounds of the soldiers who had been pursuing him, but all he could hear was the sound of his heart beating. He hoped that he'd managed to lose his pursuers, and began creeping forwards again.

Write your example in your notebook.

Phrases

Phrases aren't sentences and you will often know if you've written one on the computer, because if you have your spell check on when typing it will often indicate that it is wrong. Writers use a lot when writing dialogue for example:

> The grocery boy arrived with the delivery for the dinner party. Mrs. Beaton was busy experimenting with a new recipe and bellowed at the boy in a most unfeminine fashion, "Put them in the larder." (This is an adverbial or adverb phrase telling where the action takes place or is done.)

Paragraphs

These are sets of sentences (sometimes just one) about a topic or idea. From your reader's viewpoint long paragraphs are quite hard to digest. They were more popular in the 19th century, but less so today.

Tip

Unless you are genuinely interested in the technical details of what and how the rules of grammar work then try not to get bogged down in details unless you intend to write an historical novel about a great historical lexicographer such as the Frenchman, Pierre Larousse born in 1813, the American Noah Webster (1758-1843) or a grammarian like Dr. Robert Lowth, who was a bishop and a professor of poetry at Oxford University, in 1762, his *Short Introduction to English Grammar* (1762) famously suggested that sentences ending with a preposition for example "What time do you want to meet at?", or "What have you come here for?" were only suitable for informal writing and speech!

Chapter 14 – Technical Awareness

Punctuation, grammar and sentence structure are all part of developing a sense of technical awareness, but for the purposes of this guide presentation is also included. How will your short story look when it arrives on the desk of a magazine editor? What will the agent or publisher think when your manuscript arrives in their in-tray?

If we lived in a 'perfect' world then your story and your writing would be enough, and it wouldn't matter what it looked like. Today the way it looks does count. Agents, publishers, and editors are all under incredible pressure and their time is precious. They work in a professional world and are looking for professional writers, because publishing is a business. It needs commercial authors who will sell books and magazines.

Therefore you need to give your work the best chance possible of being read and even considered for publication. This means proofreading your work carefully, but also making it look 'nice' and 'feel nice' when you send it off, in order to take you one step further towards publication. It also means that if you have not got access to a computer and are not on-line you will need to find a way around this first and major stumbling block. For instance use the facilities available in libraries or at work, and if all else fails pay someone to do the work for you. However, the harsh reality is that writing for publication requires the tools of the trade. If you were a plumber you wouldn't be able to work without a spanner, wrench, or screwdriver, and if you want to be a commercially published author, your own email account, website or blog and computer are becoming essential to publishing success.

ACTIVITY

14.1 Identifying what looks good and what feels good

Objective   To raise your awareness of what the written word looks like on the page (which publishers commonly refer to as folios)

Your task   Go to a library or bookshop and pick out three historical fiction novels at random and select two pages somewhere in the middle of the books. Ask yourself the following questions:

*   Do I like the feel of the paper? Does it feel cheap, fragile and as if it will tear at any moment or is it smooth and pleasant to touch?
*   What do you notice about the margins? Are they wide or narrow?
*   What does the layout or the page look like?

When you've carried out this task it should help to enlighten you as to what your own manuscript should look like when you submit it for consideration. Why should you do this? Perhaps at some distant point in the past authors were treated as a rare breed by publishers who would cosset them and do almost everything for them, but today we live in a do-it-yourself, time and money conscious world.

Below is a checklist of points to keep in your mind when completing your manuscript for submission:

1   Check the publishers', magazines' or agents' websites to find out if they accept emailed submissions (in the UK it is still rare for book publishers, magazines and agents to accept submissions made in this way).

2   Carefully read the information on these sites about their submission requirements in the same way that you would do if reading the rules of a competition.

3   If in doubt phone them up and ask to speak to someone who can clarify their submission requirements. Don't start telling them about your novel in detail. Simply tell them that you've written a historical novel that you'd like to submit, and ask them whose attention you should address it to and if they have any submission guidelines.

4   If you are thinking about submitting your work to more than one publisher or agent at a time, you will need to ask if this is acceptable to them. It is more acceptable in the USA than in the UK.

5 Print your manuscript (sometimes referred to as typescript) on good quality A4 paper. Don't be tempted to photocopy it even if it is cheaper and don't print on both sides of the paper.

6 Print out a fresh copy every time you send your manuscript out. You can recycle the old one by starting to draft your next story on the back of it!

7 If there aren't any specific guidelines for submissions then don't forget to:

  ♦ Create a title page which hasn't got a number on it. Make certain that your last page also carries your contact details in the bottom right hand corner.

  ♦ The title page should include such information as word count, name or pseudonym etc.

  ♦ You will also need a covering letter.

  ♦ Number your pages sequentially throughout your whole manuscript.

  ♦ Ensure that all your pages (Folios) are in order.

  ♦ Leave a good margin all around the text of a minimum of 3cm.

  ♦ Justify your text on the left hand side only.

  ♦ Double space your manuscript.

  ♦ Always start your chapters on a fresh page.

  ♦ Use a font such as Times New Roman, Arial, Veranda or Tahoma, but avoid fancy fonts and colour.

  ♦ Indent the first line of every paragraph a minimum of 2 spaces. Do not indent the first line of your novel or chapters.

  ♦ Blank lines should only be used to indicate a change of subject and not between paragraphs.

  ♦ For rules about dialogue see **Chapter 13**.

  ♦ Grammar, spellings, capitalisation and subheadings - remember to check for consistency e.g. a historic event is used in informal writing and also when we speak, but an historic event is grammatically correct. Once you've decided if you are going to use 'a historic event' or 'an historic event' then stick to it.

  ♦ Don't staple your work together, but attach it with a bright clean paper clip if it is a short story. For a novel, use a wallet type folder clearly showing your name, contact details and the title.

  ♦ Above all don't forget to include an envelope for the return of your manuscript and the correct amount of postage. You should also enclose a self-addressed stamped postcard and ask the publisher or agent to kindly send the postcard back to you to acknowledge the receipt of your manuscript.

Tip

Michael Jecks

"And finally, bear in mind that if you have already sent your manuscript to one publisher, by the time it comes back rejected, it will have smudges and folds where it oughtn't. No editor is going to be so taken with a manuscript that looks as though it's been passed around fifteen slush-piles compared with the next one that is pristine and clearly unseen by anyone else.

Both may have been read exactly sixteen times each, but if you reprint more often, you will help your chances of being accepted."

www.michaeljecks.co.uk

Chapter 15 – Historical Accuracy and Planning

Timelines and event lines provide a fixed framework for you to write your story. They provide milestones, which anchor your storyline to the historical period that you are writing about. Accurate, detailed time and event lines make writing your story much easier. They provide a check point of reference to enable you to keep track of exactly where you are and when. Timelines also place your character in a specific historical context. By creating period, event and character timelines, you can uncover key information that can be of great significance in the lives of your characters. Your character may be affected by local events, but these in turn may be the consequence of national or even international events such as new technology, wars, famine and natural catastrophes.

For the purposes of this book, timelines are defined as a chronological list of events with specific dates. Event lines are also chronological, but chart key events, for example, in the town or city that your novel is set, or where your character lives.

How you want to display and organise your time lines will depend on your personal preference. One of the simplest ways is to use a database template or to draw a table yourself. The advantage of entering all your information into a timeline in this form is that you can include as much detail as you like initially. Then, when you have finished your research, you can make a second copy of your timeline, which contains only the dates that are relevant to your characters and your plot. You can then print this final version out, and even increase its size by having it photocopied in a larger format, so that you can display it on a wall near your work space, or in a file.

You may prefer to keep your time lines in a series of notebooks, one for each year that is relevant to your story. It might suit you to have time lines for specific topics e.g. sea battles, which are kept in files divided by markers for each year or event. What is of paramount importance is that even if your historical novel is set on one day e.g. the battle of Waterloo, Sunday 18 June 1815 near Waterloo, or over the period of a year or two e.g. the Great Plague (1665-1666) you make a detailed timeline or event line. It acts as a plan, a chart that enables you to keep track of your characters in the historical context of the period you decided they will inhabit.

Timelines

The models 1, 2 and 3, below are simplified extracts of a timeline and event lines that were researched and used by Myfanwy Cook as part of the John Taylor *Canals, Copper and Historical Creative Writing Workshop*, held at the end of November 2009 as part of the John Taylor Festival, and which was supported by the Royal Society, TAVI (Tavistock and Villages Development Forum, the Marine Biological Association, LEAF (Local Enterprise Action Forum) and Riverside Creative Projects. The first (1) is a character time line, which might be used to provide the chronological background for a biographical historical novel about John Taylor. It could also be used as the basis for a secondary character profile, or to highlight the key events that might have an impact on the life of the character that you have created.

Model 1 – Character timeline

Below is an extract from an outline character timeline. It is designed as a model to illustrate the type of factual information that you might wish to include when building up a character profile. When writing historical fiction it is also vitally important to keep track of your sources. Perhaps you may need to refer to them again. It certainly saves time if you record the sources you've used as you go along. One way of doing this is to highlight them in some way (see below). Whenever possible use at least two different sources when drawing up timelines. It would be nice to assume when you read a non-fiction book or even a primary source like an account of a battle, that the facts are 'true', but unfortunately sometimes they aren't. Assumptions and mistakes can be made even by the most meticulous non-fiction writers and researchers. However, if three sources give the same date for an event, then you can be 'almost' certain that most probably the date is correct.

Character timeline

Date	Name: John Taylor
	
	Sources:
	Booker, F, *Industrial Archaeology of the Tamar Valley,*
	    Newton Abbot, David and Charles, 1967 (secondary source)
	Burt, R, *John Taylor 1779 -1863 Mining Entrepreneur and Engineer,*
	    Moorland Publishing Co., 1977 (secondary source)
	Lyson, Devon, 1822 (primary source)

1779	Born on the 22nd of August, Norwich from a modest background. A family of Unitarian ministers. John was one of 7 children (none died). The youngest was Sarah. Their mother Susannah Taylor darned her son's socks. He was related to the reforming Martineau family of Norwich. John Taylor's grandfather lost most of his fortune as the result of the Lisbon earthquake of 1755 and John's own father died when John was 12. John's mother brought her children up with a strict moral code –honesty, trustworthiness and propriety, meticulous attention to financial matters and a determined avoidance of debt, which may have accounted for John's unflinching honesty as a business person in the mining industry, which was notorious for roguish practices. John's mother encouraged the children to study arithmetic, grammar, foreign languages and for John she bought mathematical instruments and a turning lathe 'to encourage his boyish taste for mechanical pursuits'. John had a private tutor, but then went to a day school run by Dr. John Houghton and Rev. Houghton. They were strict, but the curriculum they taught included 'modern' subjects like chemistry. Susannah apprenticed all her sons. John was apprenticed to a land surveyor and engineer.
1799	
1800	Taylor was sufficiently confident in his own ability and judgement to take a direct financial interest in re-opening Wheal Crowndale copper mine. He was aware of the canal mania that was sweeping the country, and may also have been influenced by the technical writing of John Smeaton (who built Smeaton's tower) but it was the costs and distribution problems at Friendship and Crowndale, which were primarily behind the Tavistock canal scheme. There was no wheeled traffic and packhorses had to be used costing up to 12s per ton a mile. The overall cost therefore wiping out much of the profit.
1801	He initiated a complex construction of leats, which made Wheal Friendship's dressing floors the most fully mechanised in the South West and therefore one of the most profitable copper producers in the area. Taylor used the principle that would hallmark his work. This was not to go for a quick profit with a minimum outlay, but to increase the mine's long term profitability by investment in the latest technology.
1802	

1803	On March the 16th 1803 Edward Bray, the Tavistock Steward of the Duke of Bedford, called a meeting at the old Tavistock Guildhall. It was to consider the best means for 'prosecuting' a canal from Tavistock to Morwellham. In 1793 a proposal for a canal from Morwellham via Tavistock to Launceston, had been rejected because of the cost. Edward Bray, however, was able to demonstrate that a 'navigation' to join the booming mining area and the river Tamar was financially viable. Final plans for the 4½ mile canal from Tavistock were put to Parliament It was clearly understood that the situation and the direction of the tunnel were chosen "for the express purpose of cutting all the tin and copper lodes in Morwelldown" and "To work them in the most profitable way". The total cost of the project would be increased by taking this route, but the idea was to recoup the costs from working with new deposits (Crowndale and Crebor). The estimated cost was £40,000 including a branch to the Mill Hill Quarries. Parliamentary Sanction was obtained and work started in August 1803. Most of the capital needed amounting to £40,000 in shares was subscribed locally, but the Martineau family held at least 65 shares and the Birmingham Copper Co, 50 shares. The 4½ mile long canal was to run from Abbey Bridge (taking water from the Tavy) with wharves and warehouses along its opening stretches (see the Wharf Arts Centre, Tavistock). Then south-west towards Crowndale, crossing over the river Lumburn by aqueduct, under Morwell Down by tunnel and re-appearing 240 feet above the Tamar at Morwellham. A 'cut' to serve the Mill Hill Quarries joined the canal near the aqueduct. Taylor was appointed engineer in charge, but he took no personal financial interest until 1817, when he purchased shares, which he retained throughout his life.
1804	
1805	Taylor married Ann Pring from near Honiton. Philip, his brother, went back to Norwich where he joined Dr. Fitch in a large chemist and drug business, and set up a factory for making pill boxes with machinery. The Tavistock to Crowndale stretch of the canal completed.
1806	
1807	
1808	Taylor's son John was born. Taylor designed and installed new ventilation machine to overcome tunnelling difficulties, which operated on the principle of combined evacuation and induction. Taylor was appointed to represent 9 local mines in negotiations with the Duke of Bedford, to secure a reduction in mineral royalties consequent on the disastrous wartime fall in copper prices and the increase in mining costs.

1809	He succeeded in obtaining a reduction in duty from one eighth to one tenth of the total production.
1810	Taylor's son Richard was born. The Society of Arts awarded him a medal for the new ventilation machinery, and details were published in their 'transactions' in 1810
1811	The Tavistock Penny or token was issued. These were not coins of the realm, but tokens. The Tavistock Token or Tavistock Penny is a typical example of tokens used by companies as a substitute for legal tender in response to a shortage of royal copper coinage. Between 1788 and 1796 numerous tokens were issued by individuals, traders, industrial and mine owners and local councils. Then between 1811, and c.1815 another spate of coins was issued, which may have been a consequence of the Napoleonic Wars. The Tavistock Token seen in the illustration was issued in 1811 and is typical of the period. It has the scene of a Devon mine, possibly Wheal Friendship at Mary Tavy on one side, and the plume or feathers of The Prince of Wales on the reverse. These tokens could be redeemed by the mine workers, shop owners and innkeepers at the mine accounts department or Count House. His youthful compassion for the hardships of the children, bal maidens and men who worked on and under the ground, stayed with him throughout his life, and he was well aware of the subsistence level that they lived at. An existence where not just pennies, but farthings and halfpennies were precious, particularly as hard rock mine workers were paid a month in arrears, it was vital that they were paid on time. The main companies were often late in sending the mine the money it needed to pay the workers, owing to shortages of minted coinage, transport difficulties and sometimes indifference and greed. To prevent discontent amongst his workforce, John Taylor with an astuteness that became one of his trademarks, instituted the system of tokens or chips to ensure that his workers were paid.
1812	Taylor resigned all active commitments in the Tavistock area. He left the area to join his brother Philip and helped to establish a chemical works at Stratford in Essex. The Martineau and Ricardo families invested in this venture. On leaving Tavistock he received a tumultuous farewell from hundreds of miners and their families, whose respect and regard he'd earned for his fairness in the running of the day-to-day affairs of the mine.
Additional background information	John Taylor's achievements rank him alongside Josiah Wedgewood and Richard Arkwright, but not as an inventor, rather as an improver, innovator, manager and because he was able to marry the worlds of science and technology. He did have some failures (e.g. in Mexico), but working both nationally and internationally his input into the world of mining was to implement practical and financially viable solutions. When he died on the 5th of April 1863 his estate was worth £40,000.

Your template to complete chronologically for your 'famous' historical character for a 10 year period

Date/Years	Name: Sources:
Additional notes	

Your template to complete for a one year period for the person that you have chosen

Date	Name: Sources:
January	
February	
March	
April	
May	
June	
July	
August	
September	
October	
November	
December	
Additional notes	

ACTIVITIES

15.1   Timelines for the characters that you create

Remember that you may photocopy these tables if you wish, or alternatively we suggest that you fill them in using a pencil, which means you will be able to use them again or rub out any copying errors.

Objectives   To give you the opportunity to experiment with building up a simple timeline for a character that you have already invented, or one of the characters that you created in **Chapter 7**.

Your task   **A**   Construct a chronological time line for your character just noting down key events and milestones in their life over a ten year period.

B   Select one year from their chronological timeline. Create a month by month or week by week time line for the person that you've selected.

C   Select one day from the year that you have just created a timeline for, and pick a day. Create an hour by hour timeline for the person that you've selected. In the other information box you might like to add additional information such as what the weather was like that day, and if it was a Sunday or a day of religious celebration. All these minute details must be checked to the best of your ability if you intend to use them. Writing that it was August and your character was basking in the sunshine may be creative and fit your character mood, but an astute reader will no doubt quickly inform you that on that day in the particular place you are writing about, there is a newspaper account, a letter or a diary that exists which says that it rained so hard that day that several people died as a result of flooding. Part of the craft of writing historical novels is trying to ensure historical accuracy (see **Chapter 17**) when describing events.

Your own character timeline by year

Date/Years	Name: Sources:
Additional notes	

Your own character timeline by month

Date	Name: Sources:
January	
February	
March	
April	
May	
June	
July	
August	
September	
October	
November	
December	
Additional notes	

Your own character timeline hour by hour

Year, Date and Day	Name of your character:
12 midnight	
1am/3am	
4am/5am	
6am	
7am	
8am	
9am	
10am	
11am	
12 midday	
1pm	
2pm	
3pm	
4pm	
5pm	
6pm	
7pm	
8pm	
9pm	
10pm	
11pm	
12 midnight	
Additional notes	

15.2   Your own mini event line

Objective   To provide you with practice in drawing up a chronological event timeline.

Your task   To research and draw up a mini event line for a period that you would be interested in writing about covering ten years (not necessarily a decade).

Model 2 - An extract of a chronological event timeline

This compiled and used by Myfanwy Cook as part of the John Taylor *Canals, Copper and Historical Creative Writing Workshop* held at the end of November 2009 as part of the John Taylor Festival, and which was supported by the Royal Society, TAVI (Tavistock and Villages Development Forum, the Marine Biological Association, LEAF (Local Enterprise Action Forum) and Riverside Creative Projects.

Date/Year	World/ National Events
1798	French Revolutionary Wars – Bonaparte's Egyptian Expedition, Irish Rebellion, Wordsworth and Coleridge – *Lyrical Ballads*, Bleaching powder discovered
1799	9th January Income tax introduced by William Pitt, 12th July repressive legislation against political associations, Sandhurst Royal Military College founded, Royal Institution founded
1800	British capture Malta, Foundation of the Royal College of Surgeons, use of high-pressure steam – Richard Trevithick, electric light first produced by Sir Humphrey Davy
1801	Pitt resigns and Addington becomes P.M., Napoleonic War battles of Aboukir and Alexandria, June 29th the publication of the first census
1802	Ceylon becomes a British colony, First British Factory Act
1803	War in India, British declare war against France, Semaphore perfected by Admiral Popham, 1st Edition of Debrett's Peerage, Early locomotive – Richard Trevithick, 1st Public Railway from Wandsworth to Croydon
1804	Pitt P.M. again until 1805, Napoleonic Wars continue, War in India, foundation of the Royal Society of Painters in Watercolours, Construction of the Caledonian Canal in Scotland begun by Thomas Telford completed in 1822, Opening of the Rochdale Canal – John Rennie

1805	Battle of Trafalgar- Nelson dies, Armour plate first proposed for ships by William Congreve. Completion of the Grand Junction Canal (begun 1793), Jacquard's loom weaves embroidered fabrics, Sertumer (German Chemist) finds pain killing morphine in opium
1806	Death of William Pitt the Younger, Ministry of 'All the Talent' formed under Grenville and including Fox (resigned 1807), Death of Fox, Britain declares war against Prussia, Carbon paper patented by Ralph Wedgewood (7th Oct.)
1807	Tory ministry – Portland and Perceval, Bill passed by the British Parliament to abolish the Slave Trade, first recorded journey on the Mumbles Railway, Swansea, the oldest British passenger Railway. Ascot Gold Cup horse race initiated
1808	All-iron plough – Norwich, Peninsular War
1809	Appert wins a prize for preserving food in glass jars, Perceval becomes P.M. (until 1812)

Donkin makes iron/tin cans. Opening of Dartmoor Depot (Prison) for French Prisoners of War, Christian Tract Society founded, Two Thousand Guineas horse race first run at Newmarket, Study of Aerodynamics founded by Sir George Cayley |
| 1810 | Peninsular War, Mauritius taken from French by the British, Foundation of the Independent Order of Odd Fellows temperance society founded in Manchester, Orange Free State, South Africa first settled, The Luddites (machine wreckers) active until 1818 |
| 1811 | King George III incapacitated by insanity, the Prince of Wales later George IV becomes Prince Regent, Peninsular War, appearance of the Primitive Methodist Sect, First ichthyosaurus to be brought to scientific notice by Mary Anning, first county cricket match played by women t 3rd October |
| 1812 | The London Gas, Light and Coke Co. sets up first gas street lights, Assassination of Spencer Perceval by Francis Bellingham in the House of Commons on 11th May. Liverpool P.M. until 1827,Goodwood Cup first run,

Childe Harold's Pilgrimage-by Lord Bryon, Peninsular War – the Battle of Salamanca, June 18th 1812 war declared between Britain and America |
| Additional information | 1813 Publication of *Pride and Prejudice* by Jane Austen |

Your ten year timeline

Date/Year	World/ National Events
Additional information	

ACTIVITY

15.3   Keeping it local – Local event timelines

Objective   To provide you with practice in drawing up a local chronological event timeline.

Your task   ♦   To select a town, village, street or a specific district or area in a city;

♦   To research and draw up a mini event line for the place in the period that you would be interested in writing about, covering ten years (not necessarily a decade).

Model 3 - An extract of a local chronological event timeline

Below is a simplified extract of the local time line compiled and used by Myfanwy Cook as part of the John Taylor *Canals, Copper and Historical Creative Writing Workshop*, held at the end of November 2009 as part of the John Taylor Festival, which was supported by the Royal Society, TAVI (Tavistock and Villages Development Forum, the Marine Biological Association, LEAF (Local Enterprise Action Forum) and Riverside Creative Projects.

Local event timeline

Date	Place : Tavistock, West Devon, England
1800	The Mount Foundry Parkwood established
1801	Tavistock – Inhabited houses – 472, Families – 804, Inhabitants – 3,420
1802	
1803	Tavistock canal started
1804	Tavistock Turnpike Trust sets about replacing a stretch of road between Tavistock and Horrabridge, completed in 1822. The Mount Foundry was taken over by the banker John Gill
1805	Tyrwhitt, Bouverie and Alexander meet to decide on the site for the Dartmoor Depot
1806	
1807	
1808	
1809	The Dartmoor Depot receives its first prisoners
1810	
1811	Tavistock – Inhabited houses – 495, Families – 1,026, Inhabitants – 4,723
1812	

ACTIVITY

15.4 Picking and mixing relevant information from your timelines

Objective   To provide you with practice selecting relevant information from timelines. It is very easy to be swamped by facts and events that 'might' be useful. It is important that you select only the historical background information that will help to set the scene for the actions of your characters, or influence their actions and the outcome of your story.

Your task   **A**   Look at the three model time lines **1**, **2**, and **3** and identify three common themes illustrated by the events that are common to all of them. You can check for possible answers to this on: **www.myfanwycook.com**

          B   To look at the model **3** timeline and the figures about the number of houses and the population given for 1801 and then 1811. Can you come up with any explanation for the population increase without doing any further research, but based simply on the information that is in the timeline? Would you need to do additional research or not? For an explanation of why the population increased just refer to the 'Answers page' on **www.myfanwycook.com**

Tips

Start your timeline before the date that you intend your story to begin. This enables your characters to refer to the past, or make comparisons between the past and the time they are living in.

You may also find it useful to extend your timelines after the period you are focusing on, so that you are able to keep track of what happens to your characters after your novel or story ends. This information will also be helpful if you are planning on writing a series about the same character, or intend to create stories that centre on minor characters you have introduced, and that you wish to be the main protagonists in your next work of fiction.

Chapter 16 – Things to Avoid

Clichés

Clichés are often difficult to avoid when you are writing, because they are often idioms and popular phrases that have been over used. They are defined as expressions, words, ideas and actions that have become trite and lost their power through overexposure. The origin of the word comes from the French 'clicher', which means stereotype, and clichés are exactly that: they are stereotyped words and phrases that have lost their impact. In terms of writing that means side stepping descriptive phrases such as 'her hair was like burnished gold', 'his eyes were cornflower blue' and it means putting a new slant on tired clichéd phrases, proverbs and idioms.

ACTIVITY

16.1 Refreshing clichéd expressions

Objective   To refresh old used clichés

Your task   To create new idioms, expressions or catch-phrases and proverbs from old over-used ones

Model

Clichéd phrase – 'All that glistens is not gold' (alternative versions are 'all that glitters isn't gold' and 'all that glisters is not gold'). It means that all that glitters/glistens may not necessarily be valuable. We tend to associate it with Shakespeare's play *The Merchant of Venice* where it appears as 'All that glisters is not gold', but even as early as the 12th century a French theologian Alain de Lille had used a similar expression.

Transformed phrase – 'All that is tasty is not healthy'

Your task is to transform the following three clichéd expressions into new powerful phrases that convey the same meaning, but in an exciting and interesting way.

1   'Between the devil and the deep blue sea'. The origin of this expression may date back to Greek mythology; alternatively it could refer to 'a devil', which is the

name of a type of watertight seam on a wooden sailing ship. It means that you are caught between two difficult or dangerous choices.

2   'Don't look a gift horse in the mouth' A Latin version of this expression was used by St. Jerome in 420AD and it means that you shouldn't be critical of a gift.

3   'Fight fire with fire'. The concept was used as early as 1597 by Shakespeare in reference to King John. It means to respond to attack by using similar methods to one's attacker. It took shape as a verbal expression in 19th century US pioneer settler's set 'back fires' to guard against major grass or forest fires. Its earliest use in print is 1852.

Useful sites for phrase, idioms, proverbs and their meanings

www.phrases.org.uk

www.english-for-students.com

Tip: Anachronisms

Bernard Knight

"Anachronisms are a difficulty, for any book placed before the fourteenth century cannot avoid a primary linguistic anachronism, as modern readers would not be able to understand it if it was written in the contemporary language of the time. My 12th century novels about Devon would be unintelligible, as then the population spoke Early Middle English, Western Welsh, Norman-French or Latin! So it is pointless trying to write with an 'olde worlde' flavour, using 'gadzooks' and 'prithee' unless you are in the 18th century! One must use modern English, though I try to make it sound a little formal, to give a hint of antiquity. Some historical novelists go to the other extreme and use very modern slang, such as the entertaining books of David Wishart, based in Roman times.

Another problem with language anachronisms is the use of words which could not have existed at the time of the story. For example, can you legitimately use 'sadistic' or 'mesmerised' in a plot set before the 18th century, as de Sade and Mesmer were not yet born? I recently decided not to use 'thug' in one of my medieval books, as this Indian term would have been unknown

> then. But given the fact that, as mentioned above, much of the language we use for the books is anachronistic, perhaps it doesn't matter. However, I feel that we should not put such words into dialogue, as the character could not have spoken them in those days."
>
> **bernardknight.homestead.com**

Too much detail or not enough?

Readers of historical short stories and novels often enjoy the factual information about a period that is incorporated into an author's writing. However, having every 'i dotted and t crossed'[*] can easily swamp a storyline. A work of historical fiction can easily be transformed into a work of non-fiction.

   For example you as a writer may be personally fascinated by cooking and recipes, but you need to ask yourself does the information I am including add anything to the story? See the example below.

Setting: Paris a café on the place Saint-Michel c.1921

Main character: Ernest Hemingway

> He wanted somewhere to sit and think, but above all to savour the flavour of his favourite cake of La Galette des Rois. He seated himself at a table and began to write in a blue notebook with his pencil. His eye was caught by a young woman all alone at a table by the window, but his stomach rumbled with anticipation at the culinary delight that was about to appear on his table. He thought about how the Galette des Rois was made. He thought about its ingredients, the 450 grams of crème d'amandes; 750 grams of pâté feuilletée and of course the water and the 100 grams of sucre semoule. He could visualize it being cut into rounds and cooked in a pre-heated oven...

---

[*] **Crossing your 't's**: A variation of an idiomatic expression the origin of which possibly comes from a naval manoeuvre in battle.

Hopefully, you get the picture or rather your reader won't get the picture, because it will be hidden beneath a morass of detail. If you are determined to include factual information about things like recipes, military encounters etc. then you can include them at the end of each chapter or at the back of your novel or short story as an appendix*, which would mean that the description above could read as follows:

> He wanted a somewhere to sit and think, but above all to savour the flavour of his favourite cake of la Galette des Rois. He seated himself at a table and began to write in a blue notebook with his pencil. His eye was caught by a young woman all alone at a table by the window. Ernest's stomach rumbled with anticipation at the culinary delight that was about to appear on his table, but his heart watching the pretty girl whose face was as fresh as a newly minted coin, filled him with a different kind of longing.

Tip

You only need a pinch of factual information to add flavour, atmosphere and colour to your story.

* **appendix** (plural – appendixes or appendices): a separate section of additional explanatory or documentary material at the end of a book.

Humour that isn't funny

Before adding in any jokes or comic scenes, you need to ask yourself if you are just including them because you think they are funny, witty or clever, or if they fit the tone and subject of your story and the scene that you are including them in. If you are writing about a troupe of wandering players whose job it is to entertain then you could involve farce and comic situations. If you are writing a take-off, **spoof** or even a **pastiche** then you may well be using a lot of humour, but even then it is a good idea to consider what type of humour. Are you going to use **farce, satire, irony, puns**, or **slap-stick**?

The choice is yours, but it might be useful to write a couple of the scenes that use humour or humorous situations, and let at least six different people who read fiction look at them. You don't necessarily need to tell them that you wrote them, but just ask them if they think the scenes are funny and if not, why not.

Tip

Remember that if you decide to use today's 'in-jokes' in a historical setting they will date.

farce	a broadly humorous play or episode in a work of prose that is based on the exploitation and manipulation of 'unreal' or improbable situations.
irony	the humorous or mildly sarcastic use of words to imply the opposite of what they mean. It is often used to draw attention to incongruity. The art of using ironic humour is exquisitely demonstrated in Jane Austen's *Pride and Prejudice*.
pastiche	a work that mixes styles.
puns	word play that deliberately uses the ambiguity of words and their origin. Also called *paronomasia.*
satire	a way of shaming people about their views etc. It is a form of humour that is supposed to be funny, but also acts theoretically as constructive criticism.
sarcasm	sharp, biting humour that is mocking, contemptuous and intended to be insulting or scornful.
slap-stick	a type of comedy that is based on exaggerated violence e.g. as found in a pantomimes and some children's cartoons for example Tom & Jerry.
spoof	a send up or a parody. Today the word has a broad meaning is used to describe a work that pokes fun at or mocks another original work, style or person using satire or irony.

Not letting your reader use their imagination

In other words 'show, don't tell' your readers (see also **Chapter 10**). If you don't give your readers the opportunity to use their own imagination and their own skills of prediction, then they may not become totally engrossed with your plot. This doesn't mean cheating them by leaving out chunks of vital information until the end, but it does mean 'drip feeding' just the right amount of information without them losing track of where the story and characters are going. Give your readers the chance to enjoy the journey that your story is going to take them on, and don't lecture them (unless that is part of the plot). Too much detail can cause mental overload and the aim of writing is to entertain your reader and possibly to make them think, but certainly not to exhaust them. Accurate facts conjure up a sense of the past, but do remember you aren't writing a work of non-fiction, and that you can add historical notes at the end as a separate chapter for those who would like more detail.

Danger! Children's historical fiction

One of the main dangers of writing children's historical fiction is using an adult perspective and not taking into account the viewpoint of the children who may read it. It is easy to assume that children will enjoy something when they won't. What you need to take into account before embarking on a work of historical fiction for children include the following:

♦ Are you writing a book for younger children that will be read aloud to them by adults?

♦ Decide on the reading age of the children that you would like to write for. In order to do this you will need to carry out some intensive research. Firstly if you are writing for the UK market you would benefit from checking out sites such as **www.direct.gov.uk**, and finding out what teachers in primary and secondary schools perceive to be the average reading ability of different age groups. Alternatively, befriend a teacher who teaches in a primary school or English in a secondary school, and pick their brains. What you need to establish is sentence lengths, vocabulary, punctuation etc. that children will have been introduced to and are considered appropriate for that particular stage of their language development. You will also need to research which are the popular authors, and most importantly from a historical point of view which topics are studied in which years. What does this mean in practical terms? If you are writing for very young children the books will be mainly pictures with a few key words, as they get older the complexity of the sentences and the vocabulary will increase and the number of pictures will decrease, so that it is text only. However, at this point it should be mentioned that manga-style books for all ages are very popular at the moment. These originated in Japan with Kanagaki Robun and Kawanabe Kyosai who created the first manga magazine in 1874. Manga are rather like comics and are often lavishly illustrated.

- If you haven't any direct contact with schools or children of the age that you think you might want to write for, then go along to your local library and visit the children's section. Look at all the books in the section for the age group that you are interested in writing for, and select at least three from that category. Take out the ones that the librarians say are borrowed regularly. Then just as with an adult novel, you need to read them and analyse what you think it is about them that appeals to the audience they've been written for e.g. stories with animals in, overcoming adversity etc.
- Danger! Remember you are writing a book for children and the main characters therefore should be children. Adults take a secondary role.

If you are interested in writing for the children's market and have been inspired by authors who write novels set in the past for children, such as Tim Severin, Michael Morpurgo and Caroline Lawrence, then you would benefit from experience from the experts in the genre. The Society of British Children's Book Writers and Illustrators (**www.britishscbwi.org**) may provide useful tips and guidance. SCBWI (**www.scbwi.org**) is an international organisation with branches in many parts of the world; it was founded in 1971 and has its headquarters in Los Angeles. In the UK also see the *Children's Writers' and Artists' Yearbook* (A & C Black Publishers) and the Society of Authors (**www.societyofauthors.org**).

SECTION 3

The Special Ingredient: Research

Chapter 17 – The Special Ingredient: Research

A love of research and finding out about the past is, for many professional writers, the part of the process of writing a novel or story that they enjoy the most. When you read through the tips and suggestions of authors in **Chapter 19**, you will be able to gauge and understand how important most writers feel research is, even if they may disagree on the amount of factual detail that is required. It is, dare one use the word, 'fun' to pore over books, search through the internet, talk to people who are experts in a particular field, or for more recent historical research carry out oral history interviews. Many well-known writers also feel it is essential to visit the country or place that they are writing about.

What are the sources that most historical research is based on? You will already have been introduced to some of these in Andrew Thompson's contribution in **Chapter 6.**

1 - Primary

Books, artefacts (artifacts), documents such as wills, court rolls, paintings, maps, photographs, letters, diaries, memorabilia, recordings and interviews with people who took part in the events, or as close as possible to the event, or time when the person you are writing about lived.

When using primary sources it is often useful to apply the journalistic approach when interpreting the material ,which is to make certain that you verify <u>who</u> wrote it, <u>what</u> it is, <u>when</u> (exact date if possible), <u>where</u> and <u>why</u>, what its purpose was e.g. a contract, an edict etc. for the primary source you are consulting.

2 - Secondary

Accounts of events or documents etc. relating to the event, person or place that are not first hand or primary sources, for example a book which examines the primary source material. Biographies and autobiographies can be primary sources as well, but if written a long time after the event then the accounts may not be as accurate as, obituaries, oral history or family memories that were recorded at the time of the event.

3 - Tertiary

These sources are similar to secondary ones, but often present a simplified or general picture of the events, and are used to give an introductory overview of the event or period e.g. in encyclopaedias and textbooks. Tertiary is sometimes also used to cover catalogues and bibliographies* about the period.

Autobiographies can be primary sources as well, but if written a long time after the event then the accounts may not be as accurate as a firsthand account recorded at the time. Memory plays tricks, and what happens is that it becomes selective and we forget some things and exaggerate others. Furthermore when written at a distance from the particular event, then it is easy to be influenced by the current ideas that are held about it, rather than those of the time.

*Bibliography: a systematic list of sources such as books, articles, maps etc.

ACTIVITIES

17.1 Which sources should I use? Which sources can I use?

Objectives
- To provide you with practice at identifying and listing primary, secondary and tertiary sources
- To enable you to compile a basic bibliography* of sources relating to the period that you are interested in writing about, and to assist you in managing the historical research that you carry out

Your task
Draw up a list of specific sources that you might use to research the period of history that you are keen to write about. While you are doing this, try to identify which ones it will be possible for you to access easily, and also grade them on how important and relevant they will be to your research e.g. Do you need to go back to the primary sources or can you mange with secondary sources?

Use the following headings to create your list:

Primary, Secondary, Tertiary

17.2 Keeping track and acknowledging your sources

Objective To ensure that you keep accurate records of your sources, and to acknowledge where they came from and who wrote them.

Your task Acknowledging other writers, helping your readers to locate the sources that you used and demonstrating where your knowledge came from are good practice, but also today they can provide useful additional background material to put onto your web site or blog. Keeping details systematically will also enable you to be able to refer back and find the sources that you used, and means that if you wish you can include details of the sources that you used at the end of your novel.

Go back to the activity that you've completed above and make certain that you've used some form of citation or referencing system. Try to stick to the same pattern for all your references. There are two main systems used in academic circles currently, one is the Harvard, which is also referred to as *Name and Date* and the other is the Numeric. What it means is that however you decide to record the sources that you have used, you need to note down the author, date, title, publisher etc.

Tip

Citing References, which was written by David Fisher and Terry Harrison and published by Blackwell[*], is an inexpensive publication which is designed as a guide for University students and is an ideal introduction to the subject.

[*] **http://bookshop.blackwell.co.uk/jsp/id/ Citing_References/9781853779923**

17.3 The historical fiction writer as a detective

Some aspects of writing such as proofreading and editing can be a chore, but the research shouldn't be. If you want to captivate your reader then you must be captivated by the subject that you are investigating. You need to become a hunter of intriguing facts and illuminating detail. Unfortunately you will often only be able to use a tiny proportion of the fascinating details you uncover, but the ones that you do include will add an authentic 'ring' to your story.

Objective   To uncover three unusual facts, or background details about the period that you are keen to write about from a primary source such as a diary, journal or collection letters.

Your task   A   To make notes about the three interesting facts or details you've uncovered.

B   To incorporate one of these pieces of information into a scene of no more than 500 words that you might be able to use in a story or novel.

Examples:

1   In Gilbert White's – *The Garden Kalender and Naturalist's Journal, 1751-1793* not only does he comment on the weather and the wildlife such as field mice, but on treats such as hot house 'cantaleupes'.

2   In the letters of Jane Austen's cousin Eliza de Feuillide, she mentions that in June 1792 she was staying in London at the 'Metropolis', when she was caught up in a public demonstration aimed at preventing some houses being pulled down. Her carriage was going through Mount Street when she was caught in a battle between the mob and guards on horseback. "The noise of the populace, the drawn swords and pointed bayonets of the guards, the fragments of bricks and mortar thrown on every side, one of which had nearly killed my coachman, the firing at the end of the street which had already begun, although in short alarmed me so much, that I have never really been well since." Le Faye, D.,

(2002), *Jane Austen's 'Outlandish Cousin' – The Life and Letters of Eliza de Feuillide*, p.113, London: The British Library

3   On Active Service (Private A.T. Cook, Berlin to G.M Cook, Devon, UK) – Postmarked 31st of October 1945, * L of C Troop W/S, R.E.M.E., B.A.O.R

"My dear Sweetheart,

I was very pleased to have such a long letter from you today. I was only able to write a short note last night. I think I mentioned that the operas on Sunday were wonderful. Probably the most surprising thing was to find that the singers could act. Karina Kutz gave a terrific emotional display in *Cavaleria Rusticana*. I've seen her off the stage two or three times, and she's not much to look at, but on stage she's really great. Joseph Metternick who was in both deserves his international reputation. He's a fine actor as well as a first rate tenor (almost a baritone). He has a slight build, but sings very robustly...I should like to bring back a little orphan. Just round the corner is a 'Kinderheim' and sometimes I see them out for a walk – crocodile fashion – all of them are very tiny and many pretty and so solemn..."

17.4 How to explain 'interesting' or 'unusual' words

While researching you will come across a wide-range of 'curious' words, idioms and colloquialisms that are specific to the period you are writing about. While most historical novelists would agree that it isn't a good idea to use too many of them, used sparingly they can enhance your dialogue and descriptions. You do need to check before using them that they were used during the time that you are writing about.

Objective   To practise explaining 'interesting' or 'unusual' words to your reader by using them in context as an alternative to giving a definition of them in a glossary.

Your task   Below is a list of unusual words. If you wanted to use these words in your story how can you show what they meant without giving an exact definition? Don't forget to place these words in an appropriate period. Do remember not to overuse unusual words that you uncover during the course of your research. The appropriate use of one from time to time can make your reader sit up and pay more attention to what you are writing, but keep them to a minimum otherwise it may interrupt the flow and pace of your writing and irritate your reader.

Example

Cark: a verb meaning to worry or to be burdened with worries. The word is derived from Norman French c. 13th century and from Late Latin carricāre "to load". It isn't to be confused with the Australian slang use of 'cark' as in the man 'carked it' (died).

Model

Eleanor was as carked with matters of state as was her husband Edward, but at least he had the power to take action and tackle his worries whereas she did not.

Your turn

deblaterate

goddard

energumen

lallygag

Supplementary Task

Find three examples of words, expressions or idioms that were commonly used during a specific historical period. Research their origin and use, and then try to place them in a sentence or scene that will demonstrate their meaning without directly telling your reader.

A warning from your potential readers

Do remember that you are writing to be read and that for many readers historical inaccuracies can irritate them to the point where they abandon the book that you've written and never read a book or story written by you again.

Darryl Harrison

"There is nothing more I like to read than novels set during the Battle of Britain, a period and subject I know well. What could be more thrilling than a story set at the point in the history where the future of civilised society hangs by the narrowest of threads? Unfortunately, however, I am usually disappointed: potentially fine stories are all too often ruined by careless inaccuracies that destroy the illusion of reality that the author is trying to create. No matter how gripping the plot, realistic the characters, or finely crafted the dialogue, gross errors of fact have caused me to stop reading a book (or stop taking it seriously) on more than one occasion.

Inaccuracies can start with the jacket illustration. Not every Spitfire, Hurricane or Messerschmitt flew in the Battle of Britain: the aircraft of that conflict were of distinctive appearance, both in shape and in the markings applied, a fact that seems to elude most publishers (of both fiction and non-fiction). I recently had the opportunity to check the cover illustrations of 93 books set during the Battle of Britain (most of them non-fiction), and found that 76 of them featured images inappropriate for the period. I appreciate that we shouldn't "judge a book by its cover" but the fact is that we do. Given the huge amount of effort that goes into writing a book and bringing it to market, it seems incongruous to me that authors and publishers should risk alienating knowledgeable buyers by selecting cover illustrations so lackadaisically.

Inaccuracies also crop up in the text. I have read novels set in the Battle of Britain which feature:
- aircraft which didn't fly until two years later;
- wholly fabricated (and quite incorrect) descriptions of cockpit layouts, flying drill, and bail-out techniques;
- incorrect operational characteristics of aircraft, such as speed, range, or ceiling;
- incorrect unit designations and characteristics;

- ◆ incorrect or inappropriate tactics;
- ◆ grossly simplified accounts of what it was like to fly an aircraft in combat at that particular time (by far the most common – and most irritating – error).

And that's just the aeroplanes. Add in social details such as local geography at the time, contemporary vehicles, recreational activities, popular music, pastimes and hobbies, prices of things in the shops, social structures, peculiarities of wartime life such as rationing, restrictions on movement, air raid precautions and so forth, and the potential for irritating readers by sloppy or incomplete research is very high.

Fortunately, some authors do their homework properly and the result is enthralling!"

Darryl Harrison is co-proprietor of ActiveSprite Press and an avid reader of historical fiction and non-fiction.

www.activesprite.co.uk

Tips

Edwin Buckhalter

"Dates and facts need to be right, obviously, and historical accuracy is paramount. That said, a little licence can be taken for the sake of the story - but should be explained in a preface or epilogue explaining what is true and what is invention for the sake of the storyline.

Make the reader have a feel for the period and characters early on, but don't try to emulate the speech of the century in question. Our speech today would sound strange to their ears, and (by way of exaggeration to make the point) too many pseudo "forsooths" and "gadzooks" or longer anachronisms and styles really don't sit well for today's reader - and impede the flow and enjoyment of the story line...

Read the novels of Ronald Welch if you want to see how it is done properly, albeit written for a younger audience. I learned more history from those books, and a greater understanding of people, customs and lifestyles, than in years as a history undergraduate and postgraduate. (And I am sure other readers would add further distinguished writers such as Rosemary Sutcliffe)."

Edwin Buckhalter is Chairman and founder of Severn House Publishers Ltd

www.severnhouse.com

Margaret Donsbach

"General Background Research

Aspiring historical novelists can find lots of good information at www.HistoricalNovels.info to help them write novels that will keep readers' lights burning into the wee hours. The "Writing Tips" page discusses the type of background historical novelists need to be successful: credentials are less important than a love of history, a lust for research and the persistence to keep honing one's writing skills. Recommendations are included for books on writing fiction generally and historical fiction in particular, along with links to some especially helpful websites. But the "Writing Tips" page is only the beginning.

To write any type of novel well, a writer needs to read widely and deeply in the category he or she hopes to succeed in. With over 5,000 listings organized by time and place, writers can use this website to develop a reading list for novels of the specific type they hope to write. Historical fiction has many sub-categories, from thoughtful literary novels to fluffy romances and tense action-adventure stories. Most of the brief descriptions indicate the style of the novel, and over 200 reviews give more details. Writers can also scan the lists to see what subjects are over-represented and therefore less attractive to publishers (the world may not need another novel about Queen Elizabeth I, unless it offers a really unusual twist) and what subjects are still unexplored terrain. While it's always best for writers to follow their own passions rather than attempt to tailor a book to the rapidly changing marketplace, knowing the market can help you present your novel to agents and editors in the most favorable light."

Margaret Donsbach is proprietor of www.HistoricalNovels.info. 2875 SW Raleighview Dr., Portland, Oregon 97225, USA

www.HistoricalNovels.info
mdonsbach@q.com

C.C. Humphreys

"HISTORICAL TIP NO.1: RESEARCH, OR GETTING YOUR FEET WET

I am full of this one right now, having just returned from Byzantium… Constantinople… ok, Istanbul. I went because the novel I am writing deals with the Turkish conquest of the city in

1453. Once more I was thrilled by what I learned, touched, felt, saw, heard.

There are writers who write wonderful novels and never leave the house. Probably my favorite all time author is Rosemary Sutcliff and she never left her wheelchair, yet conjured visions of Bronze Age Britain that were fabulously rich in detail, in flora and fauna and geography. And now we have the internet... why go to the expense?

I will tell you why. There is memory in stone, in places where the characters you hope to conjure trod. There are people there, descendants of those who walked, loved, fought in the era you are writing about who will say something to throw you back in a way a photograph cannot do. And if the vista is now blocked by a high rise or a three lane road, the place where you stand helps you see with the inner eye, beyond the layers time has laid down. A certain type of bird calls. A bug flies into your face. A flower catches you with its scent. And you see your character hear it, feel it, sniff it. And they do something differently, your book changes.

Examples: on the battlefield of Saratoga I watched a heron pass over me and fly straight into my novel as a recurring motif. Climbing the cliffs at Quebec my feet slid down shale, as the British Light Infantrymen's would have done in 1759, as Jack Absolute's would have done. In Vlad's ruined castle of Poenari, I heard how ravens bark, not cry. Last week in Istanbul, in a fishing boat that took me out where three waters meet – the Bosphorus, the Golden Horn and the Sea of Marmora – I found that the calm I'd imagined when the wind dropped wouldn't have gentled my battling ships... the sails would have dropped but they still would have bucked like broncos.

I could go on and on. Because what I have always discovered is that research isn't so much about getting the facts right – what are 'historical facts anyway? – research is about finding things that act as springboards for the imagination and bounce your plot and characters into places you could not have foreseen.

My tip? Sell the children, mortgage the house, pawn the family silver... and Go!"

C.C. Humphreys author of the Jack Absolute series and *Vlad the Last Confession*)

www.cchumphreys.com

SECTION 4

Historical Crime Fiction

Chapter 18 – Historical Crime Fiction

Perhaps the love of puzzles, riddles, competitions and competitive games that many of us acquire as children, is one of the reasons why crime fiction as a genre is so popular. Along with an interest in games and competitions of any kind, comes a competitive streak that engages us consciously or subconsciously, when we read this genre of fiction. We want to see if we can solve the crime or murder before we reach the end of the novel. We want to find out who did it, and many readers don't just want to have the story gradually unfurled to them without any effort. The reader is scanning for clues as they read and trying to predict who the villain or villains of the story are. Crime fiction is one of the most interactive genres of fiction, because although you may never meet the author face to face, you can learn a lot about the way their mind works through the way they plant clues throughout their stories, and build into their novels cliff hangers and predictable and unpredictable dangers for their main characters. Your role as a reader is not simply to read about how the main character or characters solve the crime, but to become a 'side-kick' and assistant in solving the crime. Crime fiction at its best is an intellectual challenge and a riddle that is packed with red-herrings that keep you 'on your toes' metaphorically speaking, but nonetheless with your eyes firmly fixed on the page.

In order to establish a sense of pattern and to learn the craft of building up suspense as a writer, you would benefit from reading at least three novels written by three masters of general crime fiction, and concentrating on the devices that they use to give their novels pace, suspense, and make them engrossing reads. What is it about their style that has made them best-selling authors? Is it their style or is it their main characters, that have created the kind of gripping read that you just can't put down? For instance read three of Agatha Christie's novels written at different periods of her writing career, and try to identify if the pattern she is using to entertain and engage her readers has changed. Try a novelist like Dick Francis whose novels were written over a long period of time, and also a contemporary writer like Michael Connelly. In Michael Connelly's case start your reading with *The Black Echo* and then read at least one in the same series, written at a later date.

Why in a book about the craft of historical fiction writing are you being recommended to read crime fiction that isn't historical? It is to enable you to disassociate yourself from historical details that may fascinate you.

To allow you to avoid being enticed by the historical subject matter, rather than focusing on the skills that the authors are using to write compelling crime fiction novels. The historical background detail is just that, it is a background. It is the way the story is written that is paramount. Do best selling crime novelists use a formula to create suspense? If so can you identify it? If you can, do not under any circumstances try to copy or plagiarise their work. However, you can try to emulate it and aim to produce something which is equally as good, if not better.

Historical crime fiction is a genre in its own right. It combines crime and history. It requires tight plotting, careful planning and a sense of timing that will catch your reader unawares. You should be able to shatter the illusions or sense of comfort of your reader, in a few sharp sentences. Crime fiction is written not to lull you off to sleep, but to keep you awake.

What you must not do is cheat! Cheating means that you don't give your reader any clues, or that the clues you give them are unfair. You've got to give your reader a sporting chance of solving the mystery. If you suddenly introduce a relative from some corner of the world, whom you've never mentioned before, as the murderer, then that is cheating. That kind of deception will only result in one thing, readers might give you a second chance and read your next novel, but they most probably won't.

Crime fiction like all the other genres has a host of sub-genres, some better known than others, such as detective style thrillers, cosy crime and psychological crime fiction. Historical crime fiction also embraces some of the other popular forms of crime fiction writing such as 'religious' thrillers of which Umberto Eco's *The Name of the Rose* (1980) is an example (see **www.umbertoeco.com**).

However, whatever the sub-genre of crime fiction you would like to try to write, what you need to keep in your mind is that you need a 'hero' or 'heroine'. This is as true today as it was when Homer wrote the epic poem the *Odyssey*, which was written possibly in the eighth century BC, and is considered by some as the earliest example of a 'thriller'. The Odyssey's main character Odysseus, who may be a hero, isn't exactly pleasant, and in fact he might be described as quite ruthless and selfish in many ways, which interestingly would also appear to be a hallmark of quite a few of the 'heroes' of crime fiction series, that have become firm favourites over the years.

Your own hero or heroine must overcome obstacles, which requires tough, determined characters. The story you write must also be driven forward by a plot that enables your main character to succeed in their quest, while at the same time creating suspense and fear. The type of fear that makes you want to re-check all your locks at night before you go to bed. Historical novelists may in this respect have an advantage, because they can create fear that is at a great distance. Readers can tuck themselves up in bed at night, safe in the knowledge that the crime took place in the past. Historical writers can provide a 'safety zone' for readers who can't cope with mass murders set in supermarkets, very like their own. They are less frightening perhaps in some way, than those that have been set in the present day, which for many readers is a positive quality.

How to murder someone

In an historical crime fiction novel, you couldn't have a character who is murdered by gas poisoning in London in 1795, but you could in Cornwall. William Murdoch finally managed to light (illuminate) his house in Redruth in Cornwall , using gas produced from coal in 1792. You would have had to wait until about 1813 or later, to murder someone using gas in London. The first public street lighting took place in 1807 in Pall Mall, and by 1813 Westminster Bridge was lit by gas. It may only be a little over a decade of difference, but if you are writing an historical novel you should aim to make it as accurate as possible. For writers thinking of using a similar theme set in the USA, curiously it was Baltimore that had the first gas streetlights!

ACTIVITY

18.1 How to commit a murder?

Objective	To create a list of possible ways to commit a murder which would have been possible during the period that you are interested in writing about.
Your task	1 Select a period and make a list in the 'How to commit a murder?' table below of at least ten ways that it might have been possible to murder someone. Make a detailed list e.g. Strangled with a silk scarf that they'd been given as a birthday present. Ask your friends to contribute suggestions. Beware that such a suggestion will no doubt result in great fun and laughter, and some very unlikely methods of murdering people, but it can also come up with some extraordinary, but perfect ways of carrying out a murder e.g. death by laughter. This idea came from a dentist who pointed out that if you wanted to set a murder in the early Victorian period, laughing gas (Nitrous oxide), could have been a possibility

because it had been used for anaesthesia in dentistry since the 1840s. A hairdresser suggested nail varnish or nail polish as an instrument for murder. At first her idea might have sounded a little bit contrived, but a quick piece of research proved that the idea was a possibility. The Chinese used to lacquer their nails with a mixture of Arabic gum, egg whites and beeswax, and it is even mentioned in Ming manuscripts. Women in the 17th century polished if not coloured their nails, and in the 19th century recipes for making 'nail paints' were included in both American and English cookbooks.

2   List the methods under different headings. You might like to jot them down in a small notebook and then transfer them onto your computer or to the table below. However, do beware of carrying notebooks - a friend, while having a cup of tea in a cafe in a well-known department store, wrote the description of how to murder someone and left it behind. She never had the courage to reclaim it!

3   For those writers who are interested in writing about earlier periods of history this task is going to be more difficult, as theoretically you are more limited in your choice e.g. hitting someone with a heavy object, strangulation, starvation, poisoning, pushing someone off or into something, stabbing them, drowning, cutting their throat etc. However, fear is also another weapon, and so driving people to take their own lives could be another option. Try to think about the health issues of the period, and if you get stuck, browse through some history books or use the web to research examples of crimes of the period. Shakespeare was brilliant at using 'true life' crimes in his plays, for instance George Duke of Clarence who in 1478, it is believed, was drowned in a butt of malmsey wine.

How to commit a murder?

When and where	Example of how to commit a murder
Middle Ages	A rabid dog is given as a present to the victim. The dog bites the victim who dies several months later. Rabies has been known since 2000BC.

Crime scenes and forensic practice

Bernard Knight's (**bernardknight.homestead.com**) first novel was published in 1963, and since then he has become identified with his popular medieval Crowner John mystery series set in Devon, with *A Plague of Heretics* the most recent in the series being published in April 2010.

He became a Home Office pathologist in 1965 and was appointed Professor of Forensic Pathology at the University of Wales College of Medicine in 1980. He has contributed to a range of textbooks, edited medical journals and was Managing Editor of Elsevier's *Forensic Science International*, the leading international publication in the field. Bernard Knight wrote *Murder, Suicide or Accident, the Forensic Pathologist at Work* in 1971 under the pseudonym, Bernard Picton. In 1977 Bernard published his best-seller *Autopsy: The Memoirs of the World's Greatest Medical Detective* (Harrap), which is the biography of the Chief Medical Examiner of New York City, Professor Milton Helpern. This was also published in book club and paperback editions. He also qualified as a barrister, and has written numerous articles such as *Crowner: Origins of the Office of Crowner* (Prof. Bernard Knight, CBE, **www.twbooks.co.uk**). During his career as a renowned Home Office pathologist, he worked on cases such as that of Fred and Rosemary West in 1994. He is currently writing a series based in the 1950s set in the Wye Valley, whose central character is a retired forensic pathologist Richard Pryor. He still finds time to be part of The Medieval Murderers (The Crime Writers' Association, **www.thecwa.co.uk**) who have produced a series of books together and give presentations at literary festivals, libraries and bookshops to promote their work amongst the public, and he is a regular reviewer of crime books (see *Tangled Web*, **www.twbooks.co.uk**).

This brief biography of the career of Bernard Knight is to help you to put into context the opening paragraph of an article, which he wrote for *The Historical Novels Review* (**www.historicalnovelsociety.org**) Issue 43, February 2008:

> "One of the problems that a forensic pathologist has in writing historical mystery novels is resisting the temptation to use one's own expertise in the stories. My long-running Crowner John series about a 12th – century coroner naturally contains a profusion of murdered corpses, but I have to restrain myself from using even the most elementary 'scenes of crime' technology if I want to preserve even a vestige of **authenticity**. No autopsies, no thermometers, no blood groups, no DNA –nothing apart from looking and prodding!"

The word **authenticity** has been highlighted above, because it is essential in historical and other forms of crime fiction writing, that in order to faithfully capture the period that you are writing about, you need to use authentic detail. It is possible to assume certain things for example "It must have been realised from prehistoric times that a body cools down progressively after death – though even today, accuracy in determining the time of death by this method exists only in the minds of novelists and script-writers. I usually let Gwyn (Sir John de Wolfe's officer) flex the limbs to see how much 'death stiffness' remains, though this could tell him only that the victim did or did not die within the last few days. The degree of decomposition would also have to be self-evident, though margins of error are enormous." So be careful to research exactly what and what was not possible in the period that you are writing about.

You can do this by reading about the history of the development of forensic medicine. Bernard Knight explained that, "The story of forensic medical investigations and autopsies is interesting in itself – I detest the modern misuse of the word 'forensics', which the media has forced upon us. 'Forensic 'is an adjective, not a noun! There is forensic medicine, forensic pathology, forensic psychiatry etc., but 'forensics' is meaningless. The word has a Roman origin from 'pertaining to the forum', where the lawyers used to ply their trade in the city's main meeting place."

The History and Development of Forensic Medicine

This is another potential pitfall for the budding historical novelist. The story itself is a fascinating one, and it would be easy to fall prey to all the tantalising details. However, should you intend to include any details about forensic medicine, it is important to keep in mind, as Bernard Knight pointed out, that "...until relatively recent centuries, the forensic examination of corpses was only external and that autopsies were rare or even prohibited, especially in the English speaking countries. In ancient China, going back well before the time of Christ, there were magistrates similar to coroners, whose duty it was to attend scenes of death and make detailed investigations including an examination of the corpse, but again this was only an external view. A comprehensive handbook for coroners, including the requirement to issue reports in triplicate, was published in 1247 and is still in print!" If you are interested in the history and development of forensic medicine there are numerous sites that can fill you in on the chronology (some examples are at the end of this chapter). However, just to stimulate your curiosity here are a few landmarks:

- 44 B.C. Antistius, a physician, having examined Julius Caesar, reported that he had been stabbed twenty-three times, but that only the second one was fatal.
- In c. 250 B.C. Erasistramus, a Greek royal physician and anatomist, observed that patients pulse rates increased when they were lying. Erasistramus and a fellow physician Herophilus founded a school of anatomy in Alexandria.
- 1156 Bologna Medical School was founded. Autopsies began to be performed, not for anatomical investigation, but for forensic reasons. In 1275 a Bolognese surgeon, William of Saleice carried out the first recorded 'autopsy'. This was followed in 1302 when surgeon-physicians carried out an autopsy at the request of a magistrate, to establish if a man named Azzolino had been poisoned.
- c.1247/1248 a book was published attributed to Hsi Duan Yu, that describes cases such as the case of a person murdered with a sickle, which was solved by a magistrate who worked out that a sickle had been used by testing various blades on an animal carcass, and comparing it with the wounds on the person who had been murdered. He instructed everyone to bring their sickles to one location and flies, attracted by the smell of blood were attracted to a single sickle blade. *The Washing Away of Wrong* also provided advice on how to determine if a death was caused by murder, suicide, or was an accident.
- 1507 *Codex Bambergensis* was extended in 1532 becoming the *Consitutio Criminalis Carolina*, which necessitated medical expertise in all cases of violent death.
- Auguste Ambroise Tardieu (1818 -1879) published a book on forensic toxicology, which marked an important step forward in forensic medicine.
- c. 1879 Alphonse Bertillon developed the science of Anthropometry, a system of personal identification, based on taking a series of body measurements to facilitate distinguishing one individual from another, and with the invention of photography was able to use it in criminal investigation. Then in 1881, he began to take standard pictures of all French criminals and archive them in the Bureau of Identification in Paris.

- 1899 At the University of Lyons, Alexandre Lacassagne a professor of forensic medicine compared the numbers of 'lands and groves' to match individual bullets to a gun barrel.
- 1903 Systematic use of fingerprints (forensic dactyloscopy) to identify criminals began in New York State prison.
- 1910 Albert Osborn published 'Questioned Documents', which outlined the developed fundamental principles of document examination.
- 1910 Bernard Henry Spilsbury (16 May 1877 – 17 December 1947) an English pathologist gave forensic evidence in the trial of Dr Crippen about the identity of the human remains found in Crippen's house, and concluded that a scar on a small piece of skin pointed to Mrs. Crippen as the victim.
- 1910 Edmond Locard, known as the Sherlock Holmes of France, championed the Principle of Exchange (every contact leaves a trace), which is a cornerstone of forensic examination of physical evidence. He set up a police laboratory in Lyons and later founded the Institute of Criminalistics at the University of Lyons. The Belgian detective crime fiction writer Georges Simenon attended his lectures.
- 1953 Francis Crick and James Watson published a paper identifying the structure of DNA.

Beware

The list of events above is designed only to give a glimpse into the history of forensic science. The detailed study of forensic history can provide the writer with a range of possible ways to rid oneself of characters, and a rich resource of 'red herrings', which can hinder the investigation of your main character or throw your reader off the 'scent of the villain'. What it can also be is the ultimate 'red herring' for the writer. Instead of focusing just on the period, country or method of murder that you intend to include in your novel, you can be lured into the mire of fascinating detail that you will come across. You can become bogged down in all the curious detail, the result being that you may try to include all the knowledge that you've acquired about the subject you are writing about or that your research takes up all your time leaving you no time to write. You have to take the surgeon's approach to this type of background research, and cut out and save only what you need to. Your reader is expecting an exciting story underpinned with selected information that is relevant, and not random interesting facts dotted throughout your novel or story.

Suggestions

If you become so absorbed in your research and want to share the knowledge that you've acquired, you might consider adding an extra chapter at the end of your work of fiction, giving some background about the period that you've been writing about, or information about the history of a place or subject that you've researched etc. You could add in footnotes as you go along, but this can be very distracting for the reader.

   Another possibility is to consolidate your research in a separate book or an article. Nicola Thorne (**www.nicolathorne.co.uk**) did this with great effect when she published *In Search of Martha Brown*, which consolidated the years of meticulous research that she'd carried out to write her novel *My Name is Martha Brown*, which is based on the story of Martha Brown, whom Thomas Hardy saw hanged. She was the last woman to be hanged publicly in Dorset in 1856.

ACTIVITY

18.2 Vocabulary your reader might not know

Objective   To explain concepts or vocabulary which may be unfamiliar to your readers without using a glossary or historical notes at the end of your novel or story.

Your task   Below are two brief descriptions of the difference between two types of autopsies. Your task is to turn these descriptions into an imaginary scene in an historical novel set in any period that you think might be appropriate, to provide your reader with an explanation of the differences between them.

> **Model**
>
> **Description:** Autopsies can be carried out for legal or medical purposes, and a forensic autopsy takes place if the cause of death may be a criminal matter. Clinical or academic autopsy is performed to uncover the medical cause of death, and is used in cases of unknown or uncertain death, or for research purposes.

Example

Rembrandt was not sure how to capture the anatomical detail on canvas. The cause of Aris Kindt's death was not being investigated by Dr. Tulp, Amsterdam's official anatomist. Kindt had been executed by strangulation early that day for armed robbery. After all, it was not an autopsy for medical or legal purposes, but a lesson in anatomy. Public dissections were only permitted once a year, and so on the 16th of January the theatre that had been hired for the purpose was packed with paying students, colleagues and those members of the public who could pay to attend the event. The preparator who had prepared the body for the lesson would not be included in his picture, because instead he had to incorporate those who had paid him to include their portraits as spectators in his work. This was after all one of the social, as well as medical events, of 1632. It diverted everyone's attention away from the winter weather and the boredom of city life.

He opened the textbook on anatomy *De humani corporis fabrica* by Andreas Vesalius and then turned to compare what he was reading with his preliminary sketches of the muscles and tendons he'd drawn. Certainly it wasn't what he'd envisaged that he'd be doing in his twenty-sixth year, but he had to earn a living through his talent as an artist, and it was quite fascinating in a repulsive way.

Write your description in your notebook, and don't forget to keep it somewhere safe as you never know when you might want it.

Where are you going to murder your victim?

If you watch any of the American CSI programmes on television, then you will notice that they quite often use the words 'primary crime scene'. This is because the place where the body is found may not be the place where they were murdered. This is an important point to bear in mind when you are writing historical fiction. Is the victim going to be discovered where they were murdered, and if not are you going to start with a crime scene that is littered with clues but no body, for example a room that has been ransacked or a cottage that has been burnt to the ground?

It is equally important to be aware that "Wherever he steps, wherever he touches, whatever he leaves, even without consciousness, will serve as a silent witness against him. Not only his fingerprints or his footprints, but his hair, the fibres from his clothes, the glass he breaks, the tool mark he leaves, the paint he scratches, the blood or semen he deposits or collects. All of these and more, bear mute witness against him. This is evidence that does not forget. It is not confused by the excitement of the moment. It is not absent because human witnesses are. It is factual evidence. Physical evidence cannot be wrong, it cannot perjure itself, it cannot be wholly absent. Only human failure to find it, study and understand it, can diminish its value." - Paul L. Kirk. 1953. *Crime investigation: physical evidence and the police laboratory*. Interscience Publishers, Inc.: New York.

ACTIVITY

18.3 Describing a crime scene without a body

Objective   Crime scenes can be any location where evidence is found, and not necessarily where it is committed, and so your objective is to practise setting a scene which will create the impression that a murder has been committed there, but without a body.

Your task   Pick a period and place of your choice and write a scene of no more that 300 words that will create in the mind of your reader the idea that someone might have been murdered there, but without the visible presence of a corpse.

Model

Even by the flickering light of the lamp, he was able to see that the inside of the carriage had been the scene of a battle. The leather upholstery had been slashed by a knife blade. The cuts were deep and committed with a degree of ferocity that did not leave much hope that the passengers had escaped unharmed. That is if there had been any passengers. The carriage with its horses had been found in the coaching inn courtyard as if abandoned, and was spotlessly clean except for the gouges in the upholstery. The only trace of recent human

---

> occupation was the slight whiff of musk and lavender. It was a scent he associated with ladies of pleasure, pretty as butterflies, but only attracted out at night like moths...

Write down your scene in your notebook

Discovering a body

If the victim of the crime is going to be discovered you will need to describe the scene. In the past in rural areas hiding bodies would have been a lot easier than it is today. A body buried in woodland might lay undisturbed for centuries, whereas today bodies are more likely to be discovered. If you want your victim's body to be found, then you need to decide who is going to find it, and where. Is it going to be found by an innocent bystander, a character who is going to play a part in your narrative or the hero or heroine who will be acting as the 'detective' and who solves the crime?

ACTIVITY

18.4 Discovering your victim

Objective To give you practice in writing the same theme from three different viewpoints.

Your task To write a scene set in an historical period of your own choice, where a body is discovered. Using no more than five hundred words for each, write the same scene three times, but describing it through the eyes of three different characters, a bystander, a character who is going to play a part in your narrative, and lastly your crime solving hero, heroine or detective.

Model

> **1 Bystander**
>
> Tom the gardener's son, clutched the letter that he'd been asked to deliver by Reverend Huckworthy in his grubby hands. The white snowdrops in between every grave made him realise how dirty his hands were, and worse still how the grime from his hands had transferred itself to the letter he was carrying.

The school master would not be pleased. He stood at the door of the church that also acted as a school for the moorland children, and wondered if he should knock or just go in. He knew that he'd be told off for not washing his hands, and so he decided that he might as well get shouted at for not knocking as well.

The door was well oiled and didn't creak as he opened it. The brightness of the spring day vanished as soon as he went through the door. The chill damp of the unheated church and the smell of damp made him shiver. In the gloom he could just make out the shape of Mr. Martin bent over the desk. Tom's hands were trembling as he walked towards him. He was waiting for Mr. Martin to turn towards him, but he didn't. Tom kept his eyes on the granite floor, but the closer he got to Mr. Martin the more he started to shake. He'd noticed that the floor had splashes of ink all over it. Mr. Martin would be furious. Tom raised his eyes and looked towards Mr. Martin. He was black. His back was covered in black ink and so was his fair hair. Tom couldn't call out to Mr. Martin to ask him if he was all right. He'd never been able to speak, but as he moved closer still his mouth dropped open. Mr. Martin's face was stained with black ink and his distorted dead face looked just like a smoked pig's head.

2   Important character

Charlotte picked up her skirt as she walked through the pocket sized churchyard. The snowdrops surrounded the graves like garlands. The ground underfoot was moist and springy. Her heart was as light as the spring breeze that ruffled her hair. In her reticule she carried a letter from Reverend Huckworthy to Mr. Martin, the schoolmaster. Her very own dear, sweet John Martin to whom she was soon to be married, despite her uncle's refusal to give his permission.

The granite built church also acted as a school, and at the back of it were rows of desks bought by donations collected from the moorland farm owners.

The well-oiled door opened without a creak and she went it. The smell of damp and candles surrounded her. She was determined to surprise John, and so she crept on tiptoe to the corner where his desk was. He was bent over and appeared to have fallen asleep. She inched her way towards him, but then a shaft of light pierced the gloom and she noticed that she was walking on black ink. The hem of her dress was already stained.

"John, wake up. You've knocked your ink pot over. Just look at my dress." Her hand reached out to touch his shoulder, but she withdrew it quickly. His jacket was wet. She looked at her hand. The palm was stained with black ink. Her best beloved John was covered in ink. His dark hair was coated with it, and his face was as black as coal and contorted into the grimace of a mummer's mask. She turned her face away and was sick. Sick at the shock of her discovery, but also sick with relief in realising that it wasn't John, but a stranger.

3   Detective or crime solving hero or heroine

Reverend Hunter Huckworthy walked in a slow and leisurely way through the pocket sized churchyard. For once Hunter was not in a hurry, and as he infrequently had the opportunity to visit or preach in this part of his parish, he intended to enjoy himself. Being a vicar of a market town on the edge of the moor he had imagined would be a pleasant sinecure, but instead he found himself acting as an unpaid investigator for the local coroner.

Hunter's curate would ride out on Sundays to give the sermons. Perhaps, he thought, it would make a refreshing change for him to come out himself and preach to the loyal flock of moorland famers who regularly attended the services in the roughly built granite church.

The snowdrops surrounded the graves like garlands. The ground underfoot was moist and springy. Hunter's heart was as light as the spring breeze that ruffled his hair. It made him remember what it was like to be a schoolboy once again and suddenly he wanted to forget his meeting with the schoolmaster and to go hunting for birds' eggs. However, Hunter knew his duty, and he was only too aware that the conscientious itinerant school master was not a man to complain and wouldn't have written to him unless he'd seen something that had troubled him. John Martin taught at three small schools in churches, but this Hunter believed was the prettiest.

The well-oiled door opened without a creak and he went in. Coloured light streamed in through the church's one small stained glass window and made Hunter happy. The musty damp smell didn't bother him as all the churches he'd ever attended had the same scent. What wasn't so attractive were the large patches of black ink that were dotted all over the granite floor slabs. He followed the trail towards the back of the church. Sitting bent low over his desk was John Martin. Hunter was about to call out a greeting to him when he realised that it would be futile to do so. On the floor surrounding the desk was a pool of black ink; a stain that would be impossible to remove. The blood it was mixed with could be washed away, but the image of John drenched in coal-black ink and blood from his fractured skull, would Hunter knew, stay with him for the rest of his earthly life.

Write your scenes in your notebook:

1   **Bystander**

2   **Important character**

3   **Detective or crime solving hero or heroine**

Motives

What is your killer's motive for murder? What emotions will your killer feel? What actions might your killer or the person committing a crime want their victims to feel? The lists that you compile below can also be applied to crimes such as robbery, fraud and blackmail.

ACTIVITIES

18.5 Motives for murder

Objective   To enable you to build up a store of possible motives for your killer.

Your task   Make a list of all the motives for murder that you can think of and ask any friends who enjoy reading thrillers to contribute their suggestions as well. e.g. revenge, spite, greed, mental instability, because they believe that they are on mission, or that they are a professional assassin etc.

Write your list in your notebook

18.6 Emotions

What emotions will your killer feel? What actions might your killer or the person committing a crime want their victims to feel?

Objective   To enable you to add emotional depth to the characters that you create.

Your task   1   What emotions will your killer feel e.g. excitement, pleasure, power, lust, satisfaction?

                2   What actions might your killer or the person committing a crime want their victims to feel e.g. pain, fear, and shock?

Write your list in your notebook

Serial killers

The World Wide Web has various sites devoted to serial killers both individuals and gangs, including Jack the Ripper, William Burke and William Hare (19th century Edinburgh), Gilles de Rais (French 15th century Satanist and child killer), Peter Stumpp (in Germany in the 1500s proclaimed himself a werewolf and killed 15 people), Hélène Jégado (a French domestic servant who poisoned, between 1833-1851, at least 23 people), Mark Jeffries (who was a Tasmanian penal colony escapee and was executed in 1826 for murdering four people), John Ball, the Alligator Man (killed at least twenty people in Texas in the early 20th century), the Bloody Benders (a family in the USA who in the late 19th century killed guests in their inn in Labette County) and Thug Behram (who was executed in India in 1840 for allegedly having murdered 900 people) etc.

The list of gangs that have been involved in organised crime and murder are also well documented particularly for cities such as New York with gangs like the *Forty Thieves* (1820s) and *The Roach* Guards (a 19th century Irish street gang) being examples. The Sicilian mafia in Calabria and Camorra developed steadily between 1500 and 1800 providing an earlier example.

The list of individual, family and groups of serial killers is frighteningly long, but also provides a remarkable source of inspiration for the writer of historical crime fiction.

ACTIVITIES

18.7 Portrait of a killer

Objective   To provide you with practice of giving motives to murderers.

Your task   1   To research a serial killer who lived during an historical period that you are interested in and to create a plausible motive for your killer.

Model

Research Profile

Name: Nikolayevna Saltykova (1703-1801)

Nikolayevna was a Russian noble woman whom married young. She was a widow by the time she was 26 and inherited a large estate. She lived there with her two sons and a large number of serfs. She was

---

well connected with those who held power at the court of Empress Catherine the Second, as a consequence of which the rumours and complaints about the alarming number of deaths of mostly women and girls on her estate were ignored. That is until relatives of the murdered women were able to bring a petition before Empress Catherine the Second. Nikolayevna was arrested in 1762 and held until 1768. During this time the authorities carried out a thorough investigation including examining records of the Saltykova estate and interviewing witnesses. The final total was 138 suspicious deaths. Nikolayevna was found guilty of having killed 38 female serfs. She had beaten or tortured them to death.

In 1754 the death penalty had been abolished in Russia and so the Empress was in a difficult position. The solution was, that having chained Nikolayevna to a platform in Moscow for one hour with a sign around her neck that read "This woman has tortured and murdered" she was then imprisoned for the rest of her life in the basement of a convent.

Motive: Jealousy, envy and spite

Nikolayevna had married young, and had no choice in who she married. By the time she was widowed she had become jealous of anyone who appeared to be more attractive or better liked by any man than she was. However, even as a child she'd been spiteful and set out to avenge herself on anyone who she thought disliked her. She also derived pleasure from bear fights and found it amusing to watch serfs being punished for minor wrong-doings.

2 To write a description of the killer as if you were an eye-witness writing an article for a newspaper (or broadsheet). The suggested word count for this piece is c.100-500 words.

Model

"This woman has tortured and murdered"

Flocks of people made their way to see the murderess Nikolayevna Saltykova, owner of the Saltykova estates, chained on a platform today wearing a sign that read: "This woman has tortured and murdered" around her neck. She will now be imprisoned in the basement of an undisclosed convent until she dies.

It was as if all of Moscow had turned out to see this monster. The nobility dressed in their finest clothes even turned out for the event. It was almost as if they needed to convince themselves that one from within their own noble ranks could be convicted of savagely beating and torturing 38 women serfs, and worse still possibly murdering another 100 serfs who died, according to the Collegium of Justice, "in suspicious circumstances." I was amongst the crowds and could not believe, even though I saw it with my own eyes, not one single tear fell from Saltykova's eyes. She did not utter one word, but stared out at the crowd with a look of disdain, as if none of us were of any worth. For the relatives of the murdered women justice has been seen to be done, but it would have been more satisfying for them to see her executed. One can only hope for the sake of the souls of those who died, that the nuns will ensure that her every waking moment will be spent in some form of penance for her cruel, spiteful and envious acts carried out on her defenceless serfs. May each whip lash come back to haunt her.

You can write your article in your notebook

Additional activities that you might like to try

1   Write an account of the killer and his (or her) victims as if you were re-telling the story to a group of friends or relatives.

2   Write an article about an organized gang and their victims, which might have appeared in a broadsheet or newspaper at the time. Alternatively, you could write an account as if you were telling the story in a letter to friends or relatives.

3   If you are thinking about writing an American style novel, you might like to design a wanted poster, and then write a scene where one of your sub-characters sees the poster and realises that he's got some information that might help the villain or villains be brought to justice. If you are writing about an earlier period you could write a proclamation that could be read out, and which you could incorporate in a scene where a listener in a crowd discovers that they know something about the perpetrators of the crime.

18.8 Alibis

Objective   To make a list of possible alibis that a killer might use.

Your task   To compile a list of ten common alibis that your killer might use.

> **Model**
> Drunk, asleep, out of the country, kidnapped etc.

Extra follow up Activity

Using the research that you have collected about the killer of your choice, you might like to try to write a short story about them or to write a synopsis for a novel.

Historical psychological crime thrillers

This genre often focuses on the characters, rather than the plot for the story development. It involves being able to create vulnerable, and helpless characters, who may or may not be able to overcome the challenges that they are facing.

If you are considering writing a novel that falls into this category, you might benefit from reading novels such as Andrew Taylor's *Bleeding Heart Square*, and also try to watch films that have been released in this genre even if they are not historical, for example *The Machinist* with Christian Bale playing Trevor Reznik. This genre is not for the 'faint hearted'!

ACTIVITY

18.9 Create a detective

Using the character that you invented in **Activity 18.4 (C)** turn him or her into a three dimensional character that your readers might be able to identify with. However, if you prefer you can use a character that you've already created and that you are planning to use in your own work of fiction.

Objective	To create a 'detective' whose character will be memorable and immediately recognisable, if you were to write a series of stories led by this 'heroic' character.
Your task	Use the profile template in **Chapter 7**, but add in extra information about your character's habits and mannerisms. You can either do this in note form or whole sentences. Notes are sometimes more accessible if you are trying to refer back to your character sketch to find out a piece of specific information, but this is a matter of what you, as a writer, feel comfortable with.

Model (Use the profile template in **Chapter 7**)

Extra details (habits, mannerisms and specific details that you can use as a hallmark to make your character stand out):

Character name: Reverend Hunter Huckworthy

Habits: He stutters, which is a great disadvantage when giving a sermon. The stutter becomes more pronounced when he is under stress.

Mannerisms: After physical exercise drags his left leg a little. This is the result of an injury that he sustained aged 11 when his father insisted that he went fox hunting, even though he didn't want to.

Specific details (e.g. likes and dislikes): Has hated fox hunting since he was a child.

Side-kicks

Although Sherlock Holmes and Poirot are not characters from historical novels, they both had side-kicks to help them with their investigations. You will find that today several of the successful historical crime and adventure novelists also have side-kicks e.g. Até, Jack Absolute's Mohawk side-kick in the novels of C.C. Humphreys. These characters are very useful devices for rescuing your main character, discovering clues they overlook and acting as a confidant* etc.

ACTIVITIES

18.10 Side-kicks in literature

Objective To make a list of side-kicks.

Your task Search your library shelves and the internet to create a list of at least 10 side-kicks used in historical crime fiction. Make notes about the qualities that these characters have that complement or make up for the shortfalls of the main characters.

18.11 Create your own side-kick

Using one of the characters that you introduced in **Activity 18.4** turn him or her into a three dimensional 'side-kick' character that your readers might be able to identify with. However, if you prefer you are welcome to use a character that you've already created and that you are planning to use in your own work of fiction.

Objective To create a side-kick.

Your task Write a profile for a possible side-kick for the detective or lead character that you created in **Activity 18.10** (see above). Just write down notes and phrases rather than using whole sentences. Use the profile template in **Chapter 7**, but add in extra information about your characters habits and mannerisms. You can either do this in note form or whole sentences, whichever you find the most convenient. Remember this 'side-kick' does not have to be an adult and if you are writing a time-slip, or gothic thriller set in the past, it could even be an apparition or a ghost.

---

* **Confidant**: the origin of this word is French and came into use in English in the 17th century. It means a person to whom personally and private matters are confided.

> **Model**
>
> **Character name**: Tom Conebere (Gardener's son)
>
> **Habits**: He steals anything that is edible from fields and hedgerows as he is always hungry.
>
> **Mannerisms**: He keeps rubbing his eyes. He never washes his face or hands unless forced to and as a result is often prey to sore eyes and conjunctivitis.
>
> **Specific details** (e.g. likes and dislikes): He hates washing. Tom is physically very agile and loves climbing trees, riding and swimming and hates school.

Extra activities:

After you have read the tips and suggestions of the professional authors below your might like to experiment with the following:

1 Using the victim that you described in **Activity 18.4** (above) write a background profile for the person who was murdered including name, age, physical description, likes and dislikes etc. Also include the reasons why he/she was killed.

2 Following on from **Activity 18.4** create a suspicious character that might have killed the person you've described above, but in fact is innocent.

3 Using one of the scenes that you described in **Activity 18.4** as an opening scene for a short story and the characters that you have already created try to continue what you have written and transform it into a short story of about 1,000-1,500 words. For this particular activity don't plan ahead, but just see where the characters lead you.

4 Try to write an opening scene c. 300-500 words where a crime has been committed that is in a country, city or town and at a past time that you know very little about. Don't do any research before you write the scene. After you've written it carry out some research to see if your imagination and hunches have any grounding in historical fact.

5 Write an opening scene c. 300-500 words where a crime has been committed that is in a country, and at a past time that you know very little about, but which takes place in a rural area e.g. a desert, goldfield, highlands of Scotland, a jungle etc. Don't do any research before your write the scene. After you've written it carry out some research to see if your imagination and hunches have any grounding in historical fact.

6   Building up suspense can be one of the most difficult elements of crime writing for writers who are just starting to learn the craft. Try to write the opening of a chapter (c.200-300 words) where one of your characters feels threatened. Begin the chapter with a noise or sound that might create a sense of foreboding.

> **Model**
> The doleful sound of the Chapel bell echoed through the empty, dark abbey cloisters. While the rest of the monks slept Brother John waited and watched from the alcove he'd concealed himself in...

Remember

When writing crime fiction that is set in the past you need a strong lead character who is going to solve the case. The motives of your murderer have to be **plausible,** and the way in which your 'detective' discovers who is responsible for the crime or crimes has to be **credible**. The evidence that you provide your readers with, and the clues that lead to the detection of the criminal need to give the illusion of being hypothetically possible.

Your story has to, above all, create suspense, and a desire in the reader to predict what will happen next. If you are writing a psychological thriller, then your job as a writer is to catch your reader unawares, by adding unexpected, but **plausible** and **feasible** events, that make them re-check that they've locked their door before going to bed.

The adjectives **plausible**, **credible** and **feasible** have been highlighted, because you need to keep them constantly fixed in your mind when writing historical crime fiction. The motives, clues and alibis have to be valid in the eyes of your reader, as well as the historical background and setting.

American Historical Thrillers

If you would like to try your hand at writing a crime novel set in a rural and pioneering environment, below is some advice courtesy of Ann Parker who specialises in writing historical thrillers set in America.

Ann Parker

"Writing a Western Historical Mystery? Check the newspapers!

If your story is set in the "Wild and Woolly" days of the American West, you're in luck. All the big cities (and many of the smaller towns—particularly if they were "boom" towns) had newspapers. Additional bonus—these days you don't necessarily have to hunt them down on microfiche: Many historical newspapers are now on line, with more being scanned and brought into the digital realm every day. So, from the comfort of your home (or local library) computer connection, you can access sites such as Colorado Historical Newspapers:
(**www.coloradohistoricnewspapers.org**) or the Wyoming Newspaper Project (**www.wyonewspapers.org**). Not sure where to start? A list of historical newspaper and indexes for many states (including those in the West) can be found at: **www.researchguides.net/ newspapers.htm** as well as at the Library of Congress' "Chronicling America" project: (**www.chroniclingamerica.loc.gov**).

Read articles not only for a sense of the large, sweeping events, but also for those wonderful "telling details." For instance, a November 1880 article from the Leadville, Colorado, *Daily Herald* provides great details about the fashions of the day. (Examples: Mrs. W. R. Phelps in "light blue striped silk trimmed with satin of the same shade, and white lace, cardinal flowers at the throat and waist" and the rather tongue-in-cheek description of Mr. Howland in "a lovely toilet of tweed over red flannel; pants and coat were separate, but worn together.") You can also get a sense of the language and slang by a careful reading of quotes and descriptions. Telling details abound in journalistic "word pictures" of street scenes, church socials, cattle drives, and, of course, in the enthusiastic journalistic renderings of murders and misdeeds. As a mystery writer, you'll find much "fodder for fiction" in the newspaper accounts of the crimes of the day—be they banking swindles, knife fights in the alleys, stagecoach robberies, panel thieves, and so on.

Last word of advice: Be sure to read the advertisements (Tolu "Rock and Rye" tonic, anyone?). "

Ann Parker is the author of the Silver Rush historical mystery series set in 1880s Colorado. Her latest book is *Leaden Skies* (published by Poisoned Pen Press).

www.annparker.net

How do you check your historical facts?

Simon Dell

"The success and believability of an historical crime novel will depend greatly on the quality of research and the accuracy of simple facts within the narrative. Once a period of time in history has been identified then many simple errors can totally destroy an otherwise good plot. To avoid such errors slipping into your story simply 'ask' is the key and don't be afraid to ask. Having a simple enquiry at the local police station from an author is not as rare a visit as you might imagine! You might not get the immediate answer from the enquiry officer behind the desk but if the question is asked in the right way then most officers know who, in the force, is likely to be able to answer the question. Most police forces have a museum or archive or even just simply someone interested in its history and it isn't too difficult to identify that person. If a museum doesn't exist then all forces have press and media departments who will probably know who will be able to answer a question of historical curiosity.

Once you find the contact, he or she will probably be able to direct you through the many shortcuts. A good first point of contact is the 'Police History Society' (PHS) who have members all over the country and indeed internationally. The PHS acts as a focal point to direct enquiries to the various archives and museums and experts in your subject material. They can be located at **www.policehistorysociety.co.uk/phsframe.htm** and there are a number of useful links from that site. Another good national resource is at: **www.open.ac.uk/Arts/history-from-police-archives/welcome.html** where Professor Clive Emsley (a member of the PHS) has detailed much information about force histories and archival researches on the Open University site.

If your story concerns procedures of a historical nature within living memory of retired police officers, many former officers delight in being asked such things. The National Association of Retired Police Officers (NARPO) has branches all over the country and often get such requests for historical information of the not-too-distant past. NARPO can be contacted through their website at **www.narpo.org.uk/** and your enquiry can be directed to the appropriate area. The Police Memorabilia Collectors Club (PMCC) at **www.pmcc-club.co.uk** is also a useful contact as is the London **www.met.police.uk/history/site**.

The **www.constabulary.com/history.htm** site is also a good source of links to various aspects of policing.

Many ledgers, beat books and other archival material concerning types of crime, methods of murder, styles of policing etc are held in police museums and collections. Some forces may possess little and many forces have donated their collections to the county record offices so don't discount the local record offices as being repositories of crime files.

Writing up force histories has become a common feature of policing and most police forces have been involved in publications following the numerous 150th anniversary celebrations that have taken place at the turn of this century following the introduction of county constabularies in the 1850s. Whilst on that subject, police force names of the 21st Century bear no resemblance to the original titles of the police force of yesteryear. For example, the Devon & Cornwall Constabulary is a force which covers an area which once had over twenty smaller borough, city and parish constabularies such as the Tiverton Borough which was subsumed into the Devon County Constabulary in 1943, which in turn was taken over by the Devon & Cornwall Constabulary in 1967. Make sure you get the correct name for the police force for the right historical time of your novel. Uniforms also differed tremendously, and the local museums and history societies will be able to put you on the right accurate track in that respect. Little idiosyncrasies crept in over such things as trivial as which breast pocket a whistle chain would lead to, and whether chin straps would be worn down or up in summer months. It's easy to get it wrong but not too difficult to get it right.

If asking about specific officers or incidents, don't be surprised if you get some reluctance because of general and understandable confusion over the more complicated aspects of the Data Protection Act, and an unwillingness to make an unwitting error. However, if you keep your enquiry more general you should meet with success.

Receiving an enquiry from a researcher is a real diversion from perhaps the more regular aspects of policing; so don't be put off asking for fear of rejection. You might be somewhat surprised by the reaction you get when you are enquiring about something a bit out of the ordinary!"

Simon Dell, MBE, Devon & Cornwall Constabulary, may be contacted through **www.myfanwycook.com**

A tip from a contemporary crime fiction writer

Simon Hall

"Crime scenes are usually one of the most important parts of a book in the detective / thriller genre, and commonly a foundation of the novel.

They're also some of my favourite passages to write, as there's scope for good description, creativity and interlacing of clues, but they're equally easy to get wrong.

Firstly, it may sound obvious, but it's vital to have a completely clear idea of your scene and what you want to convey. Plan it carefully, both with a physical drawing and an outline of its intended resonance in the book.

Was this a subtle crime, where the room, for example, shows nothing strange apart from the obvious issue of a dead body? There's no evidence of a break in, the only oddity is a still warm teapot or cup, and the knife protruding from the corpse's neck. So, perhaps the victim knew the attacker, let them in and liked and trusted them enough to turn their back and start making some tea...

Or, to the other extreme, where the door's been kicked in and all is an utter mess, with broken ornaments and furniture strewn around. Clearly the mother of all fights took place here.

Or perhaps it was staged in an attempt to make it look like that...

Reading the scene is what investigators instinctively do, be they historical or contemporary. And from the rocks of the observable facts, they can move on to the fun part of speculating on the possibilities or even likelihood of what happened. From there, the momentum of your book grows, as you test your hypotheses and draw the reader in to who may have committed the crime and why.

I'd strongly advise getting yourself a medical adviser. You've already got one of a sort - your GP – so that's a good place to start. It's perfectly possible to kill and leave only minimal blood, if indeed any. Some crime scenes are covered in so much gore it feels like an attempt to redecorate. Introducing a medical character who can comment on the anatomical quirks of a killing adds authenticity. But don't make the common error of overdoing it – this is mass entertainment you're writing, not a medical textbook.

To keep your GP onside, always acknowledge them in whatever it is you're writing, and send them a copy. Mine used her acknowledgement to break the ice in a job interview – "I don't just save lives, I advise on how to take them, only fictitiously, of course" - and got the position!

One more thought - in my view, many descriptions of crime scenes concentrate too heavily on what you can see. Hit the other senses too. Smell is evocative, and according to scientists, the sense most strongly linked to memories. And scenes smell. Blood does, corpses do, particularly after time, and even the sweat of a struggle lingers if you get there soon enough. Most detectives will tell you death has a distinctive scent as well.

Sound also helps. The ticking of a clock, the dripping of a tap, even the breeze through the trees if you're outdoors, all this crowds the scene in and makes it claustrophobic and tense. And touch too – the cold dampness of the wall, the bark of a tree, the sharpness of a knife, or the thickness of the carpet or bogginess of the ground. Details are an author's precious and powerful allies in helping to make a scene real."

Simon Hall is a BBC Crime Correspondent and contemporary crime fiction writer

www.thetvdetective.com

Writing historical crime fiction by Bernard Knight

Any historical period can provide the background for a story, though some are more turbulent than others. Once you have decided on an era, then you need to learn everything you can about it, well before starting to hammer the word-processor. Your reading should extend well beyond the immediate time and place of your story-setting, to get the feel of the period and to know as much as possible about matters not necessarily directly relevant to your plot.

The actual year of the story must be determined and the season or even the month established for the start. Unless it is to be a saga across generations, unlikely in a crime novel, then the time-span of the action should be as tight as possible, given the limitations of travel and communication, and the danger of real historical events overtaking your story.

Sources

Read everything you can about the century you are going to use, bracketing both sides of the time of your action, so that you can set the story within a longer-term context. Standard history books, monographs and biographies of major figures of the period are obvious sources - and of course the Internet. There is a tendency to scoff at learning from websites, which can be inaccurate. How are you to know that some description of 15th century York was not cobbled together by a spotty youth in Idaho, rather than a genuine historian? However, I have found that most of the stuff on Wikipedia and in the thousands of other sites delivered by a web-search, are very useful, as long as you cross-check the facts with other accounts.

Story format

You need a general theme for the story – is it to be about palaces, lords and ladies, an abbey full of monks or a feud between master-craftsmen? Many historical mysteries are grafted on to real historical events and personalities, using an actual political or martial drama as a background.

Decide whether you are going to write in the first person or the third. Though the first has more immediacy, it is more difficult, as you cannot legitimately describe anything happening outside the knowledge of your narrator. Try to avoid flash-backs, other than a Prologue – and do not succumb to this daft modern gimmick of writing in the present tense!

You need a leading character, with whom the reader can identify, the person who is going to sort out the problem, whatever it is and the one through whose eyes the readers is going to follow the action.

It is always more convincing if he/she has a legitimate reason for investigating crime – if the story antedates the founding of the police or their equivalent, then a magistrate, Keeper of the Peace, sheriff, coroner or someone with authority to see justice done, is preferable to yet another addition to the hordes of unlikely amateur detectives like Miss Marples or gardeners Rosemary and Thyme!

Your lead character must have someone to talk to, as a means of getting across facts and ideas to the reader. Holmes had his Watson and Morse had his Lewis, so one or two side-kicks are almost indispensable.

Make them as different in physical appearance and attitude as possible, both from the leader and each other. My dour Crowner John had a large, insensitive and cheerful Gwyn as his officer and a weedy, intellectual priest as his clerk, which seemed to work well enough through fourteen books.

Storyline – the plot

This is where you are on your own, as it's your yarn! If you have nothing in your mind at the start, only a desire to write a mystery, then you have to synthesise a plot. If you already have a strong lead character visualised, then you need to write a story relevant to his profession, whether he or she is a soldier, abbess, magistrate or whatever.

Some writers just sit down and start at Page One with 'It was a dark and stormy night...etc' and take it from there, making up the story a paragraph at a time, but personally I find this a disaster unless I can see quite a way ahead before I begin.

I advise devising some kind of framework or skeleton on which to hang the flesh of words, even if it is only a single page 'flow-diagram', even before you have decided on your characters and their names.

Virtually all mystery novels revolve around a murder, so call the victim 'X' and then assume that he/she is killed by 'Y'. The diagram then needs an arrow which denotes the motive – a limited range, usually lust, money, hatred, jealousy or revenge. Then you need other characters 'A, B & C', loosely called 'red herrings', who could have been the killer and whose arrows towards 'X' suggest potential reasons for becoming suspects.

Even at this early stage, it is useful to look ahead towards the ending, as many good stories fail at the last fence from a weak or unsatisfactory conclusion. The types of possible 'outcome' will be discussed later.

Once enough of a synopsis has been summoned up, then add your character names to 'X' and the others. If possible, pad out this brief summary with as much additional action as possible, even if when it comes to the writing itself, you deviate markedly from the plan. I always had to submit an outline to my publisher for approval by the commissioning committee, but usually, the finished book bore scant resemblance to what I had originally proposed.

Avoid coincidences as they feature all too often in some books and make the story less credible – and never use the corny old ploy of identical twins!

Characterisation

You need to work up considerable detail about all the characters you are going to use, especially the major ones. Start an alphabetical file with a page for each one, for this saves time when you have to refer back halfway through your script, needing to know if Billy Blogg's father had a moustache or was married twice. This is especially so if you are lucky enough to get a series out of your efforts, for nothing is more exasperating than having to search hundreds of pages to recover some detail of a character used in a previous book.

The fictional biography of each character needs to be expansive, especially of the main people, even if you do not use half of it. Just as spy-masters used to devise a 'legend' for their agents, so you need a full 'back-story' to flesh out your actors. Describe every detail of their physical characteristics, their mode of dress, their habits, their dislikes, their prejudices, until you know them as well as your own family- or better! Invent their own antecedents, the date of birth of their relatives and a potted history of their family background. Even if very little of this gets used, it helps you get to know them intimately. Of course, you needn't do this for every 'bit-player', but anyone who makes a significant contribution to the story needs to be written 'in the round', to avoid having characters like cardboard cut-outs.

Their behaviour needs to be constant throughout the book, unless some reason is apparent for a departure from the mould. A chap who is sullen and violent at the start cannot be portrayed later on as being filled with sweetness and light, unless the change is relevant to the plot.

Character names

Names are important in two senses. Firstly, the names must sound right for each individual character, as in any form of fiction. A dark, brooding villain is hardly likely to sound convincing with a name like 'Percy Philpot'. Thankfully, with word-processors, one can ring the changes right throughout the book, even at the last minute, if you think another name would be more suitable.

The other aspect is the historical authenticity, as names have temporal associations. There was an abrupt and radical change after the Conquest, when Norman names replaced Saxon, certainly in the upper echelons of society. There are plenty of sources for names in every era, both in the standard histories and in more specialised documents, such as the court records, which will also give you names for the peasants and traders, rather than the aristocracy that tend to fill the textbooks.

Try to make the names, especially of the leading characters, as varied as possible, to allow the reader to identify them more easily. Unfortunately, the post-Norman names were rather limited in range – Henry, William, Robert, John, Richard, but there are enough of the less common ones to be able to avoid confusing Hubert, Herbert and Henry.

The number of characters should not be overwhelming. It is a convention in crime writing that the suspects should not exceed about half-a-dozen, and the whole range of names should be kept manageable. I have reviewed a number of books where the author dumps a dozen or even a score of names upon the reader in the first chapter, sometimes in solid pages of text at the expense of dialogue. Feed the names in bit by bit, to give the reader a chance to assimilate and identify them, without having to scroll back through the pages to recall who Joe Soap was.

Authenticity

In my opinion, historical accuracy is vital, though some writers feel that being entertainment rather than education, a good measure of 'literary licence' may be applied. I have had many letters and emails pointing out errors and anachronisms – even one complaining that I had used wood-screws in the 12th century, though they were not invented until the 14th!

Certainly all political events should be verified and efforts made to get the geography, distances and timings of your action correct. Much of the pleasure of historical writing is in the research, and details such as costume, living conditions, weapons, and food all add that air of realism to the writing. There is plenty of source material out there, in books and on the Internet – I came across a typical example in a handbook of household management from the Paris of 1390, full of menus and kitchen advice!

Be careful, however, of using too much of your accumulated research to the point where you may bore your readers. Having done all this work, there is a temptation for the author to stuff it down the reader's throat, perhaps thinking that it was too good to waste and that it confirms you as such a learned person. One ploy is to have a 'Historical Postscript' or 'Notes' at the end, where you can enlarge upon the history, without obliging the readers to wade through it all. Better still, put some of the more relevant matters into the mouths of your characters, who tell others about these issues – I used to get my 'nerdy' clerk Thomas, to lecture the coroner and his officer, if I needed to get across some particular facts.

Wherever possible, the writer should 'walk the territory' so that he or she has actual experience of the places where the story action is taking place – again, this adds reality to the text.

The writing

As with the plot, this is where you are on your own. When you've got the general thrust of the plot in your head – or even the first part – you sit down and write. Don't strive for any particular 'style', a much over-rated concept. Never try to ape someone else, the artificiality of that will soon become apparent. We can't all be Somerset Maugham or Graham Greene, but we don't need to be, we need to be ourselves. Write what naturally comes into your mind, though of course there are general rules, grammatical and others, that you need to observe.

There are as many different ways of writing as there are writers. Personally, I sit at the keyboard and write a description of a video (DVD) that is playing in my brain. It is said that there are two kinds of writer, those whose imagination is mainly visual and those who have auditory input. I think I am the first, as I tend to see a silent film in my mind and then have to synthesise a sound-track over it. Others say that they primarily hear the dialogue and add the visual effects, rather like the difference between writing scripts for radio as opposed to television.

It is best to write down what you see fairly quickly and then edit it into shape afterwards. If the story is flowing, it is a pity to interrupt it just to correct spelling mistakes. Keep the sentences short, though not so extreme as be staccato. Ration your sub-clauses and every time you use the word 'and' decide if it would be better to use a new sentence. Try to avoid colons, semi-colons and phrases in brackets, as usually a new sentence is preferable.

Avoid endless repetitions of 'he said, she said'. I made up a list of alternatives to 'said' and have it stuck on the wall above my computer - about fifty variations from 'admitted' to 'yelped'. These structural nuances can be added on the first editing – my practice, common to many other writers, is to begin a day's work by reading what I wrote the previous day and then carefully revise it. Sometimes, it may all be rubbish and needs to be scrapped, but usually sensible editing will knock it into shape. This process also gets you in the mood to carry on with the next section, as starting 'cold' can sometimes be difficult and liable to be postponed by 'displacement activities' like a cup of coffee, to put off the evil moment when you actually have to start writing. A spell of editing is rather like an aircraft that has to taxi down the runway before it can take off.

Some writers try to end a day's work at a 'natural break' like the end of a chapter or a section – others say it is better to stop when you are in the middle of a sequence, so that you have something to pick up on recommencing.

Dividing the work into paragraphs, sections and chapters is rather arbitrary, but should be done when the sense of what you are writing comes to a conclusion. Chapters are more drastic, in that it is best to end when there is some radical change in the action or a point of suspense or a marked shift in the venue of the action.

The editing that goes on in small bursts on a daily basis is of course far from final and one or more complete read-throughs will throw up many more places where improvements can be made and errors spotted.

If you are fortunate enough to get your story accepted for publication, then probably an editor and a copy-editor will have further goes at it, sometimes through draconian eyes!

Writing aids

We have mentioned a directory of characters, to store all the details of each of the actors, but some other lists are helpful.

A chronology record helps, where you note the date or day of the week when each major event occurs, especially the start of each new chapter. This is to keep the time-scale correct, for one sometimes reads a book where if you tot up the alleged time or date of various happenings, the story gets well out of synchronisation by the end. I reviewed a book recently that was two weeks adrift by the finish.

Also, unless one keeps an eye on the calendar, you can find yourself holding a court on a Sunday or Saint's day, or having roast pork on a Friday.

Maybe this is carrying authenticity a bit far, but is surprising what your readers will spot, as I know from their feedback.

A list of chapters with their page numbers is also useful, as I often get the chapter number wrong without a memoir. Putting the page number helps to get back to it quickly when needed, without endless scrolling through four hundred pages. If you feel really keen, use this list to note important events, like a murder etc, so that you can get back to them easily. It is surprising how often you need to go back to check something and it's frustrating to have to waste time wading through half the book to find it.

The ending

This is often the hardest part of any crime novel, as there are only a limited number of 'outcomes'. Assuming that it is a murder story, then it is conventional, though not legally binding, that the culprit is identified.

The Hercule Poirot style of denouement, where everyone is assembled in the drawing-room for the great man to disclose the answer, is both outdated and highly unrealistic, but unmasking has to be done, unless the story is not a 'who-dunnit', but a 'how-it-was done'.

The killer can be arrested, killed, commit suicide, suffer a fortuitously fatal accident or escape. You need to anticipate one of these well before the end, as you may need to seed the story with situations that will allow this to happen. Many a good book has proved a disappointment due to a weak finale.

Conclusion

Writing is a very personal, individual process and any rules or advice are quite arbitrary. The only way to write a novel is to buckle down and do it, though maybe the few pointers above may help to avoid some of the pitfalls.

The book has to be interesting to the author, for if it begins to pall, then it will be equally dull for the reader. You need to grab their attention on the first page, which is why a Prologue can be useful, as you can immediately have a dramatic or blood-thirsty scene as a 'teaser', without having to compromise your slower build-up process in Chapter One, where you introduce your location and main characters.

Devise a strong plot, robust characters and know your period inside-out, then just grab you pen or your keyboard and go for it!

Tip

Ariana Franklin
"In the case of building up tension whether in a thriller or anything else, the 'pathetic fallacy' is a good rule. As most of you will know, this is giving inanimate objects or weather an atmosphere that fits the circumstances. If it's good enough for Shakespeare (Macbeth's witches on their blasted heath; Hamlet's father stalking the rampart; or Dickens with his use of fog) it's good enough for us.

And, certainly in the case of a thriller, indicate very early that it IS a thriller. Too many writers start by scene-setting and character-describing in the first chapters instead of building them as they go along, and don't get on with the plot. All right, I know Tolstoy didn't do that in 'War and Peace", but (a) he was a genius and (b) we're aware that Napoleon's on his way to ruin the lives of his characters. Grab your reader by the whatsits from the very beginning." |
| Ariana Franklin is the author of the *Mistress of the Art of Death* series
www.arianafranklin.com |

Useful sources for background information:

Web sites:

www.crimezzz.net

www.thrillingdetective.com

www.hmns.org
> This site provides a simplified chronological history of Crime Scene investigation.

www.csitheexperience.org
> This site is simply for fun!

www.wikipedia.org
> Wikipedia is a good starting point for you investigations into crimes committed in the past.

www.britannica.com

www.sciencemag.org

www.aafs.org
> American Academy of Forensic Sciences

www.santoshraut.com
> History of Forensic Sciences

Articles

- Knight, Bernard. *Forensic Practice in Ancient and Medieval Times*, Historical Novels Review. Issue 43, February 2008, p.3-4
- Latham, Bethany. *Strange Bedfellows, Historical Fiction and Forensic Medicine*, Historical Novels Review. Issue 43, February 2008, p.4-7

Books

- Lyle, D.P., M.D., *Murder and Mayhem, USA*: Thomas Dunne books, (2003)
- Mariani, S., *How to Write a Thriller*, How to Books, (2007) (see www.scottmariani.com)
- Turner, B., *The Writer's Handbook- Guide to Crime Writing*, Macmillan (2003)
- Wynn, Douglas, *The Crime Writers' Handbook, Great Britain*: Allison & Busby, (1997)

SECTION 5

Before you start writing

Tips from top professional historical novelists on writing short stories, novels, sagas and series

Chapter 19 – Tips from Top Historical Novelists

Please note that the copyright for all the tips from novelists and other professionals in this chapter and throughout this book belong to the authors who have written them.

Introduction:

These tips are arranged by author name and in alphabetical order. You will have already read extracts from these tips in previous chapters, as they have been used to complement the descriptions of the tools you need to tackle different elements of historical fiction writing. Some authors do not feature in this chapter: Bernard Knight and Andrew Thompson, whose tips have been used to illustrate key skills in other chapters, and Frank Tallis whose tip forms the postscript to this handbook. Chapters 1-4, 8, 17, 18 and 21 feature contributions from other authors not featured in this chapter: Margaret Donsbach, Andrew F.Gulli, Sarah L. Johnson, Bethany Latham (Chapters 1-4), Elizabeth Maslen (Chapter 8), Darryl Harrison (Chapter 17), Simon Dell MBE, and Simon Hall (Chapter 18), and Dr. Ann Pulsford (Chapter 21).

   All the tips have been generously contributed by the authors to help you to write historical fiction that you will be satisfied with, and that will also satisfy your readers. The contributors come from the UK, USA, Australia, Canada and New Zealand and for that reason you will notice a difference in the spelling of certain words, as we have retained both the English and American spellings that were used, and also the layout provided. They are sharing their experience and knowledge with you. They are the experts and each has a different approach to the tools and skills you need when writing. What should stand out for any aspiring writer is that many of these tips overlap. They revisit the same problems that you may encounter or challenges you may face in writing stylish and interesting historical fiction in different sub-genres. Tips kindly provided by professionals associated with writing historical fiction Bethany Latham, Sarah Johnson, and Richard Lee are dotted throughout the book as appropriate.

ACTIVITY

19.1 What makes an interesting and effective story?

Objective   To help you as a novice writer to pinpoint the key skills, pitfalls and ingredients that professional writers from the widely experienced to the debut novelist have identified through experience as being essential to their craft and success as writers.

Your task

1   Read all the tips through once.

2   Read them through a second time and first of all highlight or underline in pencil the tips that these professional authors shared with you that you think apply to historical fiction in general. Then use a different colour to highlight the tips that are relevant to the subgenre of historical fiction you are interested in writing.

3   Did you notice if any of the tips the authors suggested were similar? For example the fact that several authors went out of their way to draw your attention to these points means that they are 'essential' ingredients to include, or pitfalls to avoid when writing historical novels. Summarize on a piece of card the tips that more than one author has mentioned and keep it somewhere you can refer to when you are writing.

Tip
Experiment with the tips that you have been given and see which work for you and which don't.

Tips from historical novelists in alphabetical order

Malcolm Archibald

Historical Fiction and settings – SCOTLAND: Observation and atmosphere

Watch for the differences in light: Edinburgh's light is vastly different from Glasgow's and the East Coast has dawns that rise silver from the sea, while the west coast has spectacular sunsets. This has probably not altered through time

If writing about any historical area, visit it at different times of the day to capture its 'living' atmosphere. Town centres are usually bustling, busy places, so visit them on a Saturday afternoon to catch the lively atmosphere, but on a Sunday morning to see the historic buildings at their best. Edinburgh's High Street (Royal Mile) is incredibly atmospheric in the early morning, but a vibrant, living boisterous place on any weekend evening.

Don't ever forget the weather: a place that looks dismal in rain can be glorious in sunshine, and most towns look their best in a period of sunshine after rain. Rain would also carry soot from factory and house chimneys.

Likewise, the sense of smell is important. Until recently, most homes were heated with coal fires, so every street would have smelled of smoky fires, particularly if the wind drove the smoke downward. Market towns would smell of animals, people did not wash so often, food was probably stronger smelling.

If you are writing about the Victorian or later period, find a photograph of the place where your book is set. Look at the people: choose one and see the scene through his or her eyes. Walk into the photograph, listen to the carriage wheels and the voices, smell the horses, feel the paving stones and the texture of your clothing. Is that boy going to pick your pocket? Is that man with his thumbs in his waistcoat your husband, or a man to whom you owe money? Is that young woman across the road your sweetheart? These are real people, with the same feelings as you and similar worries and dreams; treat them with respect.

Archives and libraries will hold a stock of newspapers from the 19th and sometimes 18th centuries. Use them to see what the contemporary topics of conversation would be. We read history as politics, art and wars. People do not live in historical times; they live in their present so paying the bills and jogging along with the wife/husband is more important than Bonaparte's invasion of Prussia or the invention of some new fangled motor car. The newspapers will tell you what shop sold what, what scandal women would discuss, how much a house would cost to rent, and it can be used as a bridge between the reader's current world and the one into which you will take them:

'According to the newspaper, Lady MacSnuffin visited Queen Victoria.'

'That's fascinating dear; last time I spoke to her, she wore the most beautiful crinoline; I do wish you would buy me one.'

That short conversation introduces the reader to:

1 The period (Victorian)
2 The class – upper middle, to have a personal conversation with a titled lady
3 The status – probably married
4 Taste – fashion and crinoline
5 Household – husband has leisure to read the newspaper and interest enough in his wife to relate snippets that may interest her

And if the snippet is taken from a genuine newspaper, the writer has the touch of authenticity that all good historical authors seek.

www.malcolmarchibald.com

Carole Baldock

Why bother entering writing contests – isn't submitting work to magazines enough of a competition as it is? But just imagine: that amazing moment when you win a prize, and how many doors could open when it's a prestigious award.

And no entrant loses out because that alone encourages motivation, organisation and inspiration. There again, as editor of *Kudos* (formerly *Competitions Bulletin*), I would say that...

www.kudoswritingcompetitions.com

Edmund Bohan

A few words from New Zealand

The New Zealand historical novel is in a generally healthy state at present, but for too long languished because of academic disdain and intellectual snobbery. Mercifully, common sense, a more mature sense of national identity and enhanced literary sophistication, have all resulted in New Zealand writers taking new inspiration from our history. Such themes as Maori and European contact and conflict since the 1760s; the Land Wars of the 1860s; the nineteenth century gold rushes; the rigours of colonial life - for women especially; and the social upheavals of the early twentieth century and the depression of the 1930s have dominated. But increasingly our novelists are reaching out into the wider world for themes and settings and no longer feel bound by the constraints of place formerly imposed by inward looking and narrowly nationalistic local publishers.

Strangely, and in contrast to our Australian neighbours, the Boer War and the two World Wars that have crucially shaped our ideas of nationhood, have received comparatively little attention.

My own first two novels were written while I was based in Britain as a professional concert and operatic tenor: *The Writ of Green Wax* (1970), was set during Jack Cade's rebellion of 1450, and *The Buckler* (1972), in the Borders after the Battle of Flodden in 1513. So the first question my publishers at Hutchinson asked was whether I could guarantee the accuracy of the historical backgrounds. All they knew about me then was that I was a tenor - and hadn't a famous Italian diva declared tenors generically stupid because the ringing of their top notes in their heads damaged their brains? Their relief when they found I had an honours degree in History, had been a research assistant for New Zealand's Parliamentary Historian and had already published academic papers and articles on nineteenth century political and social history, was palpable.

Their concern was reasonable enough. The aspiring historical novelist must get the historical background right, and for that research is essential. The other requirement, of course, is a feeling for the period and the places in which one sets one's stories.

Since my return to New Zealand, my series of O'Rorke novels - *The Opawa Affair* (1996), *The Dancing Man* (1997), *The Matter of Parihaka* (2000), *The Irish Yankee* (2002), and *A Present for the Czar* (2003) - have emerged from my resumed work and extensive non-fiction writings on nineteenth century New Zealand politics, and my interests in Irish, Scottish and military history. O'Rorke's fictional career is framed by the religious, political and racial tensions inside New Zealand's Anglo-Irish settler communities of the 1880s, but the interwoven plots are driven by his previous experiences as soldier, spy and rebel in the Crimean War, American Civil War and the Irish Fenian rebellion of 1867. And for *The Opawa Affair,* in which a touring opera company becomes enmeshed in a murder mystery, I also made use of my 'other' professional experience.

Using one's entire life experience is as important as reading widely as possible, and the labour of research itself, believe it or not, can be almost as satisfying as writing.

www.bookcouncil.org.nz

Jane Borodale

Though there are no hard and fast rules, I'm sure that thorough research is the bedrock of good historical fiction. How to embark on that though would be up to you. I find it helpful to prepare the ground with a broad overview of the area of interest – in the library, on the internet, at a museum – and then my queries become more specific as momentum gains. There is always a lovely point during research for a subject when the fog clears and I start to understand where the gaps lie. Trust your own progress – it sounds obvious but one fact will lead to another, and those very delicious tangents often yield the richest fodder. Be free-wheeling in your research, let it take you to fresh and unexpected places. Not being a historian I love the way I don't have to be logical in my approach – which can be instinctive and leave questions shamelessly unanswered; I can cook 17th century flummery and call it work if I like, or spend a rigorous day in a records office with a supply of sharp pencils, or catch a train to a relevant place to breathe in its particular atmosphere. I try to keep up a system of proper storage as the picture builds, and I know it sounds boring but I've found that it's vital to note down where the precious information has come from, even (or especially) from the net. Ultimately I probably only use a tiny portion of the research I've absorbed, in fact I almost try to forget all about it – but before starting to write, it all needs to be there in the bloodstream.

Jane Borodale is the author of *The Book of Fires*, HarperPress, UK, and Pamela Dorman Books/ Viking US.

www.janeborodale.com

Edwin Buckhalter

1 Dates and facts need to be right, obviously, and historical accuracy is paramount. That said, a little licence can be taken for the sake of the story - but should be explained in a preface or epilogue explaining what is true and what is invention for the sake of the storyline.

2 Make the reader have a feel for the period and characters early on, but don't try to emulate the speech of the century in question. Our speech today would sound strange to their ears, and (by way of exaggeration to make the point) too many pseudo "forsooths" and "gadzooks" or longer anachronisms and styles really don't sit well for today's reader - and impede the flow and enjoyment of the story line...

3 Read the novels of Ronald Welch if you want to see how it is done properly, albeit written for a younger audience. I learned more history from those books, and a greater understanding of people, customs and lifestyles, than in years as a history undergraduate and postgraduate. (And I am sure other readers would add further distinguished writers such as Rosemary Sutcliffe).

Edwin Buckhalter is Chairman and founder of Severn House Publishers Ltd.

www.severnhouse.com

Mary Andrea Clarke

- Historical writing offers an opportunity to become immersed in a period one loves. This will come through in the writing and research will be a fascinating occupation. Information can come from anywhere. For example, a tour of Winchester, which included Jane Austen's grave, provided the fact that women did not attend funerals in this period. This aspect makes the research process fun as well as useful.

- Historical writing is an adventure, an education and an escape to another world. While essentially, human nature does not change, a different culture can offer a strong challenge. The perspective of the modern writer will enrich the story but the opportunity to tell it will also enrich the writer.

The origin and development of a novel:

The Crimson Cavalier was born as an experiment. Set in the eighteenth century, when the lives of women were conducted under strict social conventions, the concept of a single woman investigating a crime offered an interesting challenge. Originally intended as a standalone novel, the writing process generated further ideas which have now reached the third of the series, *Debt of Dishonour*.

Georgiana Grey is an unusual lady for her time. A member of the upper echelons of Society, she is unmarried, with her own establishment and a career, as a highway robber. Having taken to the road in response to a miscarriage of justice, Georgiana discovered a talent for it and a thrill for the excitement it offered.

The logistics of Georgiana's situation offered a lot to consider. Despite being a lawbreaker, she had to remain likeable in order to capture the interest of the reader. By using the proceeds of her robberies to help those in need, she demonstrates concern for the less fortunate while her investigation of crime shows a determination that the law does not have its way at the expense of justice.

In order to be credible, not only did Georgiana's motivation to continue with highway robbery need to be justified, her living circumstances had to be explained. Most ladies of her class had to marry in order to keep a roof over their head. Those who remained single generally became objects of pity, probably facing a future of charitable works or helping with someone else's children. Georgiana's unusual independence is explained through an eccentric uncle leaving her a house and fortune. However, Society would not allow her to live completely alone, necessitating a chaperone, in the form of an impoverished cousin, Miss Selina Knatchbull.

It takes considerable guile, as well as the aid of her maid and confidante, Emily, to keep the secret. Georgiana juggles her adventures with the appearance of social convention, sneaking out after her household has gone to bed, while keeping masked and well cloaked when among the highwaymen. As she continues in the role, she must remember what information she has gathered as Georgiana Grey and distinguish it from what the Crimson Cavalier has been told. Confusing the two could create some awkward situations to explain.

Mary Andrea Clarke is the author of *The Crimson Cavalier, Love not Poison,* and *Debt of Dishonour*

www.maryandreaclarke.com

Barbara Cleverly

Historical Crime Writing

Research your period and place until you think you really know it. Research it again. Ask yourself if you are ready to spend the next year of your life with this age, these people, this place.

If the answer's 'yes' - pack your bag, ring up BA and go to the place you're involved with. It's a history you're writing and the characters are long gone, events may have swept by leaving little trace but, surprisingly often, the bones are still there. The land has the shape it ever had, the winds blow from the same direction, the same plants grow. The people who have always lived there may have the same features as their ancestors. Study the local people. (When the face of a skeleton from the Stone Age unearthed in a cave in Somerset was reconstructed and shown to the local village audience in the church hall, the spitting image of the man was there, sitting on the back row – the local schoolmaster whose DNA proved to be a close match with Stone Age Cheddar Man!) That sends a chill down the spine of a historical novelist.

You may find that the place itself inspires you. I went to Crete not long ago with an idea sketched out. Before I'd unpacked, my Cretan hostess handed me a local guidebook. In one of the chapters I discovered that on the mountainside behind my house were to be found the disputed remains of the tomb of Zeus. 'But the gods are immortal!' I remember objecting. 'How can Zeus possibly need a tomb?' Enchanted by this four word phrase (which I used as a title), I discarded all the research I'd already done and started again.

Never make the mistake of foreseeing. You know what will happen in future years but don't let your characters have any inkling – it destroys the 'reality' of your story! Of course, history will keep on repeating itself. Nine years ago I wrote a book set on the borders of Afghanistan and the North West Frontier Province in 1926 when British troops were fighting native Pashtun tribesmen, in the end paying them off and deciding to get out of the terrible place. I wondered out loud 'Have I wasted my time? Who'd be able to point to Afghanistan on a map these days?' And, sadly, every day since I've seen the awful scenes I imagined on the television news.

Your research must appear like the tip of an iceberg: only a fraction of it should be used on the page. You need the rest to support the visible bit but keep it below the surface. Don't swank! You know a lot, you have an armoury of facts, figures and snippets of information but you're not leading a tour through a museum, directing the gaze to left and right, you're telling a story. Don't slow it down. The bulk of your knowledge will stop you from making mistakes. Take reassurance from it but don't flaunt it all. [In a trial sketch of a Victorian novel I was handed recently, a sweet shop was described. Good subject! But the writer had paraded thirteen different types of sweets. The lasting effect is – overkill. The illusion of the past is not reinforced but destroyed in a moment as the reader becomes aware that knowledge is being displayed. 'Gobstoppers or aniseed balls? No, she decided on a quarter of satin cushions.' Quite enough, thanks!]

Conversation can be tricky. How did they speak in the past? You'll know because you'll have immersed yourself in contemporary texts. The trouble is – you risk losing your readers if you stick faithfully to the phrases you've collected. Avoid jarring neologisms and keep it simple. Good, straightforward English will always be pleasing and convincing. Use a few historically appropriate phrases for impact but be sparing. Ellis Peters always judges it perfectly as does Mary Renault. Read other good historical writers and deconstruct their sentences. How do they achieve their effect?

Practical advice: I couldn't manage without a year's on-line subscription to the *Times Archive*. Worth every penny!

Barbara Cleverly's new titles March 2010: *A Darker God,* Bantam (Random House), *Strange Images of Death*, Constable & Robinson — the latest in the Joe Sandilands series.

www.barbaracleverly.com

Bernard Cornwell

The first hurdle of any new writer (other than writing the book, of course) is getting a manuscript onto a real person's desk instead of onto the slush pile (the slush pile is the vast heap of unsolicited manuscripts which turn up at all publishers' offices and which rarely get read), and my advice has always been to find an agent - how do you find an agent? Go to your local library and consult *The Writers' and Artist' Yearbook* (or its equivalent in the US). Or subscribe to *Publisher's Weekly* or *The Bookseller* and read the trade columns - or write to an author you like and ask for a recommendation. But do make sure you pick the right agent. There's no point in sending fiction to an agent who only deals in non-fiction. I also object to agents who charge a reading fee. I know that many agents hate reading the vast number of manuscripts that come their way, but it's their job, damn it, and making the writer pay them to do it is cheap.

You can, of course, approach a publisher directly. No reputable publisher will cheat you, but you will not get as good a deal as you would with an agent's help. Publishing contracts are complicated, and if you don't understand the minutiae of foreign rights, discounted books, blah blah blah, then you will be negotiating from a position of weakness. Agents do understand these things, and agents also know which editors are looking out for particular books and, better still, they often have more time to nurture a new writer than a publisher might have.

If you've written a good book you'll have little trouble finding an agent, but what is a good book? The Historical Novel Society recently polled every publisher about what they were looking for in a manuscript and received all sorts of unhelpful replies - 'page turners,' or 'best-sellers', or 'originality', which is fine, but what are those things? For a first novelist, sitting at home and writing into the terrible void, it is an acute question, and I had better say right away that I do not think I can provide the answer, but hope at least to put down some markers. The cop-out response is to offer the American judge's definition of pornography; we may not be able to define it, but we know it when we see it, but that is simply not true of manuscripts. Think how many publishers rejected Harry Potter! We might produce the most sparkling, page-turning, original manuscript, and it can still get turned down (luckily for some of us the opposite is also true).

But there are some clues in the responses of the publishers to the Historical Novel Society's questions. 'An original voice', one said, while another asked for 'drive', which I suppose means enthusiasm, and if you are not enthusiastic about your book then it will show. Writing is not supposed to be a labour, but a joy. I do not speak here of literature, about which I know nothing, but the business of writing readable stories, and to the best of my knowledge no-one is forced into doing that. We do it because we think it is better than working, and because it is enjoyable, and though the production of a first (and second, or twentieth) manuscript can be a very hard labour, it must not show in the finished product. Writing is fun, honest!

Which means you have to get past the horrid stage of not enjoying it, and that is usually caused by a lack of confidence. Is the stuff we're producing up to snuff? Is the style all right? Style seems to be a stumbling block for many first novelists, and the only advice I can offer is to tell you how I overcame it. Which is not to claim that I have a fine style, only that I no longer worry about it. But when I was writing *Sharpe's Eagle* I spent hours reading and re-reading the typescript, and every time I got hopelessly depressed thinking that it was no bloody good because the style was so clumsy, and so finally I tried an experiment. I typed out three pages of a Hornblower novel, substituting Sharpe's name for Hornblower's, and then I put the pages into a drawer. After three days I read those three pages (which looked exactly like my own typescript) and, to my relief, discovered that I was just as critical of Forester's style as I was of my own. But he was published. More, he was successful, so clearly I was being too critical. The experience freed me of that worry. Try it yourself. Reproduce three pages of a Sharpe novel on your own typewriter or word-processor, then come back to it and see just what rubbish can get published!

Later on, when I had written two or three books, I learned that style is something that can be applied at the later stages of writing. The most important thing, the all important thing, is to get the story right. Write, rewrite, rewrite again, and do not worry about anything except story. It is story, story, story. That is your business. Your job is not to educate readers on the finer points of Elizabethan diplomacy or Napoleonic warfare or villainous terrorist plots, your job is to divert and amuse people who have had a hard day at work. What will get you published? Not style, not research, but story. Once the story is right, everything else will follow. Rewriting is falling off a log, the hard work is getting the story. I once wrote a 12,000 word story for the *Daily Mail*'s Christmas editions. It took eight days to get the story right and three hours to rewrite the whole thing, and that rewrite included a brand new villain. But once the story was right the piece could take all sorts of pummeling because the story was strong enough.

Kurt Vonnegut once gave a splendid piece of advice. Every good story, he said, begins with a question. Harry meets Anne and wants to marry her. There's the question already, will he succeed? But Harry is already married to Katharine, so there is your plot. Simple, isn't it? And if your opening question is right, then the pursuit of the answer will propel the reader through the book. More important, it will propel the writer through the book. I know there are differences of opinion here, but I can only speak for myself and I rarely know how a book I'm writing will end when I begin it, and even when I think I know, I usually turn out to be wrong. How can you know? Every story is new, and if it is untold, how do you know the ending? You write to discover what will happen, and it is the excitement of that discovery that should give a manuscript its enthusiasm.

And once you have your story, you must keep it moving. How do you know if one scene is too long, or whether a discursive explanation is appropriate in a particular chapter? In time it does become instinctive, and so it should, but a first novelist may well not have those instincts. In which case there is only one thing to do, something which I know a lot of professional writers did when they began, and something which rarely seems to be recommended.

Suppose you decide to build a better mousetrap. You would begin, surely, by taking apart the existing mousetraps to see how they worked. You must do the same with books. When I wrote *Sharpe's Eagle*, never having written a book before, I began by disassembling three other books. Two were Hornblowers, and I forget which the third was, but I had enjoyed them all. So I read them again, but this time I made enormous coloured charts which showed what was happening paragraph by paragraph through the three books. How much was action? And where was the action in the overall plan of the book? How much dialogue? How much romance? How much flashback (I hate flashback)? How much background information? Where did the writer place it? I already knew what I liked in the books, and I was determined to provide more of that in my book, and I knew what I disliked, and wanted to use less of that, but the three big charts (sadly I've lost them) were my blueprints. It was not plagiarism, but it was imitation. I learned to start with a fairly frenetic scene, and to keep that pace going before I slowed it down to provide necessary information. I learned, if you like, the structure of a best-seller, and then I imposed that structure on what I was writing. These days I do not think about it anymore, but in the first three or four years those analyses were priceless.

Your book must have an original voice. But it will, won't it? Because there's only one of you, but unless you are in the posterity stakes of high-class literature, you will be producing a book that is within a recognisable genre, and you will hugely improve your chances of success if you take the time to study successful works in the same genre. Why not learn from successful authors? Disassemble their books, then set out to do better. If you worry that the long scene in your chapter four is much too long, then see how other writers tackled similar scenes in a comparable stage of their book. The answers to a lot of first novelists' questions are already on their bookshelves, but you have to dig them out.

Research, how much is needed? The answer is annoyingly contradictory - both more than you can ever do and only as much as is needed. By that I mean that you can never know enough about your chosen period, and so your whole life becomes a research project into the 16th or 18th or whatever century it is you are writing about, but when it comes to a specific book there really can be too much research. Why explore eighteenth century furniture making if the book doesn't feature furniture? Do as much research as you feel comfortable doing, write the book and see where the gaps are, then go and research the gaps. But don't get hung up on research - some folk do nothing but research and never get round to writing the book.

Nothing, I suppose, can guarantee success. It seems to me that there is a great deal of luck in the whole process. I was lucky in meeting my agent (his first words to me were 'it must be a f****** awful book'), and I was lucky in finding a publisher who understood that runaway best-sellers are rarely first novels (some are), but that if she coaxed and nagged and edited me through the first four or five then the series might be a success, and I was lucky in having a wife who was prepared to keep the wolf from the door while I wrote those first books. I am also hugely lucky, twenty-odd years later, in having the same agent, publisher and wife. So luck is important, and the publishing business is capricious, and the world is unfair, but if you understand that your job is not to be an historian, but to be a storyteller, and if you take the trouble to find out how stories are told, you can hugely improve your luck.

In the end you have to write the book. Do it, remember that everyone began just like you, sitting at a table and secretly doubting that they would ever finish the task. But keep at it. A page a day and you've written a book in a year! And enjoy it! Writing, as many of us have discovered, is much better than working.

www.bernardcornwell.net

Tania Crosse

Readers (and publishers) love a strong hero and heroine, but they must be sufficiently flawed to make them credible. Likewise, developing some sympathy towards villains, or at least giving some psychological explanation for being as they are, will involve your reader far better than a totally black character. Villains really can be fun!

When carrying out research for a historical novel, try to use a primary source wherever possible. Original records, maps or memoirs are best. If using secondary sources, try to cross reference as these can sometimes be unreliable. Old newspapers are relatively accurate, but we all know that journalists often don't get things a hundred per cent correct!

If writing within living memory, try to interview people who lived through the period in the specific location if appropriate. I did this for my new 1950s series, 'Lily's Journey' (out now) and 'Hope at Holly Cottage' (due out summer 2010). It was a most rewarding experience and I have met some fascinating people this way.

Immerse yourself in novels of the era you are interested in, and see what you can learn from them.

Tania Crosse is the author of *Hope at Holly Cottage*, publ. Allison & Busby, Summer 2010, *Lily's Journey*, publ. Allison and Busby, March 2009, and *A Dream Rides By*, publ. Severn House, October 2009.

www.tania-crosse.co.uk

Lindsey Davis

Remember you are not writing history, you are writing a novel. This requires you to master plot, characterisation, dialogue, narrative tone and description. Note that nowhere in my list do the words 'research' or 'history' appear!

Lindsey Davis' current novel is *Rebels and Traitors* (Century/Arrow) *Nemesis*. She has also written *'Falco: the Official Companion'* - June 2010 (Century).
www.lindseydavis.co.uk

Margaret Duffy

Writing as someone whose father told her that a woman's place was in the kitchen and whose husband declared that he would eat his hat if I ever got anything published (I eventually put a large furry one on his dinner plate) it's vital for the new writer only to take advice from those *who really know what they are talking about.* The words of those with experience and/or right there in the book market place are the people to heed carefully. Never mind that great-aunt Agatha, a retired vet, had a paper published in the late forties about tape worms in Algerian camels and tells you that you are wasting your time, smile sweetly and ignore her.

That said you must be aware that as soon as you declare an intent to write, thus sticking your head above the parapet, people will queue up to shoot it off. This again comes mostly from the ignorant and to me seems to be a particularly English disease; the resentment of anyone with burning ambition or modest success. It is important to develop am extremely thick skin. But above all take expert advice, if an editor asks you to undertake work that amounts to a rewrite, then rewrite it, if a publisher wants it shortened, then shorten it, never have the idea that what you have written is absolutely perfect as it is. I learned this from my father who had a novel published in the fifties. He wrote another and they wanted him to shorten it. He refused and they turned it down. Completely unrealistically he had thought he was going to win the Nobel Prize with it. That is the road to failure.

Margaret Duffy's current novels are *Souvenirs of Murder*, (Ingrid Langley and Patrick Gillard, Book 13, paperback), May 2010 and *Corpse in Waiting* (Ingrid Langley and Patrick Gillard, Book 14, hardback), June 2010.

www.fantasticfiction.co.uk

Carola Dunn

Zeitgeist: The spirit or genius which marks the thought or feeling of a period or age. *OED*

Having written books set in three distinct periods, I have come to the conclusion that, important as correct historical detail may be, still more important is to understand the *Zeitgeist* of your chosen setting.

Included in this term is the status of women, the possible paths open to them, and the consequences they were likely to face if they stepped outside the conventions. Your female protagonist may do anything she chooses, but if she acts in an unconventional way for the times, you must explain why, and what she suffers as a result.

Thus, writing a mystery series (Daisy Dalrymple) set in the 1920s, I can't make my female protagonist a police detective. The UK had few women police, those who existed had extremely low status, and many people disapproved of the very concept. By the 1960s (my Cornish Mysteries), women police were more acceptable to the authorities and the general public (though the Metropolitan Police did not, officially, have female detectives until 1973), but they still took a lot of flak from their colleagues. So, as well as an amateur protagonist, I have a woman detective, the only one on my imaginary Cornish force. DS Megan Pencarrow has to struggle for respect and do her best not to overreact to slurs and teasing.

Besides sex discrimination, other attitudes that have changed significantly in the two centuries between the Regency and the present are class distinctions, racism, anti-Semitism, and anti-gay sentiment. Though all are still present, alas, they are for the most part unacceptable in modern society. However, when you're writing about characters in the past, you have to take the general viewpoint of society into account. If you want to create a sympathetic protagonist who doesn't hold such unsympathetic beliefs, you have to show him or her as out-of-step with his/her surroundings.

For recent history, I find reading novels written in the relevant period to be a more useful guide to Zeitgeist than any number of history books.

Carola Dunn is author of the Daisy Dalrymple series
www.caroladunn.Weebly.com and **www.RegencyReads.com**

Ariana Franklin

- First rule. Not too many adjectives. I don't say eschew them completely, like Ernest Hemingway did, but if the writing doesn't get over the fact that something is 'scary', 'exciting', 'beautiful', 'horrifying' etc., then adjectives are just a waste of space and seem amateur.

- In the case of building up tension whether in a thriller or anything else, the 'pathetic fallacy' is a good rule. As most of you will know, this is giving inanimate objects or weather an atmosphere that fits the circumstances. If it's good enough for Shakespeare (Macbeth's witches on their blasted heath; Hamlet's father stalking the rampart; or Dickens with his use of fog), it's good enough for us.

- And, certainly in the case of a thriller, indicate very early that it IS a thriller. Too many writers start by scene-setting and character-describing in the first chapters instead of building them as they go along, and don't get on with the plot. All right, I know Tolstoy didn't do that in 'War and Peace", but (a) he was a genius and (b) we're aware that Napoleon's on his way to ruin the lives of his characters. Grab your reader by the whatsits from the very beginning.

- Above all, the only way to write is to write and keep on writing. If you say you haven't got time, then you'll never be a writer.

Ariana Franklin is the author of the *Mistress of the Art of Death* series.
www.arianafranklin.com

Tess Gerritsen

"Read newspapers!" I found that reading news articles that were contemporary to when the story is set gave me a great feel for the language and the events of the day. I made heavy use of the microfiche department of the Boston Public Library and just immersed myself in newspapers from the 1830's. After a while, the style of language infiltrated my writing and made it much more natural.

www.tessgerritsen.com

Susanna Gregory

For anyone considering writing historical fiction, I have two pieces of advice. The first is also applicable to fiction in general, and concerns the infamous "writers' block". A lack of inspiration dogs us all from time to time -- we are tired, bored with what we have written, would rather be outside in the garden than tied to the computer, and so on. My advice is just to work through it -- grab a cup of coffee, a glass of wine, a bar of chocolate or whatever else you need, and then just start typing. What emerges will likely be rubbish, but words are going on the screen, and nine times out of ten, there will be some good ones among them. I usually find that this process clears the fog. And if it doesn't there is always the "delete" button, and I can start again. The most important thing is never to give up.

The second tip is about research. Although crime fiction is *fiction*, many readers like to know that the historical facts are accurate. Do your research, or people will write to tell you that you are wrong. And then you have to write back and apologise! For both the Bartholomew and the Chaloner series, I have had to be careful about mentioning such matters as what kind of trees they saw (lots of species now familiar to us were brought to Britain in the 18th and 19th centuries), what kind of vegetables were available (and I don't just mean the obvious ones like potatoes -- things like swedes were late imports, too), which coins were available, and even what kind of materials they used on their beds. Research is an on-going process, but it is a huge amount of fun. My advice: get stuck in to your chosen era, and enjoy it!

A Killer of Pilgrims (Sphere) is her most recent novel in the sixteenth century chronicle of Matthew Bartholomew.

www.littlebrown.co.uk/Title/9781847442987

Feona J.Hamilton

If you write historical fiction set in a specific period, you'll need to do some research. So - spend enough time and do enough research to get the facts and dates right, but don't let the effort you put into it show in your writing. The story is the most important thing - the period detail should become so familiar to you that you include it almost without having to think. As an example, I write a series of novels set in the City of London in the latter half of the 13th century. At that time, whoever was elected was the Mayor of London, not the Lord Mayor of London - that title came in later centuries.

One other thing - when I'm actually writing, I make a conscious effort not to read other people's work set in the same period. Then I don't plagiarise sub-consciously (or consciously - tut!).

E-Publishing

E-publishing is now really taking off with the advent of readers like Amazon's Kindle and the Sony Reader. If you're interested in getting your book published in e-format you'll have the advantage of getting to a global market immediately - but choose your publisher carefully! As with print publishing, if you're asked to pay anything up front, then you're probably in touch with a vanity publisher. Steer clear - you can self-publish easily enough by putting your own work up online via your website. If you want to find a reputable e-publisher, such as Boson Books, the US firm which publishes my titles, then check that they offer at least a legal contract and a proper royalties scheme. As with any publisher, make sure they're publishing the kind of books you write and that they're happy to look at your work - check under 'Submissions'.

This is an exciting time to get into e-publishing as we're at last on the threshold of acceptance for this medium. Titles are sold in e-format by Amazon, W.H.Smith and Waterstones, as well as the specialist distributors like Mobipocket. Google 'eBooks' and just look at the list of distributors that appears! Publishers which have traditionally published only in print are offering their titles in
e-format, too, such as Penguin Books, HarperCollins and Macmillan. The advantage of a smaller, reputable e-publisher is that you don't necessarily have to submit via an agent and, of course, with no warehousing or printing costs, your books are less likely to go out of print!

www.AuthorsDen.com

Lilian Harry

Researching the Second World War for fiction is both easier and more difficult than for earlier periods - easier because there is so much archive material available in so many forms (written, radio broadcasts, film and oral history) and more difficult because there can be too much! It can be very easy to be swamped by it.

The trick is to determine your own theme and concentrate on that. Once you have that clear, you can also look at other areas, which will be useful for the wider picture, but don't allow yourself to be sidetracked. Anything that is particularly interesting but not relevant may well be used in a future project, but don't allow it to muddy the waters of the current one.

Otherwise, it is not so very different from any other period. Remember every aspect of life as it was then, starting with home life and spreading out the local situation, then to the national and then to the international. In some period stories, this will be less important, but in a world war, it is vital to know what would have been going on in different parts of the world, and whether it would affect your story. Would a son be sent to the Far East and if he becomes a Japanese POW how will this affect the family at home? Would a young woman, who had never left home before, find herself nursing in Egypt, or a younger child living with strangers in a village? As soon as you begin to ask these questions, the stories begin to flow.

There are numerous sources for research - local newspaper archives, museums (especially the Imperial War Museum), film (films made at the time often appear on TV), hundreds of books, and of course the Internet. But there is one source of which you should be careful, and that is 'memory'. Oral history is fascinating and often very helpful, but memory can distort and it can be inaccurate. The Mass Observation Unit (itself a wonderful source) found that when interviewers went back to people whose experiences they had recorded at the time, and asked what they remembered, the recollections were often quite different!

There is always someone who will write to you and point out your errors, if you make them (and which of us is without blame in this respect!) but don't be too disheartened by this. If you have done your best, you won't have made many - and anyway, it may be *their* memory which is at fault!

Lilian Harry's latest novel is *An Heir For Burracombe*, pub. August 2010.

www.lilianharry.co.uk

Susan Higginbotham

Don't wait for that perfect time to start writing, for if you do, you may never get anything written. Even if you have children and/or a full-time job--and I have both--there's almost always some way you can squeeze in the time to write, even if it's just a few minutes snatched here and there.

For historical fiction in particular: If you love reading about a historical figure or an era, it's probably a good sign that you're meant to write about it.

www.susanhigginbotham.com

C.C. Humphreys

HISTORICAL TIP NO.1: RESEARCH, OR GETTING YOUR FEET WET

I am full of this one right now, having just returned from Byzantium… Constantinople… ok, Istanbul. I went because the novel I am writing deals with the Turkish conquest of the city in 1453. Once more I was thrilled by what I learned, touched, felt, saw, heard.

There are writers who write wonderful novels and never leave the house. Probably my favorite all time author is Rosemary Sutcliff and she never left her wheelchair, yet conjured visions of Bronze Age Britain that were fabulously rich in detail, in flora and fauna and geography. And now we have the internet… why go to the expense?

I will tell you why. There is memory in stone, in places where the characters you hope to conjure trod. There are people there, descendants of those who walked, loved, fought in the era you are writing about who will say something to throw you back in a way a photograph cannot do. And if the vista is now blocked by a high rise or a three lane road, the place where you stand helps you see with the inner eye, beyond the layers time has laid down. A certain type of bird calls. A bug flies into your face. A flower catches you with its scent. And you see your character hear it, feel it, sniff it. And they do something differently, your book changes.

Examples: on the battlefield of Saratoga I watched a heron pass over me and fly straight into my novel as a recurring motif. Climbing the cliffs at Quebec my feet slid down shale, as the British Light Infantrymen's would have done in 1759, as Jack Absolute's would have done. In Vlad's ruined castle of Poenari, I heard how ravens bark, not cry. Last week in Istanbul, in a fishing boat that took me out where three waters meet – the Bosphorus, the Golden Horn and the Sea of Marmora – I found that the calm I'd imagined when the wind dropped wouldn't have gentled my battling ships... the sails would have dropped but they still would have bucked like broncos.

I could go on and on. Because what I have always discovered is that research isn't so much about getting the facts right – what are 'historical facts anyway? – research is about finding things that act as springboards for the imagination and bounce your plot and characters into places you could not have foreseen.

My tip? Sell the children, mortgage the house, pawn the family silver... and Go!

C.C. Humphreys is the author of the Jack Absolute series and *Vlad the Last Confession.*
www.cchumphreys.com

Jane Jackson

Tips for writing historical romance

Choose a period that fascinates you and a theme about which you care deeply. (A theme I enjoy exploring is a woman's place in a man's world) You are going to be working on this story for up to a year, so it's important that you are captivated and absorbed by it. If you aren't, how can you expect the reader to be?!

With historical romance the love story takes precedence. But the world in which the story takes place needs to be as authentic as possible. You will come across books that purport to be "historical" but they are simply modern stories in fancy dress. This is a shame because the authors of such stories are missing a fantastic opportunity to bring the past to vivid life for today's readers.

So, how to make it "real"? Research thoroughly. Study books of etiquette and social customs relating to the period. Class was far more sharply defined in the past than it is now, and it was far harder – in most cases impossible – to cross the class barrier until the mid 1860s when, as a result of the Industrial Revolution, there was a rapidly expanding middle class who had made their money, not simply inherited it.

Ensuring your background is real and believable will give you a solid base for your love story. To make your story stand out, to make it unique, try to ensure that it could only have happened to these two people in this place at this time. How to achieve this?

I have one character already established in the location, and the other arrives as a stranger. The reason for the incomer's presence is a threat to the status quo. These two are forced into each other's company for good solid reasons (hence the necessity for accurate research to achieve realism and believability) and the threat or change the incomer represents sets up a powerful conflict deepened and complicated by the fact that this man and woman are strongly attracted to each other.

Your detailed biographies for each of your main characters will have helped you understand who they are, where they are coming from, what they want, what they are (or are not) prepared to do to achieve it, and what they are risking by pursuing this course of action. In other words, what might it cost them?

Yet though social customs, etiquette, and men's and women's ambitions may have changed over the centuries, at heart human beings have always been driven by the same needs: Security - a place where they feel safe; food; to love and be loved, to belong to a family/community/tribe/class. For women: to marry well and have a family; for men: to make their mark in the world through achievement.

By setting these universal needs against a background and situation specific to the period you have chosen, and by ensuring your writing invokes all the senses, you will create a story that draws the reader into another world, one as real and vivid to them as this one.

How to deal with having your work rejected

Read the title carefully. See what it says? How do deal with *your work* being rejected. And that is the first point I want to make. (Obviously we are talking here about standard rejection slips – the kind that tell you nothing.) What you need to remember is that it is not *you*, the person, who is being rejected. With luck it is not you, the writer, who is being rejected. It is simply that particular submission.

There may be any number of reasons why it was turned down. (I'm assuming here that you presented it professionally – 12-point font, double spacing, wide margins, a header giving the initials of the title/your initials/chapter number/page number in the right hand corner of every page, the pages clean and held together by two rubber bands. Of course you did.)

So reasons it came back to you:

1   The agent is already handling an author who writes the same kind of story you submitted.

2   The publisher has a similar story in production or recently published.

3   You sent it to an agent or publisher who doesn't handle that genre (You wouldn't do that, would you? You'd check on-line or in the Writers & Artists Handbook first. Of course you would/did.)

4   The opening pages just didn't grab *and hold* the reader's attention. Editors and agents are incredibly busy people. They have to wade

through scores of submissions every week, and those don't include work from authors already on their client lists. If it doesn't grab catch their attention on the first page and force them to turn over, then sadly, it's likely to be set aside for return.

5   It's simply not up to the high standard publishers can afford to demand because of the astronomical number of submissions they receive.

What to do next?

1   Have a little weep, chew the carpet, go for a long walk and imagine scenarios in which you can punish the so-and-so's who have chucked a year's work back at you without so much as a word of explanation. Then make a cup of tea, pull yourself together, and decide that they made a mistake, and you're going to prove it with your next book. (See No.3)

2   If you are sure your first book really is as good as you can make it, then type out a fresh title page and send it out again. Meanwhile start work on your next. (No publisher wants a one-book author. They rarely make any money on an author's first book, and need to know you can/will produce a book a year, proving their investment in you was justified.)

3   Think about what you've learned from writing the first book and vow to make this next one better, stronger, more gripping; one that fits the genre it is aimed at, with characters who leap off the page and a plot that grows out of who the characters are and what they want, not one imposed on them.

You've taken a knock. But that's life, and it's rarely fair. A real writer, a professional writer, acts as No 1 above (plus possibly indulging in a glass or two of something alcoholic) then takes a deep breath, welcomes the slow burn of excitement that warns of a new story taking shape, and gets back to work. That's what writers do – they write. So go for it. Who knows, maybe *this* time?

Nine of Jane Jackson's novels are currently available including *Heart of Stone* (Severn House, 2009), *Bonded Heart, The Chain Garden, Dangerous Waters, Tides of Fortune* and *Eyes of the Wind.*

www.janejackson.net

There is so much to consider when thinking about writing a book. Personally I'd always concentrate on the characters, with a careful eye to make sure that they're consistent.

I've found that the best way to do this is to have a whiteboard on which the characters are depicted briefly – their key features (nothing too extensive, just guidelines to remind me what they're like), so: big nose, scarred cheek, blue eyes, etc.

Before I used the whiteboard, I discovered the wonderful merits of Post-It Notes. No, not the small ones: they make enormous "Table Top" pads, which are about A1 size.

You can write on them, pull off the page and stick it to a wall, shelf – anywhere. I used to have one for each main character, with description and motives in front of me so I could refer to them whenever I needed to.

Once you have your characters sorted, now the trouble is trying to hold the plot down and keep it exciting. There has to be excitement regularly through the book, because otherwise the reader will soon get bored.

I used to keep old manuscript drafts and tear them into quarter-length strips – sort of eight by three inches roughly – and on these I'd put a scene heading, with a very short description, as I wrote them. These would go on a wall nearby with Blu-tack, so that as I was writing I could go and peer at them to figure out how the story was running so far. Then, when it was clear that there were too many slower scenes with description or questioning all bundled together, I could see that pretty quickly, and would start to shuffle the strips, moving their order, adding new ones, until the flow looked better. It may sound simple and rudimentary, but I found it worked well for me.

In fact all these have been discarded now. I have discovered a wonderful software package recommended by David Hewson, which runs on Apple computers, called Scrivener. I have no association with the firm financially or in any other way, so you can take it from me: it will save hours of time. Instead of writing all the strips of paper, it provides all scene headings, and these can be moved and reordered to your heart's content, and each time the scene heading is moved, the text of the story is moved with it. Instead of the white board, Scrivener provides sections for characterisation and motivation – but all entirely under your own control. If you have research material, put the link from the web into the "info" section or a separate "research" heading, and it'll always be there.

Pictures can be pulled in, sections of text, anything. So it's all to hand now, whenever I start to write, on the screen right in front of me.

My own crucial piece of advice, however, is: if you want to write, there is no substitute whatever for actually sitting down and writing. All the software, all the descriptions of faces, all the carefully considered plot-twists and red herrings, will achieve precisely bugger-all, without their being set down in the correct sequence on paper.

The next important thing to bear in mind is that any editor is not looking for the next best seller. In today's market, although it sounds appalling to state it baldly, editors are looking to reject whatever you offer them. My own editor and agent each receive more than ten unsolicited manuscripts every day. They physically cannot read them all.

So, the first filter for all this work, is perhaps the editor or editorial assistant. They will scan some work first to see which efforts they should concentrate on: if you have bad grammar, clunky sentences, typos, or any other errors, they will not read further than the first page or two. Trust me – they don't have time.

Sometimes they'll hire someone to come in and look at the pile. The person hired will be an English Lit student, or perhaps the son or daughter of a senior manager. They will be incredibly nervous about putting forward for consideration something that they don't feel is absolutely top-level. It is their credibility they are worried about.

In the same way, an editor needs to be exceptionally impressed before proposing a new author. All publishers have committees which consider new potential authors and works. The editor to whom you write will have to stand up in the commissioning meeting to explain why your book is ideal for that publisher. To an extent it is his or her career on the line if the wrong work is put forward at that meeting and all the others don't like it.

Moving down the food chain, the principle is identical at an agent's. The agent will be recommending your book to publishers, and if the book is not taken up, for whatever reason, that agent's professional reputation will be harmed.

All of which depressing information goes to show that your work must be the very best you can possibly achieve. Your first ten pages must have no errors; mistyped words, formatting disasters – or smudges. Make the first ten pages sing, and you'll have a better chance of getting more people to read the whole book.

To aid this, the best advice is, read it all aloud. By reading it, you get to find your own writing voice, you help the cadences of the words on the page, and you avoid too many cock-ups, like repetition of the same word three times in five pages.

And finally, bear in mind that if you have already sent your manuscript to one publisher, by the time it comes back rejected, it will have smudges and folds where it oughtn't. No editor is going to be so taken with a manuscript that looks as though it's been passed around fifteen slush-piles compared with the next one that is pristine and clearly unseen by anyone else.

Both may have been read exactly sixteen times each, but if you reprint more often, you will help your chances of being accepted.

See also: **www.flickr.com/photos/Michael Jecks**
The Bishop Must Die, 28th in the Templar Series was published in November 2009

www.michaeljecks.co.uk

Richard Lee

What draws me to historical fiction is not the history, but the fiction. People underestimate the joy and the challenge of this. The goal of all fiction is to convey a truth about people. Writers seek for moments when characters suddenly reveal themselves, reacting to another character or a situation. They reveal themselves, and we say 'yes, that's what they are; that's what people are like'. In historical fiction when they do this they also tear a hole in time. They reveal where they are related to us and where they are not: the thrill is 'Ah - so that is what they were like.' It isn't the history that counts - these moments are usually the most purely fictional, the things that history cannot show us - but they are the moments that bring history to life. So, in Hilary Mantel's recent Man-Booker winner, *Wolf Hall*, when we watch Cromwell turn the pages of his wife's Prayer Book, the punch is not just the visceral pity we feel: his lost soul-mate, his two lost children. It isn't just the rich irony of the situation: the pragmatist feeling the touch of ghosts; the reformer cherishing Our Lady's prayers; the hard politician despondent that he cannot control his tears. The real punch is the religiosity. 'His daughters are now in Purgatory, a country of slow fires and rigid ice. Where in the Gospels does it say "purgatory?"' At this moment of utmost grief, where his fingers feel the imprint of his favourite daughter's fingers under his own, his mind is still questioning the supernatural scenes of the bible, and their deeply Catholic artistry.

Richard Lee is the Publisher and founder of the Historical Novel Society

www.historical novelsociety.org

Carole Llewellyn

I have always had a passion for reading (mainly historical fiction) and in 1992 I decide to try my hand at short story and article writing. I joined Brixham writers' Group and over the next few years was lucky to achieve publishing success in magazines such as: *My Weekly, Woman's Weekly, Take a Break, That's life, Yours* and the *Daily Telegraph*.

I then looked to turn my hand to novel writing. My first, *Megan* is an historical romance. *Megan* took me four years to write (with three rewrites) and another two years to get published. Going through rejection after rejection (often made worse by such comments as – they liked it very much but...) can be a painful process. At this stage it's easy for some writers to lose heart ...I say don't! If you believe in your characters as I believed in all mine in Megan's story, then you have to stick with it. My reward came in March 2008 I heard from publisher Robert Hale Ltd , he said he really liked *Megan* and wanted to publish it (*Megan* published 29 October 2008). He also asked for the first option on my next two books. My second book *Rhiannon* published by Robert Hale Ltd 29 January 2010 (took me two years). My third '*For the love of Catrin*' is on a schedule to be finished within a year.

My writing colleagues often tell me how much they admired my determination to stick with *Megan* - worrying at it like a terrier with a bone, refusing to let go, returning to it again and again, nibbling at its very core, in my attempt to become a 'professional writer'. I never stopped believing I would one day see it in print!

www.halebooks.com

Dorothy Lumley

Keep your submission letter simple and professional - an agent needs to know what type of novel e.g. historical mystery, historical romance, Naval warfare. The length (make it clear whether this is computer count or the old-style averaging method). A couple of lines about the storyline. A brief paragraph about yourself. You can include both a short outline and a long synopsis of the novel. Some agents like one, some the other. Don't worry too much about these being perfect. And always send the first chapter, or first three chapters. Don't send random chapters.

Dorothy Lumley is proprietor of Dorian Literary Agency (DLA). Please note that the Dorian Literary Agency have their full complement of authors at the movement and are unable to take on any more.

www.writersservices.com

Karen Maitland

1   Immerse yourself in books about different aspects of the period to soak up the general background and issues, but put a strict time limit on this process. Then lock the books away and start writing your novel. From that moment onwards concentrate on telling the story, not writing about the historical period. Keep a pad beside you as you write to note down any details you need to look up, such as – *How did they fasten their trousers? What did they drink at breakfast?* Then research these facts at the end of your writing day or writing week. That way you don't waste writing time and interrupt the creative flow.

2   As in stage and film, lighting is important in creating atmosphere in fiction – where the light is coming from? Is it dazzling or soft? Today we are so accustomed to bright lights that we often over estimate how much our ancestors could see at night or even on a dull winter's afternoon. If your novel is set in the days of candlelight, experiment to see what effect this might have on your characters' activities. Get a pure wax candle from a craft fair (modern candles have a different flame quality and brightness). At night, place your candle in a safe place where it can't be knocked over or set fire to anything and then ask yourself what you can really see. *How close does someone have to be before you can see their facial expressions? How does the light change the colours in the room? What tasks could you see well enough to perform by candlelight? Reading, sewing, baking?* Now put your candle inside a glass jar and cover the outside of the jar with greaseproof paper. This gives you a similar light quality and intensity to that of a horn lantern. Take your mock lantern outside to somewhere with no street lights. *What is actually illuminated? How far away could you see a body lying on the ground? How much detail can you see of a person standing a few yards away?* Observations like this will help you to create and vary atmosphere.

3   Some of your characters, including the minor characters, will engage in work or a task such as butchering meat, brick making, spinning, early aircraft engineering, archery, horse grooming or cooking over an open fire or on a range. Use trade or craft associations to find someone local who does this now as a job or hobby in the old traditional way. Ask if you can watch that person work for a couple of hours and talk to them about their craft and how they learned it. As well as helping you to bring your scenes alive, craftsmen will often tell you about hazards and mishaps or give you tips that you

will never find mention in reference books. This may give you great ideas for dramatic new scenes and incidents.

4   Use historical terms sparingly and if you use them, make sure that readers can always guess what they mean from the context without having to look them up. You don't want your reader to be jarred away from the story and spend their time worrying about what *Outremer* or *Chevauchee* means, instead of being immersed in the action of the scene. (See how irritating those words are if you don't recognise them and have no clues!) As long as the reader can work out roughly what is meant from the story, you can always include a glossary to give the precise definition of the word or to add additional information about a term.

Karen Maitland has written a number of medieval thrillers including *Company of Liars* and *The Owl Killers*. Forthcoming in 2011- *The Mandrake's Tale*. (All published by Penguin UK and the unabridged audio books by Oakhill). She is also one of the authors of the joint Medieval Murderers novel *The Scared Stone* (published June/July 2010) (Simon & Schuster).

www.karenmaitland.com

Ian Morson

Don't be afraid to use the Internet.

When I started writing, I was reliant on whatever books I could lay my hands on. Some I bought, and had those as constant references. Some I would borrow from the public library, and make feverish notes on before having to return them. Sometimes I had to make special journeys to have access to specialist resources, such as my visit to Oxford Public Library to work with their local history collection. This entailed lots of preparatory work, and efforts to anticipate all the information I would need in the course of writing a book. Before I even began writing a story.

Now, when faced with an issue of fact, I merely go on to the Net, and look it up. My writing flow is hardly broken, and I can research facts whatever the hour of day or night. And not have to wait to the next day for when the library opened, and then find the information was not available in book format in a local library anyway.

It is quite unbelievable what is available on the Net. I am currently writing a book set in medieval Paris, and I can now download medieval maps of Paris so that I can accurately describe my characters walking through their streets. I can verify whether a bridge over the Seine was of wood or stone, and if it had houses built on it. It all adds to the sense of realism of my story, if can incorporate such background. The year is 1273, the month June. I know the Templar Grand Master died in that year and was replaced by another, but not in which month. It was a crucial issue because one of my regular characters became Grand Master. But when? I found out on the Net, and continued my story.

Needless to say, I must take care the sites I use are reliable, but honestly I don't think that is too hard to tell. Anyway, it is good to verify facts by finding more than one source on the Net. One of those bridges I was researching was said to have been destroyed in 1046, so I couldn't use it. Yet it was on some medieval maps. In another more reliable site, I could verify that it actually fell in 1406. A significant difference brought about by a simple typing error.

Tread cautiously, but improve your background by mining the Net!

Ian Morson's latest books include *City of the Dead* (Severn House, 2008), *Falconer and the Ritual of Death* (Severn House, 2008*), Falconer's Trial* (Severn House, 2009) and *Falconer and the Death of Kings* (Severn House, 2010). He has also contributed to several titles with the Medieval Murderers, including *The Lost Prophecies* (Simon and Schuster, 2008), *King Arthur's Bones (*Simon and Schuster, 2009) and *The Sacred Stone* (Simon and Schuster, 2010)

www.ianmorson.co.uk

Ann Parker

Writing a Western Historical Mystery? Check the newspapers!

If your story is set in the "Wild and Woolly" days of the American West, you're in luck. All the big cities (and many of the smaller towns— particularly if they were "boom" towns) had newspapers. Additional bonus—these days you don't necessarily have to hunt them down on microfiche: Many historical newspapers are now on line, with more being scanned and brought into the digital realm every day. So, from the comfort of your home (or local library) computer connection, you can access sites such as Colorado Historical Newspapers: (**www.coloradohistoricnewspapers.org**) or the Wyoming Newspaper Project (**www.wyonewspapers.org**). Not sure where to start? A list of historical newspaper and indexes for many states (including those in the West) can be found at: **www.researchguides.net/newspapers.htm** as well as at the Library of Congress' "Chronicling America" project: (**www.chroniclingamerica.loc.gov**).

Read articles not only for a sense of the large, sweeping events, but also for those wonderful "telling details." For instance, a November 1880 article from the Leadville, Colorado, *Daily Herald* provides great details about the fashions of the day. (Examples: Mrs. W. R. Phelps in "light blue striped silk trimmed with satin of the same shade, and white lace, cardinal flowers at the throat and waist" and the rather tongue-in-cheek description of Mr. Howland in "a lovely toilet of tweed over red flannel; pants and coat were separate, but worn together.") You can also get a sense of the language and slang by a careful reading of quotes and descriptions. Telling details abound in journalistic "word pictures" of street scenes, church socials, cattle drives, and, of course, in the enthusiastic journalistic renderings of murders and misdeeds. As a mystery writer, you'll find much "fodder for fiction" in the newspaper accounts of the crimes of the day—be they banking swindles, knife fights in the alleys, stagecoach robberies, panel thieves, and so on.

Last word of advice: Be sure to read the advertisements (Tolu "Rock and Rye" tonic, anyone?).

Ann Parker is author of the Silver Rush historical mystery series set in 1880s Colorado. Her latest book is *Leaden Skies* (published by Poisoned Pen Press).

www.annparker.net

Glen Phillips

An Australian approach and toolbox

Introduction

Historical Fiction—it sounds like a contradiction in terms. Yet the vast majority of fiction is and has to be based on recent or ancient history. Ah, you say, what about science fiction? If you think for a moment you will see that without the present and past reality, as we humans have experienced it, there would be no way to experience the fascination of finding the zany worlds of the future so amazingly different from the present.

Let me be clear from the outset, I am talking about longer works of prose fiction, in fact, the novel. Even those authors who specialise in the short story usually nurse an ambition to one day succeed as a novelist. The thing about the novel is that it is unique among literary art forms (or possibly all art forms) in requiring its beholders to spend many many hours for a first complete contemplation (i.e. reading) of the work. This makes it all the more important to see where the historical novel came from and where it is going. Of course, it is also important to gain some first principles about writing historical fiction gleaned from successful novelists past and present.

The Historical Novel

Novels as we know and buy them today are from a historical point of view a recent phenomenon. But they had antecedents in the poetic and dramatic sagas of past times right back to *Gilgamesh* in Mesopotamia and later in the epic Greek classic verse stories of Homer and Hesiod. There were also Greek prose writers such as Apulieus and even later came Roman narratives of authors such as Plutarch. These were usually composite works with a nationalistic purpose of inspiration as well as edification. Hence fact and fiction were always accepted as part of the story. In other cultures, in India, China and Japan, for example, a similar progression eventually led to a taste for the really long narrative. And when printing made it possible for the tales to escape from the limitations of hand-written or oral literature, proto-novels like the four classic novels of Chinese literature emerged—*Dream of the Red Chamber (Story of the Stone)*, *Journey to the West (Monkey)*, *Outlaws of the Marsh (Water Margin)* and *The Romance of Three Kingdoms*. Much later, in Spain, Cervantes' *Don Quixote* signalled that the true European novel would not be far off and *The Life of Gargantua and Pantagruel* by Rabelais in the 16th century was another hint of the coming of the true novel.

As far as the novel in English is concerned, the historical novel emerged along with the other novelistic genres in the early 18th century with Daniel Defoe. Although *Robinson Crusoe* was in its time more of a contemporary reality show, Defoe's *Journal of the Plague Year* and *Memoirs of a Cavalier* are the prototypes for the historical novels which Sir Walter Scott turned out abundantly in the early 19th century. With the industrial revolution and an emerging middle class in substantial numbers all over Europe, together with huge advances in paper manufacture and printing, the novel became the new cultural artefact. Dickens wrote *A Tale of Two Cities* and in Italy Alessandro Manzoni produced *The Betrothed (I Promessi Sposi)*. The 19th century was also a period for the emergence of the truly great exponents of the novel, such as Tolstoy in Russia, Victor Hugo in France and Friedrich Schlegel in Germany. Following close behind was the United States of America and other countries in the New World. But the historical novel in particular is our main concern here and we might come back to the history a little later.

It is useful, however, to remind ourselves of the common appeal of the historical novel for many beginning writers. The simplicity of a 'ready made' story is the choice of which historical events seem to offer. So the writer sees his task as an embellishment of these basic facts. But this borrowing from history must be balanced by awareness of what the novelist can do, and what the historian cannot—and that is a transformation of fact into a living narrative, where the people, places and events are re-birthed within the imagination of the novelist. It is rather like the raising of a Lazarus, the disinterred bones of past events and lives being miraculously given flesh. Think of the exhibits in the museum walking out of their glass cases and making off down the street. The novelist give himself or herself a licence for all sorts of reinterpretations, guesswork, inspiration and the feeling of real experience born out of the novelist's imagination and brilliant word-smithing skills.

Historical Fiction Toolbox

What I want to present now is my practical guide and toolbox for the aspiring historical novelist. After that I will introduce you to some of the chosen topics of Australian authors of historical fiction whom I particularly admire.

But, first, what are some of the key practical aspects of writing historical fiction? I write historical fiction and I enjoy reading historical fiction but I have also spent many years in universities teaching the writing of fiction. I have also interviewed many writers of historical fiction. The most consistent advice is that the quality of an historical novel, however imaginative its components, depends absolutely on research. And we might add, research and more research. There are two good reasons for this—first any errors of fact will certainly be noticed in a novel and will discredit even the most brilliantly composed work; and in the second place, the appeal of all novels lies in the elaboration of facts (the very thing which by their nature short stories, poetry and drama cannot afford). The novel is uniquely liberated from the absolute dictates of economy, which are the very measure of success for poetic language or to make the short story form successful. That is not to say that the novelist need not strike a balance between insertion of detail and the forward tempo of the narrative. It is a matter of relativity, I suppose. The novelist must not dally self-indulgently on details of character or landscape when the story should be progressing.

Of all novelists the author of the historical novel is probably the most in danger of digressive description (except perhaps the autobiographer). Every novelist still has to set limits on the proliferation of characters and subplots and curb any tendency to turn from storytelling to mounting the lectern! The historical novelist normally has certain obsessions with time and place and would do well not to become tediously absorbed with detail beyond necessity for setting the scene vividly. Research will always tend to provide more material than can possibly be used, so the author must become a wise and prudent judge of what to include and what to discard.

Research

What techniques of research are really useful? The first principle is efficiency. Because with all the mountains of detailed facts that the historical novelists must dredge up, it is commonplace for them to become so overwhelmed by the products of their own industriousness that the time-line for completing the novel is sacrificed. Frequently, the proposed
novel is abandoned in that litter of un-retrievable detail. The facility of research provided by the internet has only added to this problem. If your studies in higher education have included training in traditional historical research, you will be very fortunately in possession of much of the expertise you need.

But there are some down-to-earth principles to help your research to be as efficient as possible. Let us look at storage of the facts before we look at accessing information. Indexing the stored material as you go along will serve you well. But you have to decide what will be the best headings for the information you put aside for later use. First you may want to divide the period of your novel's setting into its successive decades, or even smaller time components. Apart from a chronological organisation of data, you may need to group together facts about places such as cities or towns; or cultural matters like costume, architecture, diets, dialects, religious observances, tools of work and so on. Climate and weather, means of transport and communication, medical practices, educational and legal systems and scientific facts about plants, animals (or even geology) may constitute categories worth including in your research cataloguing system. Whether you use filing cabinets, index cards or digitalised systems, the worth of your research when it comes to retrieving details for your narrative will depend a great deal on how well you decide the main headings for your collection.

A second principle is to know the full range of sources of information and how to choose the most effective ones for the historical period you are re-creating in your fiction. One of the commonest impulses we all have about the past is the desire to investigate family genealogies. There are many agencies available to help you, and public libraries often provide assistance on exploring family history. Obviously, the same services and methodologies will be useful where a historical novel is based on lives of real people. But even where the characters are fictional it could be useful to select real people to interview in the same locality. If it is recent history you could learn a great deal about life and its challenges that would be useful for your fictional characters.

In a similar way, civil and military records are often very accessible and well organised. There are many other avenues of genealogical research that can help the historical novelist as well. Municipal records, including minutes of council or committee meetings, go back in some cases for several centuries. These give you a great flavour of life in those times even though they a very formalised and often quite cryptic. Police and court records (especially daily incident books from police stations) give fascinating detail on the realities of the criminal side of community life.

There are many areas of working life where journals or logs have to be maintained. My grandfather, like most, kept a farm journal from the time he first cleared virgin bush for his wheat farm in Western Australia. Sadly, my uncles threw them down a disused well when clearing the house after his death. How valuable they would be to me now! But apart from ships' logs, many other workplaces were documented as a matter of course and some of these turn up still in family business records or in the smaller types of local museum. Again the value to the historical novelist is the flavour of the times. Private diaries (including war diaries) are for the researcher like finding gold nuggets.

While we are thinking of the survival of documentary historical evidence there is no more interesting and useful window into any past time of the last few centuries than microfilmed (digitalised or not) of early newspapers. My writing students found it amazing that they could check the local weather on their birth date (or in some cases, for those of grandparents) in our splendid State Reference Library. But much more than that can be revealed by browsing the advertisement, the movies being screened at the time, properties to let and for sale, latest shipping arrivals, births-marriages-deaths columns, the sporting pages—even before you look at the headlines to see what else was going on in the world-at-large or locally. Nowadays you can get CD or DVD discs of the back issues of popular or specialist magazines. In the case of famous motor magazines, it is very helpful to check for photos of the cars typical of certain periods. Of course this is even more relevant for movie makers for nothing is easier to fault in a movie than a model or make of car appearing which hadn't yet been built at that time. Yes, it does happen frequently. I guess this applies to many other machine age inventions and the historical novelist can authenticate a scene very easily by being able to add the absolutely correct means of transport or domestic aids.

What we have moved on to here are images in the form of photographs. Collecting these by scanning is now a very good way to have them at hand for reference purposes when you are actually working at the keyboard. Photographs only go back effectively to about the middle of the 19th century, so beyond that we rely on lithographs, etchings, paintings and drawings. Most historical libraries have collections of images but more and more are becoming available on the internet. Commercial services exist for advertisers and film makers to provide appropriate images, not that an author is normally going to be able to afford these. Newspaper or magazine images of particular interest are clipped and filed by many writers of historical but their usefulness depends on how well you can organise and index them into files or scrapbooks.

Related to photographs are old movies and documentaries or newsreels. Many now have been digitalised or can be borrowed from the video stores. If the movie research assistants did their authentication well such films provide a very rapid way to check on street scenes, interiors of houses and the clothes generally worn in that period. Since movies have only been made for about the last 100 years, you have to rely on their recreations of early times and they cannot always be trusted to be authentic. There is another way to get details like clothing correct and that is to go to the reference books used by producers of period drama in the theatres. Most costume hire businesses can also be very helpful for checking period costumes.

This brings us to reference books in general. Most useful are the countless local histories, often commissioned by local councils. They may be tedious to read for any other reason but they are remarkably helpful, if the historical novelist has a particular locale in mind. For a larger view of history, it goes without saying that the history shelves of the local library (or more specialist university or state libraries) should allow all the detail which is the national or international setting within which your fictional creation will be set. I am currently writing an historical novel that includes the notorious Nanjing Massacre in China before World War 2. I think I have now read almost every major book written on this topic. If we bear in mind that virtually every subject we can imagine has been the topic of some factual book or other at one time. With the aid of the internet it is very easy to locate the titles you need. Major library catalogues are often accessible on the net too. Don't forget that the history of the use of the internet in our daily lives is stretching back further and further every year. Emails and cellphone records will be common research sources for historical novelists even if not so often used today.

What we might call 'on-the-ground' research is the last but by far the most effective self-service historical novelists can undertake. What I am talking about first are the landscapes where the novel is set. Although long changed from what they once must have been, they have connections with the past. In creating authentic background in a fictional work I think there is no greater sense of certainty than the 'feeling' for a locale gained by having visited there. Most of us have an easily awakened nostalgia for our birth country or region. For this there is no substitute. We may not have to go out searching for those landscapes if our work is as autobiographical as, say Steinbeck's was. Thomas Hardy and D H Lawrence relied on territory that was very personal to them. When we return to such places after even a long absence we immediately experience a sensation no other landscape can really evoke.

If we intend to use places that are not part of our own backgrounds (or even places previously visited) we must visit them afresh and do more research for the purposes of writing historical fiction. We have all had the experience of a general familiarity with a distant place gained from news items, reading books or newspapers but on discovering the 'real' region through travel experienced a complete revelation. This principle applies to the novelist's ability to bring to life a locale chosen for an historical novel. There is no substitute for putting your feet on the ground in that place, however long ago the action you are going to re-create in your narrative took place.

A second 'reality check', if you like, is interviewing. This requires skill and diplomacy, as well as good technical means of recording such interviews. Nowadays you would always use a digital recorder so that you can download the recorded conversation directly. If you want to pay for transcribing you will discover the costs are mind-boggling. There are important professional protocols in making recordings of interviews and you are advised to observe local laws and customs scrupulously. Universities nowadays are super conscious of legal implications of interviewing and ethics committees review all proposals for research by interview. But remember, interviewing as a research tool is very time-consuming and can well turn into a rod for your own back if you accumulate unmanageable volumes of information. Yet, the 'authenticity' you are seeking from the descendents of those people you are writing about can greatly enhance your own recreation of their culture and individuality.

This brings me to a final topic for this toolbox section of advice to the aspiring historical fiction writer. It is the significance of legal aspects. Even if a writer is attracted to historical fiction from a wish to avoid legal problems associated with telling tales about real events, these problems still exist potentially. Grievances and ill feelings that could come out of writing about one's contemporaries and contemporary life are real risks. There is not much hope of avoiding conflicts by trying to change certain details of story, character or setting. People have an amazing ability to imagine they have been depicted in your novel. There are very serious laws of libel. In most cases, arguing you are 'telling the truth' is no defence. Even the deceased usually have surviving relatives who can take offence. The best action is to seek approval from people or institutions involved and even to offer them the reading of the draft manuscript. At least you can deal with their objections, if any. Many authors have found fears of hostility to be unfounded.

It is a common but incorrect assumption of would-be-writers that their publishers will protect them from legal action. Publishers are too smart for that in these litigious times and your contract will usually require you to guarantee that no legal risks to the publisher exist in your manuscript.

Apart from the risk of libel action, the other main likely area for legal intervention is abuse of copyright (including plagiarism). If written material in any form has a value then it is likely to be owned by someone (and not only the author) and therefore to take those words is theft. The only recourse if you must use those words is to obtain permission from the original source. Changing the words around may not be enough to avoid legal action against you. The more you are likely to profit from your use of the words or facts, the greater the likely claim against you. All I can say is, apply for permission, pay if necessary and promise to make proper acknowledgment of sources, including the oral ones. There is something known as 'the public domain' but you need the advice of a publisher or a copyright lawyer to be sure of what that is.

Finally, depending where you live and work there are some other areas of possible legal problems. As we know from the case of Salman Rushdie, some of the world's religions and political systems are exceedingly sensitive about negative comments or blasphemy. Sedition is unlikely to be a problem for historical novelists, except in a very few countries, but obscenity is not to be overlooked where there is any sort of public defence of morals through book banning or lists or prohibited books. Although it might enhance public awareness of your book to have it banned, it then won't make you any money to pay for your 'crime'. A good move is to be sure you are a member of a professional writers' organisation and get its advice.

The Writers of Historical Fiction

As a sort of epilogue, I want to tell you about some works of historical fiction of my fellow authors in Western Australia. I first became a member (and later a Life Member) of the Fellowship of Australian Writers in 1968, joining the WA Branch. That is when my real education in Australian writing commenced. At that time it was difficult to find any

Australian universities prepared to include more than the token Australian work in their courses in English Literature. Of course I grew up knowing the names of some of the major Australian authors but little else, except some of the poems of Henry Lawson or 'Banjo' Patterson recited at elementary school. It was the local West Australian authors I learned to appreciate first because they became friends and colleagues. Many of them were writing historical fiction. I suppose they were trying to put into the hands of their readers the record (so long neglected) of the unique story of the British and European settlement of this remote place in the early 19th century. Included in that would be its impact on the resident Aboriginal population, who had some 50,000 years of their own history of ownership. We have now come about 180 years since the Swan River Colony was established. Yet there were European visitors (Portuguese and Dutch) getting themselves to this coast deliberately or accidentally since the early 1600s. The 'piratically inclined' British sea captain, William Dampier visited the west coast in 1688 and French scientific expeditions came late in the 18th century. Captain James Cook was, of course, a visitor to the east coast in 1770. Largely because of Cook's explorations, Botany Bay and Tasmania, as permanent settlements, became part of the British crime 'solution' by 1778. The next matter for me to deal with is how all this history (and more) has influenced our local writers of historical fiction.

In fact, this brings me once more to the presence of the Aboriginal people in this part of Australia. Scornfully dismissed by Dampier and others as barely human, their story is told today by many gifted Aboriginal authors. The award-winning Kim Scott, a Nyungar from the South West of W.A., has told in his novel *Benang* how his people survived and inter-bred with British pioneer settlers in the late 19th and early 20th centuries. In his latest novel, *That Dead Man's Dance*, he goes back even further to the very beginnings or the Swan River Colony and King George's Sound settlement in the 1820s and 1830s. Using archival documents, diaries and oral history of his Indigenous people, he tells a remarkable story of how in the Albany area the initial encounters were marked by a friendly respect and curiosity on both sides. But such diverse cultures were bound to become part of the same tragic tale of conflict, abuse and subjugation wherever colonisation of an indigenous people has occurred. Another local author of indigenous descent, Richard Wilkes (*Bulmurn*), wrote about the more hostile displacement of the Aborigines of the Swan River Colony and their incarceration on a nearby island, which became available once the British closed down the system of transporting felons to W.A.

Archie Weller in his *Day of the Dog* relates a more recent and urban story of the subjugation of the hybrid survivors of the original Nyungars in the years following World War 2. Doris Pilkington's *Follow the Rabbit Proof Fence* (now an award-winning movie) tells another story of the policy of the white government stealing away the hybrid children from their Aboriginal mothers to bring them up in so-called orphanages as virtual prisoners of the State. In an autobiographical novel, an Indigenous professor at the University of Western Australia, Dr Sally Morgan, wrote a best seller (*My Place*) about her disadvantaged life as a 'fringe dwelling' hybrid person. Even white writers such as Nene Gare, in her novel *The Fringe Dwellers,* have also depicted the victimisation of people of part-Aboriginal descent in Western Australian country towns. The latter also became a very successful feature movie directed by Bruce Beresford.

Katharine Susannah Prichard's early works were published in Britain and her *Coonardoo* is still a favourite wherever Australian literature is studied all around the world. It was the first serious work to choose the tragedy of an Aboriginal woman as a central theme. Her more ambitious project of historical fiction was the Coolgardie-Kalgoorlie Goldfields trilogy, the three novels of which we will note in more detail in a moment. Prichard was a trained journalist and daughter of a newspaper editor of some note. She was also one of the founders of the Australian Communist Party and a campaigner for peace and against many perceived failings of society. Her journalistic skills meant she was most industrious in gathering first-hand information. She always spent time in the locales of her fiction and even travelled with a circus for some months in order to write the novel *Haxby's Circus.*

To go back a little into historical possibilities for Australian novels, we might well look at the infamous wreck and mutiny that befell *The Batavia* in 1629 off the coast of Western Australia. It has inspired many historical books, novels, plays and even an opera. Perhaps the most successful historical novel about the "Batavia" has been Nicholas Hasluck's *The Bellarmine Jug* (1984). There have been hundreds of wrecks or shipping losses off the W.A. coast so there is obviously plenty of scope there, as in most maritime locations around the globe. And, indeed, the romance of the sea has created its own sub-genre within historical fiction. My grandmother was an avid collector of the British maritime writer W W Jacobs, who wrote more about life on and off ships in the London Docks rather than aboard ships on "the Main" or in the armadas of great navies. History is everywhere you care to look.

To return to my own country, Dame Mary Durack was the great chronicler for us of the early history of the cattle industry in the north-west of Australia. The best known of her trilogy of novels on this subject is *Kings in Grass Castles* (1959) and as a friend of hers for the last 15 years or so of her life, I was able to learn much of how she approached historical fiction. Actually the fictional element was probably overshadowed by the factual since she had access to voluminous Durack family records in terms of journals, correspondence and the accounts of her family in the pastoral industry. On the other hand, another talented novelist of the north-west area of Australia was Donald Stuart, also a friend of Dame Mary, but of different political persuasion. To my mind, his two greatest feats were first to write an authentic fictional history of a certain Aboriginal tribal grouping before and after contact with the first white cattlemen and also to write a splendid series of war novels, *The Conjuror's Years*, chronicling his military service and survival as a prisoner of war under the Japanese, working on the infamous Thailand railway. The Aboriginal novels were *Ilbarana* and *Maloonkai,* while ironically, his final novel referred to above was entitled *I Think I'll Live.*

In a novel set in more recent times, *The Merry-go-round in the Sea* (1965), the highly talented W.A. author Randolph Stow (1935-2010) also told the story of the Thailand Railway (but from accounts of a family survivor rather than personal experience) as part of his largely autobiographical childhood story. Incidentally, Australia can claim one of the greatest of all World War 1 historical novelists (according to Ezra Pound, T E Lawrence and others) Frederic Manning —for his *The Middle Parts of Fortune* (or *Her Privates We*). He did live much of his adult life in Britain but among Australian writers of historical fiction, many others have chosen war history as a theme, including David Malouf and Thomas Keneally.

If we go back to the emergence of the historical novel in Australia, the doyens we could name would include Henry Handel Richardson (nom de plume Ethel Florence Lindesay Richardson) for her great trilogy *The Fortunes of Richard Mahoney* and the later Eleanor Dark with her novels of the founding of the Sydney colony and settlement of New South Wales. A particular feature of the trilogy of Richardson (actually Ethel Richardson) was its documenting of the 1850s gold rushes in Victoria. From Lawson to K S Prichard, the search for and mining of gold has been an obvious choice for the historical novelist interested in the first discoveries of gold in New South Wales and the final great gold discoveries of W.A. Prichard's trilogy was written mainly in the 1930s and the titles are: *The Roaring Nineties, Golden Miles* and *Winged Seeds*. Prichard chose another kind of mining for one of her novels—opal mining—set in the Lightning Ridge fields in Queensland. Somewhat associated with the gold rushes were novels about notorious bushrangers. A recent example would be Peter Carey's *The True History of the Kelly Gang* (2000).

While some of the above novels might have been written much closer to the authors' own times than most historical fiction, it seems rather pointless to try and define a particular interlude of time after events that would make the events 'historical'. Equally, an author need not make up his or her own mind on what time should have passed before a novel can be classified as historical fiction. It is the reader who has a passion for history recounted through fiction, who should decide what constitutes a sufficiently past tense to pass muster as historical!

It is also true that the readers of historical fiction all over the world can choose their 'home-grown' locations for novels about the past or the exotic ones of other lands. My particular favourite writer in recent years is the Indian-Swiss novelist Meira Chand, whose chronicles of Japan (where she lived for 20 years), India, China and latterly Singapore (*A Different Sky*, 2010) are exemplars of careful research and wonderfully detailed recreation of past times and places.

Special events in history are always a target for the productive authors of historical fiction. In my home state, Robert Drewe has woven a novel, *The Drowner*, around the incredible feat of engineer C Y O'Connor in constructing a 350 mile pipeline to take water from the west coast near Perth to the desert location of Coolgardie-Kalgoorlie during the W.A. gold rushes at the end of the 19th century. Some of the other well-known Australian novelist such as Morris West (*The Devil's Advocate*), Colleen McCullough (*The Song of Troy*), Thomas Keneally (*Schindler's Ark*), Peter Carey (*Jack Maggs*) and David Malouf (*An Imaginary Life*) have chosen subjects outside their own countries for historical fiction. To date, and understandably so, not so many novelists around the rest of the world have chosen to write about Australian history.

Conclusion

To conclude, I would say that thinking about the subject of the historical novel has only reinforced my conviction that this relatively modern human invention of the extended narrative as an art form is fundamentally one of marshalling the 'factional' content which is for the reader the substantial reward and pleasure, apart from the tale itself. These facts require either an extraordinary memory for experiential detail or a well-developed system of research if the novel is to succeed. It is then that the 100,000 or so necessary words of the average novel are going to provide the reader with the requisite hours of reading pleasure that he or she has paid for. Would-be-novelists are mistaken if they imagine that ignoring painstaking research the tale will be drawn out of something like a ball of knitting wool in their brains by tugging some creative thread.

Glen Phillips is a West Australian writer and is currently Honorary Professor of English at Edith Cowan University, Perth. Born in Western Australia in 1936, in the remote gold-mining town of Southern Cross, he was brought up in outback areas where he developed an early love of Australian literature. He has been an executive member of the English Teachers Association, the Fellowship of Australian Writers, PEN International (Perth), the WA Writers' Council, the WA Writers Forum, the Katharine Susannah Prichard Foundation, the Peter Cowan Writers Centre and the Children's Book Council.

He has co-edited poetry collections and English text books and his own poetry has won prizes and appeared in American, Asian, Italian and Australian journals and anthologies. His poetry collections include *Umbria-Australia, Green and Gold*, (Perugia, Italy 1986), *Poetry in Motion* (Perth, 1988 - with three other WA poets who had formed in 1985 the well-known "Poetry in Motion" performance group), *Sacrificing the Leaves* (Bangkok, 1988), *Lovesongs, Lovescenes* (Perth, 1991) and *Spring Burning* (Perth, 1999), *Singing Granites* (Devon, with Anne Born, 2008), Shanghai Suite (Perth, 2009) and *Redshift Cosmology* (Perth, 2009) .

In recent years Glen Phillips has completed a number of joint projects with composers, choreographers and painters and has received awards and commissions for his work. Currently he is completing a prose/poetry project with John Kinsella. He lives in Mount Lawley, a suburb of Perth.

g.phillips@ecu.edu.au

David Roberts

The aristocratic Lord Edward Corinth and the liberated Verity Browne make an unlikely team, but so far they have collaborated on no less than nine successful murder investigations. Creatures of the stylish but dangerous times they inhabit, they combine dash with intellectual vigour...

The iceberg is the historical novelist's most important symbol. Do all the research but resist the temptation to shove all of it down. If you do, you risk lecturing the reader which is boring. Choose the research which is essential to the plot and use that. The reader will know you could have gone on much longer and be grateful you didn't.

Secondly, if your novel is set in relatively modern times, read as many diaries and letters as possible. That will give you the speech rhythms, and read popular fiction of the time for prejudices and assumptions.

If your novel is set in the distant past, try to get a feel of what was important to people in that period. Even Cadfael can sound like a modern social worker talking about the brain and the mind rather than humours, or the soul. In medieval times, for instance, the source of passion was to be found not in the heart but in the spleen or the liver. Easy to get facts right but the feel of the times wrong!

www.lordedwardcorinth.co.uk

William Ryan

How research can change your story

It was a strange experience writing *The Holy Thief,* because the research ended up changing the story entirely, and added several key scenes that I hadn't at all anticipated. For example, I spent quite a lot of time looking at photographs, and came across one of football fans hanging from the side of a Moscow tram on the way to a game in 1936, which duly led to such a journey in the book. Another photograph showed Red Army soldiers walking in front of the Kremlin, holding large building-shaped balloons that were decorated to create an inflatable, moving collective farm, and this resulted in an episode in the final chapters, and one of my favourite images in the book. In fact, the more I found out about Moscow, Soviet jazz, the popularity of Sherlock Holmes in this supposedly classless society, the rivalry between Spartak and Dynamo sporting organisations and any other aspects of Soviet life at the time, the more the novel seemed to take on a life of its own. But the real stroke of luck came when I read about the Pope's handing back to the Russian Orthodox Church an important Icon that had disappeared after the Revolution. As novelists sometimes do, I put two and two together and made something quite different to four.

www.panmacmillan.co.uk

Tim Severin

My tip for aspiring writers of historical fiction about the Viking era is:

Look no further than the Icelandic sagas for your plot lines, characters, scenes ... the sagas are a treasure trove of riches, raided by writers from Walter Scott to Tolkien, and still far from exhausted. For my VIKING trilogy the saga tales provided me with my hero Thorgils, described in the Saga of Erik the Red as someone about whom 'there was something uncanny all life'. And they allowed me to send Thorgils to the furthest corners of the then known world - from Constantinople to Vinland to Jerusalem and to the banks of the Volga - always carried along on the mainstream of saga adventuring.

www.timseverin.net

Harry Sidebottom

The Past is Another Country

Research is vital in writing historical novels. Too many fail in one key area. While it is essential to get the externals of the period right (the clothes, food, weapons, and whatever), it is even more important also to try and get the attitudes and values of the time as correct as possible. The past is another country, they not only do things differently there, they think about things differently. The best way to avoid the problem is to read a great deal of primary source material and plenty of modern scholarship on the mentalities of your chosen culture. If you just dress up modern people as a Napoleonic general or a Roman centurion it will not convince.

Harry Sidebottom is author of the *Warrior of Rome* series (Michael Joseph/Penguin): *Fire in the East* (2008), *King of Kings* (2009) and *Lion of the Sun* (2010)

www.harrysidebottom.co.uk

Julian Stockwin

Writing a series

Writing one book, let alone a series, seems incredibly daunting to most would-be authors, and I have to confess that when I first thought about the idea I was very sceptical. Now, ten published books later, I look back on this achievement with both pride and amazement – one million words in print!

A series gives a writer a wonderful opportunity to really develop a character and to grow a readership very loyal to the world you write about. But it also poses great challenges: will you run out of steam after the first two or three titles? Have you chosen a subject that publishers/agents/readers will still care about five or more years down the line? Do you have the mental and physical stamina to take on such a commitment?

Then what advice would I give eager wordsmiths about tackling a series? Well, I think it comes down to six points.

1   Write about something for which you care passionately. For me, this is the sea which has fascinated me ever since I can remember. My mother describes a toddler bringing home dead seagulls because they stank of the sea and as a young boy I used to stare out over the cold waters of Sheerness at the low, grey, shapes heading off to who knew where...

2   Don't stint on research. Although I have a well-thumbed personal

library of maritime books, before I even put pen to paper I really got stuck into the period I had chosen to write about – the great age of Fighting Sail, 1793-1815. I sought out additional volumes, scoured the internet, and developed a system for cataloguing all my books and cross-referencing data from various sources. This is what I call the paper research – then there is location research. If you can actually visit the area in which you set your book your confidence in the sights, smells, sounds etc. will inform your writing.

3 Character, character, character. Getting the central character right is absolutely crucial. The reader must really care about him/her. Plot development, in my view, comes very much after character, and is really only the stage for your character to show his true colours. If you are going to write a series you must have a character who you will want to stay with for many books.

4 Plan your work and work your plan. This adage from the business world is vital for writers. I have a chart which describes my books in terms of the main variables – time, geographical location, the stage in life of the main characters etc. Then for each book I follow this up with a very detailed plan.

5 Master the art of back story. A big challenge in writing a series is to produce each book so that a person new to your work can experience a satisfying read, picking up sufficient information of what has gone before to understand the flow and nuances of the text, while a fan of your earlier books is not bored by too much back story.

6 Develop an editor's eye. The other side of becoming a successful author is being a successful editor (a skill quite different from writing but just as important). One excellent piece of advice I was given was to put the manuscript aside for at least six weeks before starting on the edit.

The world of publishing is very challenging at the moment – but I would never discourage anyone who is serious about writing from giving it a go. And good luck! There is nothing like the thrill of seeing *your* book in the bookstores...

Julian Stockwin's latest novel *Victory*, which is the 10th in the Kydd series, was published in June, 2010.

www.julianstockwin.com

Andrew Taylor

On Writing Historical Fiction

In 1940, Robert Graves defined the role of historical novelist: 'All that readers of an historical novel can fairly ask from the author is an assurance that he has nowhere deliberately falsified geography, chronology, or character, and that the information contained in it is accurate enough to add without discount to their general stock of history.' This we should take for granted - a fundamental commitment to the historical facts as far as they are known or may reasonably be conjectured. There are authors who don't do this, of course - but they aren't writing historical novels; they write fantasy in fancy dress.

Gaps in the record are quite another matter: they offer fertile ground for the novelist's imagination. In her wonderful novel *The Blue Flower*, Penelope Fitzgerald quoted the dictum of Novalis, the German romantic poet, that novels are made from the shortcomings of history. Perhaps that should be the second guiding principle for the novelist - the willingness to use his or her imagination within the confines of the historical record. When I was researching *The American Boy*, I remember my excitement when I discovered that so little was known for certain about the boyhood of Edgar Allan Poe. It was a perfect subject for a historical novelist.

As a general rule, I look for ways to approach history from unexpected angles. That's what fiction can do so well - and, in the process, it throws a spotlight on the dark corners of the past while entertaining and absorbing its readers.

I don't like reading or writing historical novels that are populated with characters who are essentially modern in their beliefs, from feisty fifth-century feminists to noble sixteenth-century anti-fascists. I think the novelist should at least try to inhabit the psychological universe of his or her characters, to understand what their moral, religious, political and social universe was like. This can be tricky - there were plenty of decent people even fifty years ago whose beliefs about (for example) race, class and sexuality are nowadays beyond the pale. I can remember a schoolmaster who had a black labrador called Nigger. Nowadays he would lose his job for that and possibly face prosecution. Back then, nobody turned a hair.

If your novel is going to convince as history, you have to find a way to handle this convincingly. This isn't a question of condoning past attitudes of course. But as every good historical novelist knows, for a narrative to work, both as history or as a novel, you have to be true to your material. Authors like Alfred Duggan and Mary Renault, Patrick O'Brian and Manda

Scott, show how it can be done.

It's a tall order, however, especially since no amount of research, no amount of faithful verisimilitude, will make a good novel. Once you've assembled the materials, the real task begins. As Julian Rathbone once said: 'History is to me what imagery or verse form might be to a poet. It is the scaffolding within which the structure is built or, at best, the bricks and water which gives it form.'

Andrew Taylor is the winner of two CWA Ellis Peter Historical Daggers, and most recently in 2009 the CWA Cartier Diamond Dagger winner. He is the author of *The American Boy*. Andrew Taylor's latest novel is *The Anatomy of Ghosts* (Michael Joseph/Penguin) published in September 2010.

www.andrew-taylor.co.uk

E.V. Thompson

The Historical Novelist

When giving talks, one of the most frequent questions put to an established writer is "How can *I* become an author?" There is no definitive answer, but it is said that when a young man put the question to Ernest Hemingway, his reply was, "In order to write about life, first you must live it."

To the aspiring *Historical* novelist, such advice may at first glance seem unhelpful. He or she intends writing about the past and time travel remains the subject of Science Fiction. It is not possible to transport oneself back to the time the hopeful author wishes to portray and experience life as lived by the characters in his or her book ... or is it?

In order for fictional characters to fit easily into the settings in which the author has placed them, their creator must feel as familiar with their surroundings as they would have been. He or she should walk where they walk and, if possible, look at views they would have known and try to imagine what their feelings might have been.

The need to do this, to view hills and skylines, smell the mud of a river and marvel at the vastness of a vista, as they would have done has taken me to America, Canada, Australia, Africa, Asia and many other faraway places, as well as tracing the path of Wellington's army from Portugal, through Spain to France.

But it is not always necessary for the author to travel so far from home to discover his or her characters. Close to my own home on Cornwall's Bodmin Moor, among the ruins of long derelict engine-houses built by tin and copper miners in the early 19th century I discovered a fictional family who would become part of my life and be real to tens of thousands of readers in ensuing years.

Seated on the doorstep of what was no more now than a shell of a primitive dwelling-house, I looked out on a view the occupants must have seen every day of their penurious lives and thought about the men, women and children who lived, loved and died here. I wondered how many of their miner sons were buried in the parish churchyard where the average age of the young men laid to rest there was less than twenty-one years, and imagined their daughters, put to work on the mines as soon as they were strong enough to wield an ore-breaking hammer. There, on that lonely and evocative spot a family, for *me* a real life family, was born.

The historical novelist is perhaps fortunate in the choice of genre. So much of interest has happened in the world of the past that it is often possible to simply lift an historical event from the pages of time, insert the author's own fictional characters, and the success or failure of the novel will then depend upon the writer's skill and the credibility of the men and women conceived by his or her imagination.

This is one of the most important aspects of the author's craft, to create an empathy between the reader and characters in his or her novel, whether they are portrayed as living in the past, present or future. To express through them the loves; hates; fears; ambitions; joys; sorrows and all the other emotions *we* experience in our own lives. The emotions that people – *real* people – have felt throughout the ages.

If a prospective author can achieve this and imbue the novel with his or her own enduring love of history coupled with an irrepressible urge to write and a determination to succeed, they will have doubtless lived life a little along the way and taken a positive step on the path to success as an historical novelist.

www.littlebrown.co.uk
www.fantasticfiction.co.uk

Nicola Thorne

Writing historical fiction

1 You should have a passion for history, be prepared to do a lot of research and immerse yourself in the period you have chosen so that you feel and think as though you are actually living in it.

2 Don't attempt to write historical novels, or novels of any kind for that matter, unless you have a strong sense of imagination. A novelist must be like an actor playing a part, in this case several parts. I once researched a book so thoroughly in advance (*The Daughters of the House*) that I didn't know where to begin and

nearly abandoned it.

3   Choose a period that you feel at home in. For instance I would never attempt to write about pre-history, Greeks and Romans, the Dark Ages or the Renaissance even though this latter in particular is a period I love from the point of view of art. My earliest period is the 18th Century (*The Enchantress Saga - Bonnie Prince Charlie*) and I feel comfortable from then on. I also like mid to late 19th Century and the early years of the 20th (*The Askham Chronicles, The People of this Parish* and the *Broken Bough* sagas).

4   An interest and knowledge of social history, above all attitudes, is also important: class divisions, rich versus poor, the sort of thing Catherine Cookson did so well. Find out what people wore, what they ate and how they actually lived and considered normal, things that we now view as socially unacceptable even barbaric like the death penalty and the exploitation of children, who were sent up chimneys, could be and actually were hanged for sheep stealing. My researches into 19th Century Dorset resulted in *My Name is Martha Brown*, a time when public hanging was readily acceptable, so much so that people flocked to view the occasion. There are always of course people who rebel against the customs of the day, William Wilberforce (slavery), Elizabeth Fry, Mary Wollstonecraft and the Pankhursts (feminism and the treatment of women).

5   If you are writing about real places try and visit them so that you have some idea of the topography. I did a lot of research in West Dorset for the Martha Brown novel and the Lake District for *The Enchantress Saga*, the Scottish borders for *Where the Rivers Meet*. However this is where the imagination plays a part - obviously I was not actually present at the Battle of Omdurman (1898) but believe I have been quite accurate and convincing in the first book of the Askham Chronicles *Never Such Innocence* . This is where you have to research your sources thoroughly and if you are reasonably near London and can afford it join it the London Library in St James Square a wonderful, almost unique treasure trove of contemporary literature.

6   Times change and now you can get a lot of information on the internet which we didn't have when I wrote my early novels. It is very useful, but in a strange way some of the fun and adventure, as well as the hard slog has gone from researching history!

Nicola Thorne is the author of over 50 novels, which include contemporary fiction, historical and gothic. Her latest novel, *The Holly Tree,* published in July 2010 by Severn House, has a contemporary theme about the interaction of a group of adult students attending a watercolour class in the course of a year.   **www.nicolathorne.com**

Marilyn Todd

1   Enjoy your research - you never know where it may lead. A few years ago, I discovered that the Ancient Greeks staunched their shaving cuts with spiders' webs pickled in vinegar. This set me thinking. What sort of person collects these things? How do they go about it? Is it seasonal? In the end, I worked a whole novel round the Man Who Collects Spiders Webs.

2   Worried about flitting between eras? Take a tip from Sherlock Holmes. "In rapid succession, we passed through the fringe of fashionable London, hotel London, theatrical London, commercial London and finally maritime London, till we came to a riverside city of 100,000 souls, where the tenement houses swelter and reek with the outcasts of Europe." In other words, live it, feel it, love it, breathe it, no matter what the period or location.

3   The single, most important factor when bringing the past to the present is that the subject matter *must* relate to its 21st century readers. Whether it's crime, romance, a political thriller or a rip-roaring adventure, no story/novel will get off the ground unless it appeals to a modern audience.

The third High Priestess Iliona mystery *Still Waters* was published May 2010. Marilyn Todd will also be launching a new series shortly, set in the 50s, which features a female PI.

www.fantasticfiction.co.uk

Christine Trent

Writing about Special Interests Tip

Writing about something you know makes your job easy. Writing about something you love makes it *fun*.

Introducing a hobby or special interest of your own can add considerable depth and interest to your novel, as well as giving it a unique twist. It's easy to be excited about your hobby and want to give the reader as much information as possible up front. After all, it requires almost no research on your part, unlike the rest of your book. But, as with historical detail, this has the effect of overwhelming the reader and making him feel he is in the classroom receiving a lecture. Now, historical fiction readers will appreciate a certain amount of "learning," just because the genre is, simply put, a glimpse into so many fascinating eras. But there seems to be a cliff's edge that you cannot step over without your book being relegated to that of a textbook.

So how do you balance the information in your book so that you don't fall off the cliff? By taking a very sharp knife to everything you know and determining what are only the basics that you will eventually present to the reader. Then, you very, very slowly reveal those facts to the reader. Let the reader discover your hobby much as you did.

For example, let's say your character has a passion for breeding rare parrots. In one scene we might see her working with some newborn Yellow-headed Amazon nestlings. Later, she is clipping wings and trimming toenails on a Black Cockatoo as she chats with her best friend, who thinks the bird hobby borders on obsession and will end in the character's utter financial ruin. And after that, the character visits her solicitor in order to add one of her parents to her last will and testament. Just through the events of the character's life, the reader has learned that parrots need a lot of work, are valuable, and live a long time since they must be added to one's estate.

Or perhaps your character is a dealer in ancient coins who lives in 19th century America. Perhaps your character can let small pieces of information drop in various conversations. When talking with his wife, he mentions that he sold an Athenian silver tetradrachm from the 5th century B.C. for a high price. In a later conversation with a customer, he explains that he will be receiving a new shipment of coins from his contact in London. Now the reader knows that rare, ancient coins frequently came from London, and that even two centuries ago, an Athenian silver tetradrachm was considered quite valuable. Lots of information, no lecturing.

Christine Trent is author of *The Queen's Dollmaker*.

www.christinetrent.com

Jacqueline Winspear

Writers of historical fiction are also terrific researchers of their chosen era. However, the key is to remember that you are a storyteller first - all research is there to support your story. I always use the "iceberg" rule of thumb: only 7% of your research should be visible above the surface. The rest informs every word you write.

The Mapping of Love and Death is the latest in the Maisie Dobbs series.

www.jacquelinewinspear.com

Stephanie Grace Whitson

Researching Historical Fiction

A historical fiction author as obsessive about accuracy as I am can't feed, dress, or move her characters before she researches. She can't have them talk or think, either, because women in the 19th century did not eat what I eat, dress like I dress, or move through the world the way I do. They didn't think or talk the way I do, either. I begin with a blank slate.

That being said, the problems that people face are basic to humanity. People in every age worry about the meaning of life. They wonder how a loving God can 'let that happen.' They wonder about their own place in the universe and wonder what's worth dying for. So, while the 'big picture' for my characters doesn't vary all that much for this morning's news, everything else does.

How do I make sure I get it right? Well. . . I do my best, but I know that I make mistakes. I don't have a research partner and there is a limit to how much one lone researcher can learn before deadlines finally rear their heads and demand that I put words on the screen.

Research is the foundation of everything for me, and by "research" I mean reading primary documents from the era (as opposed to calling up Wikipedia, which is fraught with misinformation). I spend a great deal of time in historical archives reading primary documents (diaries, newspaper articles, letters) that are dated during the same time a given book is set.

For my new release *Sixteen Brides*, that meant that I travelled to Dawson County, Nebraska, where "the brides" lived, to read memoirs, diaries, letters, etc., at the county historical society.

Beyond primary documents, I go to other historians' research on a given topic--research that appears in things like historical society magazines or books housed in archival and/or university libraries. These books usually include bibliographies that can also provide a treasure trove of trustworthy resources.

I've found wonderful resources in book form at historical society book stores and museum gift shops, where they can carry very narrow-focused books that don't often make it to the general book market. For example, while I was researching *A Claim of Her Own* which takes place in Deadwood, SD, I found a published diary of an Illinois man who prospected in Deadwood in the 1870s on the shelf at the local university library. When preparing to write *Secrets on the Wind,* my Fort Robinson, Nebraska, series, I learned that the curator of the museum there had written a two-volume history of Fort Robinson published by a small press.

There are no shortcuts to doing research, but research is my favorite part of writing. There's always a new bunny trail I want to hop down. I love being surrounded by the stuff of the past. I've met some inspiring women reading diaries and letters. Some of them re-appear on the pages of my historical fiction. Others linger in the "idea" file just waiting to be called forth someday.

www.stephaniewhitson.com

Sally Zigmond

PERSISTENCE

Writing a novel is not for the faint-hearted. Once you start you have to accept that you're in for the long haul. Leaving aside the time it takes to learn the art and craft of writing, every novel worth its salt takes months, even years to write—and a historical novel brings the extra burden of research and then making sure that none of it looks like research. That's a task in itself.

If writing and editing isn't time-consuming enough, it's nothing compared with the process of pitching to agents and/or publishers. Unless you are very, very lucky or the best writer ever, you are going to receive more rejections than you ever thought possible. There's no point moaning about it, or feeling hurt or angry. The reality is that there are more manuscripts floating around the system than anyone would ever want to buy. Rejection is not personal. It's just a fact of life like flies in summer.

Sometimes, however, you have to accept that your manuscript doesn't quite cut the mustard (for many reasons, most not to do with your talent as a writer) and it's best to try again with something different. That's a whole different issue but one you should bear in mind, even as you parcel it up and send it out again. There's perseverance and then there's pig-headedness. Listen to what others tells you. Get some unbiased feedback from a professional—not your mother—and if that person tells you your manuscript is publishable, keep going.

Even when you secure a publisher, it can take a year or more before your duckling becomes a fully-fledged swan. Once you've got that publishing deal, that's when the editing really begins. There's structural editing, line-editing and finally, the copy-editing. This is time-consuming, frustrating and it's darned hard work.

There will be many times you want to pack it all in or choose the easy option and email your manuscript to the first person who says he can 'publish' your novel within a couple of months. This isn't the time or place to warn against the perils of vanity publishing but I would advise everyone to think long and hard because it will almost always end in disappointment, if not despair.

So, persistence is the watchword. Because, when—at long last—you hold your first published novel to your heart, it will be all the more precious.

Sally Zigmond is a member of the HNS, having been both a reviews editor and the co-ordinating editor of *The Historical Novels Review*. For several years she was the submissions editor for QWF magazine. Her short fiction has been published widely and won many competitions. Sally's first novel *Hope against Hope* (set in Victorian Yorkshire) is published by Myrmidon Books, April 2010. She is currently writing her second novel.

Sally blogs at **http://theelephantinthewritingroom.blogspot.com**

SECTION 6

Starting Writing

Chapter 20 – Starting Writing

At school we were taught that stories should have a beginning, a middle, and an end. We may have learnt that the opening of your short story needs to grab your reader's attention and that the end needs to be satisfactory. This doesn't mean that it needs to be happy, but that your main character or character's journey has come to a believable end.

The analogy between a novel or a story and an account of an individual or group's journey through part of, or their whole life may be a model that will help you. Why? This is because often an aspiring writer will take a lot of time writing both the first and last pages of their novel, but forget the middle. The middle of the story is the filling in the sandwich. It needs to be tempting and tasty and to satisfy the readers. In **Chapter 5** we looked at the importance of planning. You may have decided to write a detailed plan for each chapter or a brief and sketchy outline. What is important is the plan. Every journey usually involves a plan of some kind, whether it is checking out the bus or train times or mentally calculating how long it will take us to walk somewhere.

A beginning to capture the imagination of your reader

Your first line on the first page of your short story or novel can be the most terrifying step that you take, but what you need to keep firmly in your own mind is that everything you write you can also change. It can be daunting because you may be aware of comments you've read and heard that tell you the first page of your novel is likely to either entice a publisher or agent, to read on, or to return it to you unread. The same may be true for the first line or paragraph of a short story.

ACTIVITIES

20.1 Overcoming your fear

Objective   To understand through analysing the work of other writers that there are many effective ways of opening a novel or story, and to identify which type of opening appeals to you the most.

Your task   Pick three historical novels written by different authors and read only the first page. Make notes on how each of the novelists has opened their novel. First look at the first sentence and then the first paragraph and lastly the whole page. If you are interested in writing short stories just focus on the first sentence and the first paragraph. Decide if they've opened their story with action, setting the scene or introducing a character. Have they done this for example by using prose description or dialogue? When you've completed this task, ask yourself which opening you preferred and why.

20.2 Just Right?

Objectives To be aware that whatever you write, you may need to change, cut out, and rewrite to enable you to get it 'just right', or at least as near perfect as it possible.

To learn that changing, editing and altering what you have written is not negative, but a positive and vital part of writing.

To understand that you have a choice.

Your task

1 Write down ten possible opening sentences for your novel or short story.

2 Select five of these sentences and write a whole paragraph for each of them.

3 Pick three of these paragraphs and continue them so that you have written the first whole page of your novel c.500 words. Set yourself a time limit for this activity e.g. a maximum of half an hour for each first page. If you are writing a short story of c.1,500 words remember that this means you have already completed a third of your story.

4 At the end of each half hour count the number of words that you have written. This will provide you with a benchmark idea of how long it will take to write your novel e.g. If you've written 1,000 words in an hour and an average length novel is c.80,000 to 120,000 words then theoretically you could write a first draft of your novel in c.800 to 1,200 hours, which sounds a lot. In practical terms it means that if you wrote 2,000 words (c.2 hours' work) a week you could complete an 80,000 word novel in 40 weeks. This does not include research time or editing time.

However, it does explain how commercially successful authors can produce one novel a year. If you are keen on writing short stories then it should also prove that an hour of your time can produce a draft story of c.1,000 words. In order to test the theory I set myself the task of writing this guide book in as short a time as possible while working and as a sole parent and therefore running a household by myself. The research had already been done, but this book was started in January and completed in August 2010. I hasten to add that I had the advantage of wonderful friends with an excellent grasp of English who proof read as I wrote. They sent their hard copy corrections back to me, which I then edited. Why did I adopt this method? In order to demonstrate how it is possible for aspiring writers to fulfil their ambitions if they are prepared to find and sacrifice 'time' to do it. This method may not match your own personal way of working, but for some people it may help them to realise that writing a story or novel does not have to involve years and years of work, although it may do.

5   The next step involves a leap of faith. You need to pick one of your opening pages and write the first chapter. Having three beginnings does give you the advantage that if at the end of the first chapter you are unsure that you've chosen the right one, you can always write a different first chapter using one of your other openings as a starting point and then compare them to see which you are most comfortable with before you continue.

6   As you complete each day's writing some people find it beneficial to read their work aloud. This provides you with the opportunity to uncover such slips as changes in tense or even re-naming your characters by mistake. When you become absorbed in what you are writing these errors often creep in, as they will do if you are typing up something that you have written by hand. Other writers may prefer to finish each chapter before they re-read what they have written. The choice is yours.

20.3 Last lines first?

Objectives   To provide you with a signpost to lead you to the end of your novel or story.

To write the last lines or last paragraph of your novel or short story first, as a reminder that you don't have to worry about an ending as you've already got a selection to pick from.

Your task   Write five possible last paragraphs or sentences for your novel or short story. By doing this you have created five possible destinations for your characters and stories to arrive at. When you reach the end of your story none of the endings you've written may be appropriate, or you may have thought of a better one. However for some writers completing a task like this is rather like signing a contract. It commits them to finishing the story that they've embarked on, even if by the end of the journey it turns about to be very different from the one they'd originally planned.

No Excuses

Finding time to commit to writing isn't easy, but making excuses isn't valid. Sometimes we all suffer from a bout of flu, or we are swamped with personal problems or too much work, but that is life and if you want to be a 'professional writer' then you will have to work around these problems. You will also have to accept that in order to achieve any form of professional status as a writer you will have to a) stop making excuses, b) devise a plan to provide you with time, c) don't make 'other' people a scapegoat for not writing, and d) above all don't feel selfish or guilty for doing something you enjoy and want to do.

By finding the time to even read a tool kit like this you have shown the desire to write, and a willingness to learn and experiment. That has involved you finding time to do it. Some people will be able to steal minutes to write in their working day. Others will record their thoughts as they are cooking a meal for their family, to type-up at a later time. Many people prefer not to have a plan, but sometimes we all get sidetracked. The activity below is designed to remind you not to get sidetracked.

ACTIVITY

20.4 Excuses, Excuses, Excuses

Objectives To provide you with a list to remind you of the excuses that you might give yourself not to find the time to write and an 'antidote' to the excuses.

To create a list of at least 10 excuses that your characters might use for not being able to do something.

Your task Write as many excuses and antidotes as you can think of in the table below.

Excuse	Antidote
No milk had to go and buy some	One day without milk is good for your health.
Too many emails to answer from friends.	Reply with one line answers e.g. Really interesting! Working will be in contact soon. Thanks, Love. You can copy and paste these to all your friends.
Asked to work overtime	Tell them you can't as you have a previous professional appointment (you have with your writing).
Too many calls on your mobile	Switch it off for an hour.

Middle and cliffhangers

The middle of a novel can prove the most gruelling part for the aspiring writer. If you are writing a short story this isn't necessarily the case, because proportionally the middle won't be much longer than the beginning or the end. If you take the analogy* of a gourmet sandwich, then the beginning and the end are the bread that holds the story sandwich together. The middle should contain a delicious and satisfying filling. If it is a crime or thriller then the filling will contain a few surprising ingredients as well. The whole story sandwich should be so tasty and well made that the reader consumes it all including the crusts, which for the purpose of this comparison you might like to consider as the harrowing or emotionally challenging parts.

   Careful pre-planning of the outline and content of each chapter will help, but so too will changing the pace of your story (see **Chapter 10**), and the use of appropriate cliffhangers. When in doubt or in need of reassurance also read a novel that you are particularly fond of, and remind yourself of how the author keeps your interest from flagging in the middle.

*
   analogy: a comparison drawn to demonstrate or highlight a similarity between certain features.

ACTIVITIES

20.5 Making your novel interesting by using cliffhangers

What is a cliffhanger (cliff-hanger or cliff hanger)? The definition of a cliffhanger in dictionaries and glossaries will vary slightly, but it usually means a situation of suspense and imminent danger that is created at the end of the chapter of a novel, story or serial. However, cliff hangers can range from creating a sense of foreboding or a dilemma for one of your protagonists to leaving your character in physical danger. Today we tend to associate them with crime thrillers, or TV serials, but as a plot device they've been around for a very long time. The tales that Scheherazade told to save her life and that we know as *One Thousand and One Nights* are perhaps the most famous example. The concept may not be new, but the word cliffhanger is. It is thought to have become popular during the era of the silent movies when films were often shown serial-style and the heroine might be left hanging precariously from a cliff waiting to be rescued in the next episode. An alternative explanation of its origin is that when Thomas Hardy's novel *A Pair of Blue Eyes* was published in monthly serial form in *Tinsley's Magazine* between 1872 and 1873, Hardy decided to leave Henry Knight one of his main characters, hanging off a cliff and hence Hardy's Victorian melodramatic climax may be the origin of the word cliffhanger.

Objective   To practise writing cliffhangers.

Your task   Go back to the plan for your proposed novel or short story and re-read it. Go through each chapter and jot down an alternative ending for each chapter except the last one. Try to make the cliff-hangers at the end of each chapter bolder and more dramatic without becoming melodramatic. Then go back to the beginning of your plan and read it through. When you've read it through decide which type of cliff-hanger fits better with the theme and tone of your novel.

20.6 Perfecting the craft of writing cliffhangers

Objective   To gain more experience in the craft of writing cliffhangers.

Your task   Select three best-selling novelists of any genre, but include at least one historical novelist. Only read the last page of each chapter and note down how they finished each chapter and the first page of each chapter. Do they for instance end some chapters on a happy or optimistic note and then plunge their reader into turmoil and drama on the first page of the next chapter? Do they usually end their chapters at a nail-biting moment and take up the next chapter where they left off? Do they follow a pattern for their chapter endings or does it appear to be random? While you are analysing their work remember that writing is both an art and a craft. If you wanted to be an expert cabinet or furniture maker you might deconstruct the work of a master in your craft to see what glue they used and how they perfected their dovetail joints. Therefore in carrying out this type of activity you are putting yourself in the role of the craftsperson.

For those writers who are more interested in writing short stories, you will need to collect back issues of at least ten examples of the particular magazine that you are interested in targeting and focus on the middle paragraphs of the story to identify if they use mini-cliff hangers and what form these come in. Remember your aim isn't just to read the stories, but to take notes as you go along as well! These notes will provide you with your own personal guidelines for any short stories that you may write at a later date. They will provide you with what the French word *aide-mémoire* sums up perfectly. You will have notes that will help or aid your memory.

20.7 Satisfying Endings

Objective   To find an ending to your story that will satisfy your readers and that you will be pleased with as well.

Your task   Using the endings that you created above in Activity 20.3, transform at least two of your endings into the final three pages of your novel. Put these two different versions away in a file either hard copy or on your computer. Resist the temptation to look at them for two weeks. At the end of two weeks print out a hard copy. A hard copy version is required for this activity, because this is the way that the majority of books are still read and sold. Read the first ending and highlight all the parts you like. Do the same with the second ending. Re-write the chapter incorporating the parts that you like from both versions and then put this version in a safe place until you have reached your final chapter. Write your final chapter again. Then compare this with the version that you stored away. Go through both versions and highlight the parts of both of them that you feel are most in keeping with your novel. Then re-write your chapter combining the best elements of both. Please do bear in mind that with all the activities in this book this is a suggestion and isn't prescriptive.

20.8 Twist and Twist again

If you would like to write short stories and to have them published, today's market favours stories with twists, double and even triple twists. You can master this art if you practise. It's rather like learning to tie shoe laces, once you've practised it enough, it becomes automatic. Adèle Ramet's *Creating a Twist in the Tale*, published by *How to Books* is an excellent introduction to the art.

Objective   To experiment with writing twist and double twist

Your task   1   To use an historical short story that you have already written and add a twist to it in the last paragraph or final sentences.

2   To then add a second or double twist.

Model — Without a twist

Southern Cross

When *HMS Formidable* was torpedoed off Start Point on New Year's Day 1915 Rose's hopes sank with the battleship. Her fiancée Tom wasn't among the 199 who survived out of the ship's company of 750 men. Tom hadn't been handsome, but an ordinary young man who'd already been in the Navy for five years when she'd met him. He was only twenty when he became a casualty of the British Navy's first major loss since the outbreak of the war.

Rose hadn't been able to understand how Europe had become caught up in the war in the first place, but now she realised that nothing would ever be the same again. The smiling face that she'd met on the day trip up the Tamar from Plymouth to Calstock on the paddle steamer *Eleanor*, was gone. His legacy to her was contained in his letters full of optimism about their future, which increased her determination to help the survivors of the conflict every time she read them. Her grandmother had always encouraged her to read and apply herself to her lessons at school. Rose loved to dream, but also realized that work had to come before flights of fancy. Her diligence had enabled her to find work in the office of the laundry in Parkwood Road, Tavistock. Rose's childhood had been a happy one even without parents.

They had both died in Timins in Canada where her father was working as a miner, and Rose had no memory of them at all. The photograph of them on their wedding day told her nothing about her parents except that she could read the love for each other in their eyes. It was the same expression that she and Tom had shared. It was her grandmother who made Rose turn her desire to help into action.

"There is no point biding your time here Rose. You can wish all you want that Tom might come back, but wishing on stars didn't get anyone anywhere. I've been reading up on it and you could become a VAD, join a Voluntary Aid Detachment. It would mean you going to live in Exeter, but that is no real distance by train, and I'm sure we could find you lodgings. It's part of the British Red Cross Society or so it says in the newspapers. No doubt they'd be pleased to have you."

Rose's grandmother was right, they were delighted to accept her help, and she quickly mastered all the general nursing skills she was taught. Exeter was on the main railway to the ports of Plymouth and Portsmouth, and many soldiers from Australia, New Zealand and Canada passed through there. The wounded would arrive at Queen Street station and often blinded by gas, would walk in a long crocodile, holding on to the man in front, before being taken to one of the Devon and Exeter's group of twenty hospitals and sixteen convalescent homes. Rose was based at VA Hospital No.1. Sometimes she would pop into a small store in Magdalen Street, close to the hospital to buy sweets, and would find the shop packed with Australian soldiers enjoying a couple of hours away from their wards. They were dressed in the blue jackets and red ties issued to wounded troops, and would chat and occasionally start singing *Waltzing Matilda*. It made her wonder what they must be thinking so far away from their loved ones and country. She was also worried about what these wounded men of all ages would do when they returned home, having fought in a war that wasn't their concern.

Rose was working so hard that when her grandmother died peacefully in her sleep the blow was not as hard as it might have been. Though she was amazed that her grandmother had left her enough money not to have to worry about her future for the short term. When the war ended Rose intended to become a full time professional nurse. She had no reason to return to Tavistock. The house in College Avenue had been rented, and if her old school friend and neighbour Alice Roberts hadn't insisted that she went to her wedding, she wouldn't have gone back. Alice had served in the British Army. She had fallen in love with Stan Hammer from Southern Cross in Australia. He'd joined the 5th Pioneers Battalion in 1916 and fought in France. They were married in June 1918 at St. Eustachius, her old Parish church.

Rose spent a lot of time talking to Stan's best man McMahon. He was an Australian, but didn't intend to go straight home like Stan. He wanted to study business in London first, before going back to run his uncle's farm. Rose interrogated him ruthlessly, and discovered that Southern Cross had wide streets and that in the summer it was very hot and could be bitterly cold in the winter. "It's some 240 miles from Perth in Western Australia. It was planned well as a town with five wide streets. When it came to naming the roads, they took into consideration the fact that Southern Cross was discovered by taking directions from the constellation Antares. Southern Cross was even named after a constellation of stars and so the Main Street is called Orion, the cross street Antares, and the Salt Lake is named Polaris. It's an area rich in gold, but short on water. You might end up cooking your vegetables in your washing water or vice versa. In the early days you'd have been lucky to have a bucket of water a day for your whole family. You use mallee roots for fires in winter and believe me you need them. The 'Cross', as we know it, is only for the hardy," explained Stan's friend and added "Stan was the first baby boy of a pioneer family to be delivered in the 'Cross' in 1895 by Sarah Morris. We were lucky to have a nurse. There still aren't enough nurses who are willing to face a life in the Outback. Stan is lucky to have found a plucky girl like Alice to move back with him.

It was New Year's Eve 1922 and Rose stood outside Alice's home in the 'Cross'. The air was parched as if all the moisture had been sucked out of it. It was just before midnight. There would be no church bells to welcome in the coming year. Rose had qualified as a nurse and was on her way to take up her job as a sister in the hospital at Kalgoorlie further up the railway track. There were flies, dust in abundance, but at night for Rose it was as if you could reach up and pick a star from the sparkling sky above. When Tom had died in 1915 and then her grandmother, nothing except work had mattered, but seven years later she had a profession. Standing as pioneers had done before her, she welcomed the New World she was now a part of. Rose turned her face upward to look for the brightest star and wished that she might find the love that Alice shared with Stan.

Model — With a twist

It was New Year's Eve 1922 and Rose stood outside Alice's home in the 'Cross'. The air was parched as if all the moisture had been sucked out of it. It was just before midnight. There would be no church bells to welcome in the coming year. Rose had qualified as a nurse and was on her way to take up her job as a sister in the hospital at Kalgoorlie further up the railway track. There were flies, dust in abundance, but at night for Rose it was as if you could reach up and pick a star from the sparkling sky above. When Tom had died in 1915 and then her grandmother, nothing except work had mattered, but seven years later she had a profession. Standing as pioneers had done before her, she welcomed the New World she was now a part of. Rose turned her face upward to look for the brightest star and wished that she might find the love that Alice shared with Stan.

Tom couldn't believe he'd survived. He was home again. He stepped off the train and almost ran down the hill into Bedford Square. He hadn't let anyone in Tavistock know he was coming back. What would Rose think? Tom knew that he should have, but for a long time he hadn't been able to remember what had happened. There'd been an almighty explosion and then blank. It was only recently that fragments of his life had started to reassemble themselves. He reached College Avenue just as the bells started to ring out the old year. He could see the lights on in Rose's grandmother's house. He knocked several times loudly on the door and waited.

Model — With a double twist

It was New Year's Eve 1922 and Rose stood outside Alice's home in the 'Cross'. The air was parched as if all the moisture had been sucked out of it. It was just before midnight. There would be no church bells to welcome in the coming year. Rose had qualified as a nurse and was on her way to take up her job as a sister in the hospital at Kalgoorlie further up the railway track. There were flies, dust in abundance, but at night for Rose it was as if you could reach up and pick a star from the sparkling sky above. When Tom had died in 1915 and then her grandmother, nothing except work had mattered, but seven years later she had a profession. Standing as pioneers had done before her, she welcomed the New World she was now a part of. Rose turned her face upward to look for the brightest star and wished that she might find the love that Alice shared with Stan.

Tom couldn't believe he'd survived. He was home again. He stepped off the train and almost ran down the hill into Bedford Square. He hadn't let anyone in Tavistock know he was coming back. What would Rose think? Tom knew that he should have, but for a long time he hadn't been able to remember what had happened. There'd been an almighty explosion and then blank. It was only recently that fragments of his life had started to reassemble themselves. He reached College Avenue just as the bells started to ring out the old year. He could see the lights on in Rose's grandmother's house. He knocked several times loudly on the door and waited. The door opened.

"Who is it, John?"

"I don't know Amy. It must have been one of the children from down the road. Drat them! I can see that it may be almost a new year, but some things aren't going to change are they?" John closed the door and was followed in by a pale grey shadow.

Your turn

    a) Without a twist

    b) With a twist

    c) With a double twist

20.9 Title, title, title

Objective   To find a title that will catch the eye of an agent, publisher, your reader and that you think encapsulates the essence of the story that you've written.

Your task

1   Write down the working title that you already have for your novel or story.

2   Set your alarm clock or your mobile to ring after three minutes. Try not to think and just write down at least five possible titles for your work. Don't cheat!

3   Re-set your clock or mobile for a further three minutes and write another six.

4   After you have written the first chapter of your novel or completed your story read it aloud and highlight any phrases that you think might make a possible title.

5   Compile a list of all the titles and print out 11 copies. On one of the copies circle your favourite title.

6   Road test your titles. Ask ten people who you know read novels (at work, baby and toddler group, library or wherever you find them) to circle the title that they think might be suitable for a historical novel on the theme of (add your chosen theme or genre e.g. historical fantasy fiction) and the period it is set in. Don't tell them the plot, because you want them to buy your novel or read your story when it appears.

7   Check the bookshops, your local library or do an on-line search to see if there are any other novels with a similar title (this isn't necessary for short stories), but it might be if your novel title is the same as someone else's even if it is in a different genre.

8   Compare your choice of title with the ones that your market research group selected and then select one as a working title.

Tip

Michael Jecks
"My own crucial piece of advice is: if you want to write, there is no substitute whatever for actually sitting down and writing. All the software, all the descriptions of faces, all the carefully considered plot-twists and red herrings, will achieve precisely bugger-all, without their being set down in the correct sequence on paper."
See also: **flickr.com/photos/Michael Jecks**
www.michaeljecks.co.uk

SECTION 7

Mixing all your ingredients together to produce a mouth-watering piece of historical fiction

Chapter 21 – Finishing Touches

Once you've mixed all your ingredients together and written your short story or novel you should be filled with a sense of elation, but a first draft is only that, and the next stage of the writing process requires more stamina and determination. It would be lovely to think that once you'd completed the last sentence on the final page that was it, and that you could then send it off to an agent who would find a publisher, and you'd become an overnight best seller. However, the reality is that even before you send it off to anyone there are certain stages that you will need to go through, and the first of these is editing your own work.

Editing

(Some of these suggestions have already been mentioned in **Chapter 13**).

Books have been written about editing and professional courses in editing are run by specialists in the field such as the Publishing Training Centre (**www.train4publishing.co.uk**). The activities below have been designed to introduce you to certain practices, which will help you to self-edit.

ACTIVITIES

21.1 Reading aloud

When you begin to edit one starting point is to read your work aloud. Often you will find that if there is an error in a text that you will hesitate or have difficulty reading the word, phrase or sentence without stumbling. The extract from the story below has been changed to incorporate a range of different types of mistakes. Your Obedient Son was originally published in October 2009 in *The West Devon Diary*.

Objective To read the extract of the story aloud and highlight any mistakes that you can identify e.g. grammar, spelling, punctuation etc. When you have read it aloud check the published version below. Even if you already have excellent proof reading skills it is still a useful exercise to carry out from time to time with your own work, as it will also provide you with an opportunity to check if your work flows, if the pace is as you intended it to be, and if it 'sounds' as you intended it to. It will also help you to indentify if your sentences are too long and cumbersome.

The extract as it was published is to be found at the end of this activity.

Your task Read the extract aloud and highlight any errors that you find.

Historical notes: The USA declared War on Britain in 1812. Britain had been impressing sailors from US ships and blockading them during the Napoleonic Wars. The USA also had deeper concerns, as it feared that Britain was attempting to colonise the North West.

The War ended with the treaty of Ghent in 1815. At one point during the conflict 9,000 American and French prisoners of war were being held at Dartmoor Depot (now known as Princetown Prison). There were also 1,500 soldiers, officers and turnkeys guarding them.

The Americans' accounts of their stay at Dartmoor Depot are both detailed and vivid. The story below is based on some of the details described in these poignant letters.

27th of May, 1815

Honoured Parents,

I have the pleasure to inform you that my time on Dartmoor is at a end and I will be returning on the brig *Albert of Portland*. Through Gods good grace I remain in good healths and pray that you, my wife Betsy and our child are in an similar state.

When on the 2nd of April 1813 I marched with men of Marblehead, from the *Spitfire,* the 18 miles from Plymouth, we were already in low spirit. We knew not what lay ahead of us, but rumours had reached us that Plymouth's prison hulk's were paradise compared to the teaming No.4 prison we was to be sent to. 'Les Capitole', as the French named No. 4 prison, already helds Frenchmen of the most brutish kind.

Text as published: Your Obedient Son

(http://content.yudu.com/Library/A1gr5v/WestDevonDiaryOct09/
resources/14.htm)

27th of May, 1815

Honoured Parents,

I have the pleasure to inform you that my time on Dartmoor is
at an end and I will be returning on the brig *Albert of Portland*.
Through God's good grace I remain in good health and pray
that you, my wife Betsy and our child are in a similar state.

When on the 2nd of April 1813 I marched with the men of
Marblehead, from the *Spitfire,* the 18 miles from Plymouth,
we were already in low spirits. We knew not what lay ahead
of us, but rumours had reached us that Plymouth's prison
hulks were paradise compared to the teaming No.4 prison we
were to be sent to. 'Les Capitole', as the French named No. 4
prison, already held Frenchmen of the most brutish kind.

21.2 Adverbs versus verbs

Objective   To reduce your word count, and tighten up your sentences
          by replacing adverbs with stronger verbs.

Your task   Go through your story or novel and highlight any places
          where you might be able to edit out adverbs, and replace
          them with verbs that are similar in meaning and that add
          extra depth to your descriptions.

Examples

He ran quickly...
She cried loudly...

Depending on the context they could be changed to:

He rushed... He dashed... He charged...
She sobbed... She wailed... She howled...

21.3 Adjectives

Objective   Adjectives[*] are often an easy way to 'tell' your reader how a place or person looks. Your task is to select examples from your writing and transform them so that you are showing and not telling your reader.

> * **Adjective**: a word which alters or modifies a noun by qualifying (adding to) a characteristic (quality, state or action) of it

Your task   To select a few adjectives that you've used to describe people and places, and try to rewrite them.

Example

Her dress was beautiful, but not as pretty as she was.

Depending on the context they could be changed to:

The heavy midnight blue velvet that her dress was made from fitted every curve of her body. The silver sequins and bugle beads glittered in candlelight and her eyes sparkled with merriment. All eyes were drawn towards her...

21.4 Replacing adjectives with nouns

If you need to reduce your overall word count another simple way is to use more specific nouns to replace long descriptions with a more precise and detailed picture.

Objective   To reduce your overall word count and to tighten up your descriptions.

Your task   To go through your work and check to see if you can replace any general nouns e.g. dog, man etc. with more specific nouns that will enable you to sharpen up your descriptions and cut out words.

Examples

A small brown bird darted in and out...
A fierce guard dog was tied up outside...

Depending on the context they could be changed to:

A wren darted in and out...
An Alsatian was tied up outside...

N.B. By using 'specific' rather than general nouns you can also help to create a sense of atmosphere and place.

21.5 Agreement of verb and subject

(This point of grammar has already been mentioned In **Chapter 13**.) When you check through your work this is one of the commonest slips that writers make. It is also often hard to identify because it means that you have to be able to identify the difference between plural subjects and singular subjects. Unfortunately, 'plural subjects' may or may not have an 's' at the end to identify them. This is where you need to make certain that you have a grammar book somewhere nearby so that you refer to it when you need to. There are at least nine different rules for this particular construction.

Objective	To read through your story or novel and pay particular attention to this common error.
Your task	To find and change any sentences where the agreement between verb and subject isn't correct.

Common Example

Anything, anybody, each, either, nobody, nothing, one, someone, something are examples of 'indefinite pronouns' which can be used as 'subjects'. Singular 'indefinite pronouns' will take singular verbs e.g.

Correct: Everyone wants to write a bestseller.

Incorrect: Everyone want to write a best seller.

21.6 Apostrophes

When thinking, writing and typing at the same time it is very easy to let unwanted apostrophes creep in. These will not necessarily show up when you run a spell check.

Objective	To focus on the apostrophes that you've used and to make certain that you haven't mistakenly used them for plurals rather than to demonstrate possession.
Your task	To go through your work and just focus on any plural forms that you've used to make certain that you haven't used apostrophes when they aren't needed.

Example

Incorrect: To go through your work and just focus on any plural forms that you've used to make certain that you haven't used **apostrophe's** when they aren't needed.

> **Correct:** To go through your work and just focus on any plural forms that you've used to make certain that you haven't used **apostrophes** when they aren't needed.

21.7 Reorganise your sentences

Jonathan Coe, Bohumil Hrabal, Victor Hugo and Marcel Proust have all been singled out as examples of the longest sentence writers in literature. If you'd like to achieve a similar accolade then that is your decision, but most readers today prefer much shorter sentences. Shorter sentences do not mean that they are less effective or powerful. They can convey as much information and have a powerful impact on the reader. Complex sentences can sometimes be difficult to follow and may result in your reader losing track of your plot.

Objective To ensure that you don't become a contender for the author of the world's longest sentence.

Your task To find a sentence that you have written that is more than 20 words long and try to reorganise it so that you lose about 25% of the words. Try not to change the meaning of your sentence, but make it into several shorter ones if appropriate.

> **Example**
>
> Augustus wasn't in any hurry as it was a sunny, golden autumn day and the moors were still and tranquil, even his horse's hoofs were barely audible and in his heart Augustus was content but hot, as he'd worn his thick coat as he'd expected it to be windy and cold. (51 words)
>
> **Depending on the context this could be changed to:**
>
> Augustus wasn't in any hurry as it was a golden autumn day. The moors were still and tranquil, even his horse's hoofs were barely audible. He was too hot in his thick coat, but in his heart he was content. (40 words)

21.8 Deconstruct and reconstruct

Objective To transform editing into a game

Your task To take a sentence or cluster of sentences you are not satisfied with, and write every word on a separate piece of paper, then lay them out in order. Try to remove words from your sentences to see if they are necessary or not. The next stage is to focus on verbs that you've used. On scraps of paper write all the similar verbs that you might be able to use, and then swap then from the verb you'd originally written (see below). Finally you can select any descriptive words or phrases that you aren't certain about and write similar words and phrases on slips of paper and then try replacing them with the one that you had already (see below).

Example

Verb: hide

Other possibilities depending on the context: obscure, cover up, conceal, disguise...

Descriptive word or phrase: big

Other possibilities depending on the context: huge, large, massive, sizable, big as an elephant, gigantic, enormous, titanic, colossal, immense, vast, whopping, enlarged, larger-than-life...

Tip: Any hard copy or on-line will thesaurus be able to help you build up a list of synonyms (similar words or phrases).

21.9 Proofreading: re-check and edit again

Objective Once you've checked your work, find at least one other person to check it.

Your task Find a proofreader

Tip: Once you've edited your work, if possible get someone else to check it from a technical perspective see **Chapter 14** in the section headed **Pay someone to check your work.**

Track Record

It is not necessarily essential, but it does help to build up a track record of work that you've already had published, if you are aiming at finding an agent or a mainstream publisher. It demonstrates a determination and commitment to be published, and provides an agent with an indication that your writing is of a standard that is considered publishable.

When compiling your track record do remember to include any non-fiction articles that you have had published as well. Don't forget to keep a dedicated list of your successes and when and where they were published. Then you can just add to the list whenever you publish anything. This both saves you time and acts as a positive reminder that you are making progress.

Suggestions:

A You might feel comfortable with starting small and working upwards: Write letters and send them off to local newspapers, national newspapers and magazines. Why? It won't use up much of your 'precious' writing time and there is nothing like seeing your own letter or article in print (hard copy) or on the web, to give your main writing project or ambitions a boost. It helps to affirm that you can do it and that your writing is worthy of publication. It also gives you experience of writing in a different style for different purposes. In addition it will help you to build up a list of possible contacts to send a press release to when your novel is published, or your short story appears in an anthology.

B If you are finding it challenging to find anyone to accept your fiction, then you might like to try writing a non-fiction article about a local site, and offer it to your local newspaper or a community or parish magazine. You may be able to turn it into a series of articles or even a regular column. Remember that being paid is a bonus, your objective is to build up a track record and to get your name known. Then when you are published you already have a pool of people locally who may buy your novel, or who will enjoy reading your short stories.

ACTIVITY

21.10 Get something published

Getting anything published anywhere is a great confidence booster. It demonstrates that it is possible to get work published.

Objective To get something published

Your task To decide if you would like to write a letter or an article and which newspaper or publication you are going to write it for. It is unlikely that this will have anything to do with the historical novel that you are planning. It could be as simple as writing a letter to a local newspaper to praise everyone who took part in a local carnival. Alternatively, it could be writing an article for a local newspaper or history society about some particular aspect of the period that you are interested in writing historical fiction about, and which relates to your area e.g. an important building or geographical landmark. Before you write the letter, or the article you would benefit from:

- Reading the word count of the average letter in the magazine or paper you intend to send it to. Make certain that the letter you send is not longer than the longest letter. Try to work out what style of letter they are looking for. Are the letters 'formal' or 'informal' are they serious, chatty or funny and are they anecdotal? Do remember to put your address and contact details.

- Check that they accept unsolicited material before you submit it. You could email them or send them a letter. If you telephone them write down what you want to ask and don't waffle. If you are nervous about telephoning people remember that they can't see your face and so you can just read the questions that you've written. Time is precious to everyone so be polite and professional. Don't forget that you will also need to establish a word count, ask if they would like photographs to go with the article and if they have a preferred house style e.g. double spacing, Times New Roman (font) etc. It is also essential that you read some of the articles that are usually published to make certain that you adapt your style to fit that of the publication.

* Many publications today will accept emailed submissions for letters and articles, but if you are sending an article by post do include a self-addressed envelope, so that they can send it back to you if they decide that it isn't suitable for their publication. Small specialist magazines do not often pay for articles and neither does on-line publication. If you are paid do keep the details of the money that you receive as you may need to declare it for tax purposes.

* Make and sell your own short story cards to local museums and visitors' attractions. Use a digital camera to take a photograph of the place that you describe in your story. Buy some thin cardboard, envelopes and plastic pockets and make them yourself. Don't forget to add in a box or space where the person who is sending the card can write their message.

Entering Competitions

Carole Baldock

"Why bother entering writing contests – isn't submitting work to magazines enough of a competition as it is? But just imagine: that amazing moment when you win a prize, and how many doors could open when it's a prestigious award.

And no entrant loses out because that alone encourages motivation, organisation and inspiration. There again, as editor of *Kudos* (formerly *Competitions Bulletin*), I would say that..."

www.kudoswritingcompetitions.com

Tip

For other writing competitions do check out **www.Prizemagic.co.uk**

Writing for magazines

Dr. Ann Pulsford

"Short stories based on local history can be a rewarding way to begin to get your writing published and build a portfolio of published work. Most regions publish free community magazines and are usually looking for interesting writing based on the local area. The *Margins* magazine was started in Tavistock (Devon. U.K.) in 2006 by local writers' groups to give an opportunity for local writers to see their work in print and more recently online: **http://www.dartmoorcam.co.uk/margins/margins.htm**

It was inspired by the beautiful moorland landscape of Dartmoor and the fascinating history of its small towns and villages. The moorland is also rich in archaeological remnants of past settlements from the Bronze Age to the nineteenth century industrial mining heritage. This rich landscape has been the inspiration for many stories and poems and articles, one of the most internationally famous being Dr Arthur Conan Doyle's *Hound of the Baskervilles*. Dartmoor also inspires photographers to record its mysterious and constantly changing panorama. These photographs embrace the spirit of the area and complement the atmosphere of the stories and poems published in the high quality *Margins* print and online magazine."

Dr Ann Pulsford is editor of *Margins* magazine
http://www.dartmoorcam.co.uk/margins/margins.htm

Getting published or self-publishing

Finding the right agent or publisher to send it to

First of all you will need to draw up a list of agents who might possibly consider the novel or collection of short stories that you wish to submit. You can do this by:

A   Making a list that you've compiled from *The Writers' and Artists' Yearbook* or *The Children's Writers' and Artist's Yearbook* **www.writersandartists.co.uk**, *The Writers' Handbook* **www.thewritershandbook.com** or a site such as **www.writersservices.com**, which lists agents and publishers in many different countries and is an excellent free resource. Other sites that may provide you with useful hints and suggestions are: **www.bookmarket.com** and **www.publishingcentral.com**. You will then need to check that the agents and publishers that you've listed are still accepting submissions, by emailing or writing to them. Alternatively, if you are feeling brave you could call them, but if you decide on this route you would benefit from making a list of brief questions that you would like to ask. Don't be tempted to launch into a long description of what your novel is about, because you need to remember that anyone you are speaking to is almost certainly overwhelmed with work and just hasn't got the time to engage in long discussions. They, like their authors, are professionals and have to work to strict deadlines.

You might like to approach your call in the following way:

Good morning, I wonder if you can help me? I'm trying to find out if you are still accepting submissions and what your requirements are?

Other questions you might want to ask are:

Do you accept (romantic/ crime/ naval/ Regency/ military/alternative history/historical fantasy/timeslip) historical fiction (novel/story collection) submissions?

What would you like me to send (e.g. the first chapter, a synopsis, an author profile etc.)?

Do you accept emailed submissions?

How many new authors do you take on every year?

I understand that you don't specialise in X type of historical fiction. Could you possibly suggest another (agent/publisher) who does?

When you finish your call do remember to thank them very much for their help and time. It is only a matter of courtesy, but also you never know if the person that you are speaking to will be the person who reads your submission!

B Research who is the agent for professional writers who are writing in a similar genre to that of your novel. You can often do this by checking out their web sites or by keying in your tool bar a question such as: *Literary Agents for (name of author).*

The market for short fiction

Finding agents for novels is a challenging task, but for short stories even if you have a collection of them, it will be even harder particularly in the UK where the genre is less popular than in the USA for example. Publishing is a business and publishers want a return on their investment, and short stories do not make big money. However, if you trawl through the internet you will find a variety of ways to publish on-line. In your tool bar key in a specific request for information such as: Publishing opportunities on-line for short fiction, and then try a different question such as sites that publish *historical short fiction on-line and you'll discover that you come up with different possibilities.* Vary the request that you put in the tool bar to uncover the possibilities, but do beware of any site that asks you for money.

It is not very likely that you will be paid for an on-line contribution, but you shouldn't have to pay, that is vanity publishing.

Writing a covering letter

Keep it businesslike and short, but include the essential details such as the word count, theme, genre, the target audience that you've written for and why you think that it will appeal to them. You will also need to give a few enticing details about who you are and your 'passion' for writing. Above all you need to sound enthusiastic about your story or novel. If you aren't it is highly unlikely that others will be.

Your profile

Write your profile or author biography as if it was a story; a very short story. Your aim once again is to catch the attention of the reader.

Presentation

Make certain when you are sending a hardcopy to an agent or publisher of magazines that you have checked everything including the presentation and your synopsis before you send it, and that you've included a self-addressed envelope and a stamped addressed postcard with your name and address on it so that you will know it has been received.

Waiting

While you are waiting for a reply to your submission start work on your next writing project and continue to research paying markets for short stories etc. through sites like: **www.writerswrite.net**

Self publishing:

If you have made the effort to research and write a novel then you are aspiring to see it published too. Your novel may have been rejected by publishers and agents, because they consider that it won't have a wide enough appeal to make it profitable for them to publish. For instance you may have set your novel in a country and time that they do not consider to have a readership for at the moment. However your novel may not technically be up to the level they require, or it may have too many characters, lack suspense or be repetitive. If this is the case then you may fall prey to 'vanity publishers' who like 'cowboy builders' will make you all sorts of promises that they don't fulfil. Before you invest money in self-publishing do invest some money in having it read and critiqued by professional editors. It may cost you several hundred pounds or dollars, but not the thousands which self-publishing your novel will do. Contact a reputable body such as **www.societyofauthors.org** or **www.sfep.org.uk** and ask them by email if they have any recommendations or suggestions as to whom to contact.

E-publishing

The way forward? Whatever one's opinion as a writer is about e-publishing and print on demand it has a market which is rapidly increasing. Keep an eye on what is happening by checking out **www.thebookseller.com** or **www.bellaonline.com**

Getting technical!

In order to see your novel privately published you will need to master certain technical skills, but there is a lot of free advice and help out there if you are prepared to invest time in research using the internet e.g. **www.ehow.com /list_6699710_self-publishing-tips-authors.html** and **www.selfpublishingmagazine.co.uk**

Marketing and selling your own publication

Don't expect your novel or collection of stories to sell itself, it won't. You will need to send press releases and market your work in as many different ways as possible. Below is a list of free and low-cost ways in which you can promote yourself and your work:

- Contact your local newspapers, magazines, radio and television stations and offer a copy or copies of your novel as reader giveaways.
- Contact all local and regional magazines and offer to write a free feature article for them on a theme that will tie-in with their publication.

- Contact any national magazine that has even the slightest connection with the theme that you are writing about.
- Contact any national arts programmes on radio and TV and ask them if they'd like a copy of your novel or story.
- Offer copies to newspaper and magazines to review. Don't send them without asking as review copies are precious particularly if you have to pay for them yourself.
- Organise an event in conjunction with your local library, bookshop, book festival or arts centre. Don't expect to be paid!
- Give a talk for a charity and offer a couple of books as raffle prizes.
- Offer yourself as a speaker for book groups, associations, colleges, writers groups, local history societies etc.
- Print some post cards or bookmarks and ask your friends to distribute them to their local libraries etc.
- Print a quote from your work onto a serviette or beer mat and offer them to local arts centre and appropriate restaurants, cafés or hotels to distribute.
- Have a few T shirts printed with the details of your novel etc. that you can wear when promoting your work, but also so that you can run a prize draw via your own web site or at events.
- Send press releases to any relevant site on the web that reviews books and ask them if they'd like to review your work.
- Organise a launch event, and invite everyone that you know including local dignitaries and VIPS in your area. They may not accept your invitation, but at least they will recognise your name. Make it a real 'fun' event e.g. ask everyone to dress in a costume, or a hat appropriate to the period that your novel or collection of stories is set in. Offer a prize for the best costume.
- Make your own posters and put them up in any local shops that you can find. Send posters to your friends in other places, and ask them to take them along to their local bookshops and libraries.
- Create a mailing list to send out press releases to, but do remember that you must adhere to the data protection act. For those based in the UK check out: **www.businesslink.gov.uk** for details.
- Volunteer as a judge for writing competitions, offer to review novels etc.
- Be charming and always remember to say thank you to anyone who helps you in any way.
- If money isn't a problem for you, you might consider paying to enrol on an MA course in some aspect of creative writing, because as one student remarked it was "a sound financial investment as it

provided the opportunity to meet agents and publishers, which you wouldn't normally be able to do."

* Join a professional association and promote your novel through their network of members and contacts e.g.
www.swwj.co.uk (The Society of Women Writers and Journalists)
www.asja.org (The American Society of Journalists and Authors),
www.asauthors.org (Australian Society of Authors),
www.canauthors.org (Canadian Writers Association),
www.writers.asn.au (The Fellowship of Australian Writers),
www.authors.org.nz (The New Zealand Society of Authors),
www.internationalpen.org.uk,
www.westcountrywriters.com

Tip: To market yourself and your work you will also need to research who is the best person to send a press release to. It is often more effective to send a press release to a contact name rather than a general mail shot style press release.

Your press release:

* Try to keep it short and intriguing. Think of what you are writing as being a mini-story that will entice your reader (in this case the newspaper, radio or TV reporter) to want to find out more e.g. it may be that your story is set in the place where the newspaper is published, or for local radio, that you were born in the area. It might be that your own personal background is of interest e.g. "Roughneck* historical novelist. X is no longer drilling for oil, but for facts instead."
* Remember not to use 'I' (the first person) in your press releases, but 'he' or 'she' (third person). It will make it sound more professional to the reader. The exception to this might be for your local paper or local radio station.
* Make certain that you have a high resolution photograph of yourself ready to email to them if they ask.

* **Roughneck:** Worker on a drilling rig.

Tip: Another route, which several current creative writing MA students have suggested is to enrol on an MA course for the sole reason of getting your work considered by a professional editor. If you can afford to pay for an MA course in creative writing that offers the option of being mentored by an editor with an established publishing house, and if you are prepared to undertake the work then you might decide to take this route.

Chapter 21

Coping with rejections

Jane Jackson

"How to deal with having your work rejected

Read the title carefully. See what it says? How do deal with *your work* being rejected. And that is the first point I want to make. (Obviously we are talking here about standard rejection slips – the kind that tell you nothing.) What you need to remember is that it is not *you*, the person, who is being rejected. With luck it is not you, the writer, who is being rejected. It is simply that particular submission.

There may be any number of reasons why it was turned down. (I'm assuming here that you presented it professionally – 12 point font, double spacing, wide margins, a header giving the initials of the title/your initials/chapter number/page number in the right hand corner of every page, the pages clean and held together by two rubber bands. Of course you did.)

So reasons it came back to you:

1 The agent is already handling an author who writes the same kind of story you submitted.

2 The publisher has a similar story in production or recently published.

3 You sent it to an agent or publisher who doesn't handle that genre (You wouldn't do that, would you? You'd check on-line or in the *Writers & Artists Handbook* first. Of course you would/did.)

4 The opening pages just didn't grab *and hold* the reader's attention. Editors and agents are incredibly busy people. They have to wade through scores of submissions every week, and those don't include work from authors already on their client lists. If it doesn't grab catch their attention on the first page and force them to turn over, then sadly, it's likely to be set aside for return.

5 It's simply not up to the high standard publishers can afford to demand because of the astronomical number of submissions they receive.

What to do next?

1 Have a little weep, chew the carpet, go for a long walk and imagine scenarios in which you can punish the so-and-so's

who have chucked a year's work back at you without so much as a word of explanation. Then make a cup of tea, pull yourself together, and decide that they made a mistake, and you're going to prove it with your next book. (See No.3)

2 If you are sure your first book really is as good as you can make it, then type out a fresh title page and send it out again. Meanwhile start work on your next. (No publisher wants a one-book author. They rarely make any money on an author's first book, and need to know you can/will produce a book a year, proving their investment in you was justified.)

3 Think about what you've learned from writing the first book and vow to make this next one better, stronger, more gripping; one that fits the genre it is aimed at, with characters who leap off the page and a plot that grows out of who the characters are and what they want, not one imposed on them.

You've taken a knock. But that's life, and it's rarely fair. A real writer, a professional writer, acts as No 1 above (plus possibly indulging in a glass or two of something alcoholic) then takes a deep breath, welcomes the slow burn of excitement that warns of a new story taking shape, and gets back to work. That's what writers do – they write. So go for it. Who knows, maybe *this* time?"

Nine of Jane Jackson's novels are currently available including *Heart of Stone* (Severn House, 2009), *Bonded Heart, The Chain Garden, Dangerous Waters, Tides of Fortune* and *Eyes of the Wind*.

www.janejackson.net

What next?

Write

Write whenever and wherever you can.

Read

Read fiction and non-fiction books about the period that you are interested in writing about.

Read books about the craft of writing.

There are so many excellent books on how to write, that it would be unfair to single out any from the most recent ones that have appeared on the market. Each takes a different approach and all of them will teach you something about the craft of writing, even if you decide not to apply what you have learnt. A few of the authors whose books on how to write changed the traditional approach to writing include Natalie Goldberg, Julia Cameron and Dorothea Brande's *Becoming a Writer*. This thin book was first published the USA in 1934. It is a 'classic' of the 'how to write fiction' genre.

Visit

Visit museums, battlefields, historic sites and houses, anything and anyplace that will add extra detail and depth to your writing.

Look

Look at the sky and observe how it changes with the weather. Observe what characterises the change of the seasons and above all study people to see how they interact with each other.

Listen

Listen to everyday conversations to help you with your dialogue or to uncover new ideas for plots or details to enrich your stories with.

Listen to experts talking about the period of history that you are interested in.

Watch

Watch out for articles in newspapers about the topics you are interested in.

Watch people to discover new characters for your novels.

Taste

Taste the food and drinks that were common in the period that you are writing about, but this doesn't mean taking it to the extreme of drinking untreated water to test the effect that it has on you!

Meet fellow aspiring writers and go on workshops

Some writers prefer not to meet with other aspiring writers while others like the feeling of community and exchanging ideas that comes with joining a writing group or attending a workshop. The decision is a personal one, but do try to go on at least one workshop just to see if it is for you or not. Libraries in the UK are excellent at offering free taster workshops if you are worried about the cost.

Beware of the hidden danger of PERFECTIONISM

Any writer who is serious about their craft will try to make whatever they write for publication as near-perfect a possible. However, just as this guide and tool-kit will not be perfect however many times it is checked and re-read, so too whatever you write can never be 'perfect'. If you are satisfied with it and so are the majority of your readers then that is 'as good as it gets'! Don't berate yourself if someone discovers that you've used a comma instead of a semi-colon. Some people enjoy finding mistakes and errors, but don't let this diminish your own sense of achievement.

To conclude:

Remember that this is a basic guide and tool-kit intended to provide you with concrete activities and suggestions. Consider it as a 'starter pack' to get you going.

Authors' definitions of what writing about 'the past' and 'historical fiction' mean will diverge, but what unites them is that they are chronicling a way of life that was significantly different from ours today. Although the problems and challenges that the people faced were similar to ours, their attitudes to them and ways of tackling them will have been different. Their hopes and aspirations such as good health, financial security, love and peace appear to have been similar to ours, but we can't be certain.

What makes writing about the past such a fertile source of inspiration for writers, is that except through diaries, literature and plays of the period we don't know what their lives were like or what they thought about their lives. Even the visual sources that are available such as maps, paintings, portraits and photographs are not necessarily 'true' representations. We know from history how easily visual and written records can be used to present the point of view of a ruling regime.

Writing about the past is like writing about space: you are stepping into the unknown. The dates of events are the stars that help to position us, but what we discover as we navigate around the past is an adventure for both writers and readers. Historical fiction should entertain its creators and its readers, but it should also provide a vehicle for the reader to escape the uncertainty and fear that surrounds the lives of so many people globally. It can also act as a glimmer of hope for the future by reassuring the writer and the reader that individuals and countries alike have suffered some cataclysmic events in the past, and still survived!

Whatever your reason for wanting to write historical fiction, the process shouldn't just be a hard slog. It should be fun and creative. Above all the process of writing should be a satisfying experience and a journey that you enjoy.

Postscript

Frank Tallis

"Many years ago, I was sitting with two writers of historical fiction discussing the role of research. One of my companions said something like, 'The important thing is the story. I always make sure I have a good story first and then I do my research after. Otherwise I end up doing too much research, most of which I never actually use.' My other companion responded, 'That's a really good tip: so very professional!' And it is a good tip, except for that fact that I don't work like that at all. I'm usually inspired by a place and a particular time frame. I then go off and read lots of books about that place and period, and while I'm doing my research, various plot ideas pop into my mind. So, which of these two methods is best? Story, followed by research, or, research, followed by story? The answer is, neither. They are equally good ways to proceed. The real issue is not so much the specific approach, but what works best for the individual. Although this might be a peculiar tip to be giving in a book of tips, my tip is - beware of tips! My guess is that all tips are – to a greater or lesser extent – helpful; however, some are more helpful than others, depending on what kind of writer you are. A tip should be treated like a hypothesis. Something that should be tested and the results examined. If a tip works for you, then stick with it. If it doesn't, just move on. Before becoming a novelist I was a clinical psychologist for over twenty years, and one thing you learn very quickly in clinical practice is that treatments are not equally effective. The same treatment will produce different results, depending on the person. A good therapist is flexible and pragmatic. A good therapist is willing to use different interventions to establish which approach works best for each individual patient. The same principle applies to creative writing. Tips are wonderful things. If you try them out and they don't work then that isn't necessarily because the tips aren't any good. Maybe it's just they weren't the right ones for you. Although this is a very basic point, it is one that is surprisingly overlooked. Just because a tip sounds good or seems reasonable, doesn't mean that it is 'right' in any absolute sense. Only use tips that are right for you. "

Frank Tallis is the author of *The Liebermann Papers*

www.franktallis.com

Glossary

This glossary has been designed to provide straightforward, basic explanations of a selection of the terms that are often used in association with writing fiction. These are not dictionary definitions, but simplified explanations of selected key words and concepts.

agreement   agreement of verbs for example a singular subject (e.g. a person, a selection) must have a singular verb form i.e. A selection of books was available. Whereas a plural subject (e.g. people, books) must have a plural verb-form i.e. Selections of books were available.

alliteration   is the use in a phrase or sentence of words that begin with the same letter as in 'Silvia's sumptuous silk sash'. However, the term alliteration can also be used to refer to the repetition of a letter within a word or a combination of initial and medial repetition 'Alison always allowing. It can also be used to describe the repetition of the same sound as in 'fierce **ph**antoms **f**ought **F**rancis'.

analogy   a comparison drawn to demonstrate or highlight a similarity between certain features.

clichés   clichés are often difficult to avoid when you are writing, because they are often idioms and popular phrases that have been over used. They are defined as expressions, words, ideas and actions that have become trite and lost their power through overexposure. The origin of the word comes from the French 'clicher', which means stereotype and clichés are exactly that. They are stereotyped words and phrases that have lost their impact.

cliffhanger   What is a cliffhanger (cliff-hanger)? The definition of a cliffhanger in dictionaries and glossaries will vary slightly, but it usually means a situation of suspense and imminent danger that is created at the end of the chapter of a novel or story in serial form. However, cliff hangers can range from creating a sense of foreboding or a dilemma for one of your protagonists to leaving your character in physical danger. Today we tend to associate them with crime thrillers, or TV serials, but as a plot device they've been around for a very long time. The tales that Scheherazade told to save her life and that we know as *One Thousand and One Nights* are perhaps the most famous example. The concept may not be new, but the word cliffhanger is. It is thought to have become popular during the era of the silent movies when films were often shown serial-style and the heroine might be left hanging precariously from a cliff waiting to be rescued in the next episode. An alternative explanation of its origin is that when Thomas Hardy's novel *A Pair of Blue Eyes* was published in monthly serial form in *Tinsley's Magazine* between 1872 and 1873. Hardy decided to leave Henry Knight one of his main characters hanging off a cliff and hence Hardy's Victorian melodramatic climax may be the origin of the word cliffhanger.

colloquial (adj.), colloquially (adv.) — a word, phrase or idiom that is used in informal conversations

expletives — swear-words or sounds that express an emotional reaction and need not have any meaning.

farce — a broadly humorous play or episode in a work of prose that is based on the exploitation and manipulation of 'unreal' or improbable situations.

idiom — a group of words whose meaning cannot be predicted from the meanings of the words alone e.g. He shot his bolt. Today this would mean that someone had used up all their resources and capabilities. Originally it referred to using up all one's short heavy arrows (bolts), which were fired from a cross bow and by the 13th century was commonly used idiomatically. A colloquial variant referring to gambling 'to shoot one's wad (rolled-up banknotes)' originated in about 1900.

irony	the humorous or mildly sarcastic use of words to imply the opposite of what they mean. It is often used to draw attention to incongruity. The art of using ironic humour is exquisitely demonstrated in Jane Austen's *Pride and Prejudice*.
narrator	the person from whose viewpoint the story is told.
narrative voice	first, second or third person.
narrative mode	the skills and devices that an author uses to write his/her plot; also called **mode of narration**.
omniscient narrator	an all seeing or god-like third person narrator (a person who can tell the story of all the characters involved in the story often in a distant and unbiased way).
parody	a piece of writing that imitates or mimics the style of another writer for humorous purposes.
personification	the origin of this word comes from the Latin words *persona* meaning an actor's mask and *facere*, to make. It means to make (an object, animal or emotion) into a person. In everyday speech we use this form all the time when we refer to a ship as 'she' or we call our cars 'him' or her' or when we use expressions such as 'Fate walked in'.
pastiche	a work that mixes styles.
plagiarism	the act of taking the ideas or work of another person and using them as if they were your own. Curiously the origin of the verb plagiarise is from Latin and combines two words, one that originally meant plunder and the other to kidnap.
protagonist	character e.g. main character or primary character, secondary character etc.
puns	word play that deliberately uses the ambiguity of words and their origin; also called *paronomasia*
satire	a way of shaming people about their views etc. It is a form of humour that is supposed to be funny, but also acts theoretically as constructive criticism.
sarcasm	sharp, biting humour that is mocking and intended to be insulting or scornful.
simile and metaphor	a simile compares or likens two different things in one or more of their properties or features; for

example 'clever as a river rat' or 'white as a freshly laundered sheet'.

Metaphors have been defined as compressed similes, because in a metaphor a phrase or word one idea or object is used in order to suggest a likeness or comparison between them for instance ' Mrs. Cutty-Smythe sailed into the church'.

slang	vocabulary or idioms that are not always appropriate in formal conversations.
slap-stick	a type of comedy that is based on exaggerated violence e.g. as found in pantomimes and some children's cartoons for example Tom & Jerry.
spoof	a send up or a parody. Today the word has a broad meaning and is used to describe a work that pokes fun at or mocks another original work, style or person using satire or irony.
story line	plot or theme (depending on the context).
style	The way that a writer uses their words, which gives their writing an individual hallmark and flavour or a distinctive, consistent manner of writing in words.
tense	A verb has several tenses. Tenses tell us when the action takes place e.g. I am talking to them. (now) I will talk to them. (future) I talked to them. (past)
verb	is used to describe an action or state of being e.g. say, read, talk, write, think.
verisimilitude	the appearance of being real or true.
voice	They way in which the author addresses their character or characters: I (first person), he/she (second person), narrator style etc.

Useful Books and web sites

There are so many useful books and web sites that are available that it is not possible to provide a comprehensive list. The books and sites listed below include a few that have been mentioned. The details were accurate at the time of publication, but may have changed by the time you read this book. We suggest that if this is the case you carry out a key word search on the internet.

Grammar books and websites:

Grammar Book:
  http://bookshop.blackwell.co.uk/jsp/id/Grammar_Book/9781853779862

Citing References:
  http://bookshop.blackwell.co.uk/jsp/id/Citing_References/9781853779923

www.english-for-students.com

www.phrases.org.uk

Magazines:

Kudos:
  www.kudoswritingcompetitions.com

Historical Novel Society Review, Solander:

  www.historicalnovelsociety.org

Other reference sources:

Roman numeral conversion :

  www.guernsey.net/~sgibbs/roman.html

  www.onlineconversion.com/roman_numerals_advanced.htm

Perfume:

  www.perfumesguide.com

  www.parispass.com

  Fragonard Parfumeur - Le Musée du Parfum , 9 rue Scribe, 75009 Paris

  Fragonard Parfumeur - Le Théatre-Musée des Capucines, 39 Bld des Capucines, 75002 Paris

Prisons:

  www.hmprisonservice.gov.uk

Books:

Brande, D. (1996) *Becoming a Writer*. London: Macmillan Reference books. (This book was first published in 1934 and the © remains with Harcourt Brace & Company Ltd.)

Children's Writers' and Artists' Yearbook. UK: A & C Black Publishers (a new edition is published every year)

Grant-Adamson, L., *Writing Crime Fiction* (Teach Yourself Educational)

Lyle, D.P., M.D. (2003). *Murder and Mayhem*. New York: Thomas Dunne Books

Ramat, A., *Creating a Twist in the Tale, How to Books* (1996)

Wynn, D., (2003). *The Crime Writer's Handbook*. London: Allison & Busby

Useful Web sites:

www.fashion-era.com
www.historicalnovels.info
www.scbwi.org
www.OldHouseBooks.co.uk

Travel related:
www.ukhrail.uel.ac.uk
www.nrm.org.uk
www.swindon.gov.uk/steam
www.talyllyn.co.uk
www.didcotrailwaycentre.org.uk
www.southdevonrailway.org
www.firstgreatwestern.co.uk

Useful Web Sites for Writers:

www.societyofauthors.org.uk – The Society of Authors
www.writersguild.org.uk –The Writers' Guild of Great Britain
www.train4publishing.co.uk
www.publishersglobal.com